IMAGES
of America

CLIFFSIDE

Portrait of a Carolina Mill Town

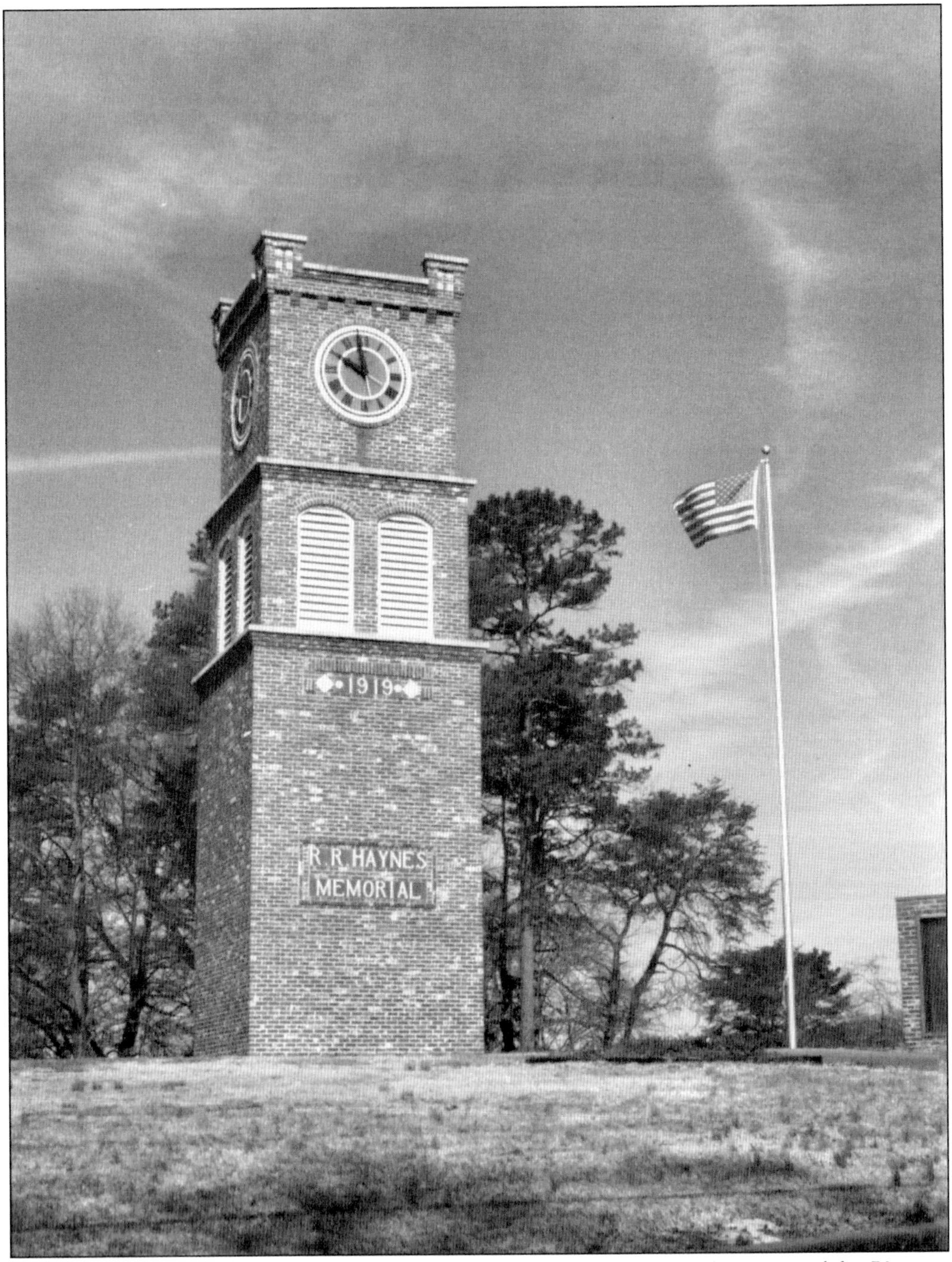

The Clock Tower. On the knoll on Main Street where the Haynes home stood for 70 years stands a more modern edifice, a tower to memorialize Raleigh Rutherford Haynes, founder of Cliffside. In effect, it is a memorial to a memorial, for the clock in this structure once chimed from atop the R. R. Haynes Memorial Building, built in 1922. When that building was razed in the 1976, the clock was installed on this peaceful hilltop. It is one of only a few remaining relics to remind us, with its stately presence and out-of-tune chimes, that a town with vitality and some importance once occupied these empty spaces. (Photograph by the author.)

IMAGES
of America

CLIFFSIDE

Portrait of a Carolina Mill Town

Alfred Reno Bailey

ARCADIA
PUBLISHING

ISBN 978-0-7385-4160-0

Published by Arcadia Publishing
Charleston, South Carolina

Printed in the United States of America

Library of Congress Catalog Card Number: 2005925652

For all general information contact Arcadia Publishing at:
Telephone 843-853-2070
Fax 843-853-0044
E-mail sales@arcadiapublishing.com
For customer service and orders:
Toll-Free 1-888-313-2665

Visit us on the Internet at www.arcadiapublishing.com

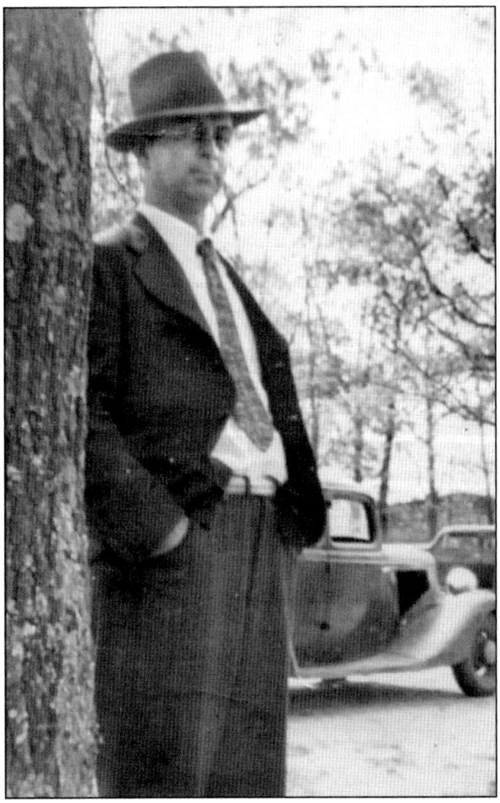

DEDICATION. His name was Byron Bailey, but almost everyone called him B. R. or "Barn." He worked all his adult life in the mill and lived in Cliffside for most of it, until he died far too soon. His gentle and unassuming manner endeared him to all who knew him, and his sly humor made him fit right in, for in Cliffside that seemed to be the most common denominator. Byron liked nothing better than to read about the old days and the old ways and to remember—and he would have worn the ink off these pages. This one's for you, Dad.

Contents

ACKNOWLEDGMENTS

Hazel Haynes Bridges deserves special recognition for sharing her collection of treasured photographs. Very special thanks go to Joyce Atkinson Hunter for her tenacious fact-finding and photograph searching and to Ginny Ann Greene Reid, who served as the Cliffside conduit, rounding up photographs from hither and yon. Grover Haynes Jr. and Judson "Bud" Crow went beyond the call of duty in researching families, landmarks, names, and old cars, and providing insights into the town and its people. Anita Price Davis dissolved our hesitation with her gentle encouragement, strong support, and sound advice.

We encourage a loud round of applause for Don Bailey, Ruby Bailey, Buzzy Biggerstaff, Jack Biggerstaff, Virginia Padgett Biggerstaff, Anne Cargill, Dena Watkins Chandler, Harold Clardy, Betty Houser Cromer, Al Dalton, Sam Davis, Patsy Ingram Dothard, Geraldine Wall Evans, Peggy Blanton Hadden, Mark Hames, Guy Hamrick, Mary Edna McCraw, Madeline Scruggs Hardin, Joan Humphries Harris, Bob Hawkins, Jim Haynes, Myles Haynes Jr., Mack Hendrick, Evelyn Hollifield Houser, Frances McMurray Houser, Ben Humphries, Charles "Red" Humphries, Lula Goode Humphries, Dr. Jack Hunt, Jim Ingram, Dot Beason Lowery, Kay Lowery, Larry McDaniel, Buzzy Moss, Todd Putnam, Louise Wall Price, Jim Ruppe, Jim Scancarelli, Mary Scruggs, Nell Deane Scruggs, Rebecca Callahan Scruggs, Gene Shuford, Juanita Davis Smith, Ben Steele, Loree Harrill Steele, Janice Bridges Swing, Marc Swing, Shirley Crawford Thompson, James M. Walker, Nancy Brown Wallace, Carolyn Greene Waters, Phillip White, Jane Winn, and Danny Wortman.

And I am particular grateful to Betty, light of my life, who kept the train on the tracks, the ducks in a row, the author in his chair, and the coffee hot.

INTRODUCTION

It was an early flight to Los Angeles about 25 years ago. I had been assigned to L.A. for a grueling, jet-lagged week of 14-hour, pressure-filled days, sprinkled with huge egos, flaring tempers, and a guaranteed crisis every few minutes. Except for that, I was eager to go. We had just left Charlotte going west when I had one of those *Field of Dreams* moments. I was drawn to the window, looked down, and was jarred by what I saw—it was Cliffside! I had never seen it from the air before but knew it instantly. It now looked old and battered, and I could tell a lot of it was gone. I could swear I heard a whisper, "*We're still here if you want us.*" Stop the plane, please. I'll be getting off here.

I had not been back, except for fleeting visits with my parents, since Eisenhower was president and had not kept up with its news or its problems. I was saddened and ashamed that, as a teenager, I couldn't wait to leave the place but so glad now to think of it again. Who is left down there? I wondered. How selfish and stupid of me, for all these years, to have ignored the place and people that were still so much a part of me.

Life went on. I was kept away by responsibilities, but I promised myself that one day I would reconnect with Cliffside and would somehow record and perpetuate its memories and history. That "somehow" turned out to be a Web site called Remember Cliffside (remembercliffside.com) and, eventually, this book.

Cliffside in days gone by was a village—a society, actually—made possible by the vision and determination of a single man: Raleigh Rutherford Haynes. It was a one-man town. Haynes, with a few silent partners, owned Cliffside Mills. The company owned the land, every house on the land, and every tree around every house on the land. It owned hundreds of acres up and down the river on which tenant farmers grew the cotton needed to produce cloth and the vegetables, fruit, and meat needed by the company stores to feed the employees.

This is not to disparage the arrangement. In 1900, it was the only arrangement that would have worked. To go out in the wilderness and, practically overnight, create an entire self-sustaining town and a mill that employed hundreds requires fierce determination and a freewheeling style. Had a consortium or a disparate collection of industry captains been involved, Cliffside would be only halfway finished by now.

The town lies in lower Rutherford County, North Carolina, hugging the Cleveland County line and only a hop and a skip from South Carolina. In its heyday in the 1940s and 1950s, its population never exceeded 2,500 people living in about 450 homes. Being company-owned, it never had city limits, laws, a town council, real-estate salesmen, or a traffic light. That may seem like a bad thing, depending on your point of view, but it also didn't have prostitutes, burglars, chiseling landlords, beer joints, crooked merchants, or unfair managers. No one locked his doors, not even for out-of-town trips.

There was no police department, only a county deputy to keep the peace. Wages were no lower—and were sometimes higher—than similar mills in the area. A family paid 25¢ a week for each room in their house, and a little extra for the window screens, which were optional. In hard times, if the mill stood idle and no wages were forthcoming, families were not thrown out. The company stores would sell them food at cost or less to keep employees going. On the other hand, if you beat your wife, were a drunk, failed to do your job properly, let your youngsters run wild or sass their teacher, or kept a dog on your rented premises, you were warned. If the infraction continued, you were fired and promptly evicted. Mr. Haynes did not like dogs, and he knew how some men would feed their dogs while their children went hungry. It is amazing how the threat of unemployment and eviction can make a man straighten up, work hard, and keep his children in line.

Short of requiring that at least one member of a tenant family work in the mill or in a business that served the town, there were no hard and fast rules, and management did everything possible to be fair and accommodating, providing all the vital services and some not so vital.

However frugal Mr. Haynes was purported to be (having workmen pick up and straighten kegs of bent nails, for example), it is told that he would get up every morning thinking of ways to provide more conveniences and comforts for his people.

The marvel of it is, this attitude—this company culture—continued for decades, long after the old man had died. It became embodied in most of us who lived in Cliffside in those years that the whole point of living is being fair, kind, and helpful to one another.

Once in the 1970s, a New York magazine writer spent a few days chasing around after Earl Owensby, one of Cliffside's few self-made millionaires, who loved movies so much he built his own film studio about 10 miles away. Soon the writer tired of hearing tales of Earl's hometown and burst out with "Cliffside! Cliffside! Cliffside! That's all I've heard around here. How can I find out what makes that place so special?" Brownlee Davis, a Cliffside boy with a razor-sharp wit, overheard the writer and piped up, "I guess you'll just have to die and go there."

One

At a Bend in the River

When Cliffside was unattractive hillsides and covered with undergrowth and uninviting to everybody else, this man by clear vision saw what it was to become.

—R. L. Ryburn, 1922

It is not clear exactly when the vision of Cliffside took hold in Raleigh Haynes's fertile imagination. He had spent the 1890s developing the mills and towns of Henrietta and Caroleen further up the river, but in 1899, as if tired of past pursuits, he began with a special fervor to found a new mill and a new town at a double horseshoe bend further down the river, the perfect place to build a dam.

He either named the place Cliffside himself, or approved the name suggested by someone else, but what else would you call a place where everything was either uphill or down, where the terrain was so steep many of the new mill houses hung onto the hillsides like long-legged spiders? Streets were carved out of the rocky landscape; wells were dug in every corner of the town; new people were hired from outside to perform the hundreds of new duties that had to be performed.

Millions of bricks were made on site to construct the big mill, but practically everything else needed to build and support this enormous effort was hauled in by mule-drawn wagons from the railroad four miles away.

The most amazing thing is not his vision, but how he fulfilled it, how he successfully found, attracted, and marshaled the expertise needed in so many fields for such an enterprise.

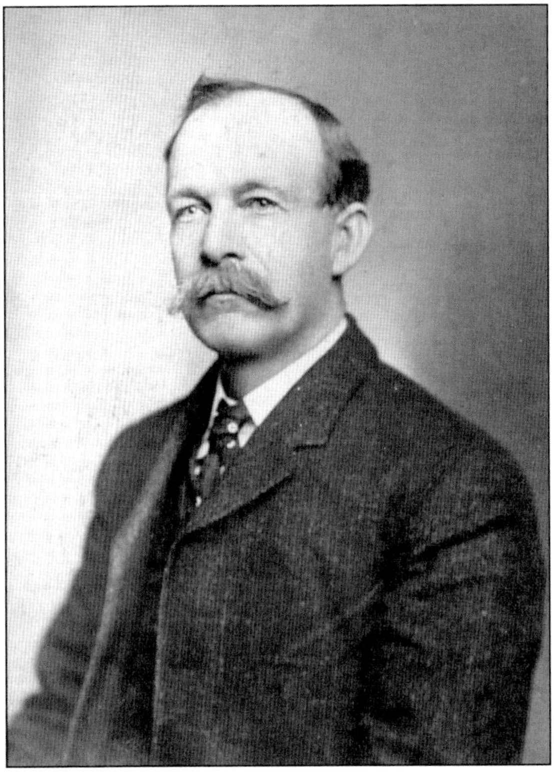

RALEIGH RUTHERFORD HAYNES. From poor farmer to storekeeper to textile tycoon, he made it all look so easy. Haynes's ability to amass the capital and attract the talented people needed to fulfill a grand vision was his genius. His compassion for and fair treatment of his employees were unusual. This photograph was probably taken around 1895, a few years before his Cliffside project got underway. (Courtesy Hazel Haynes Bridges.)

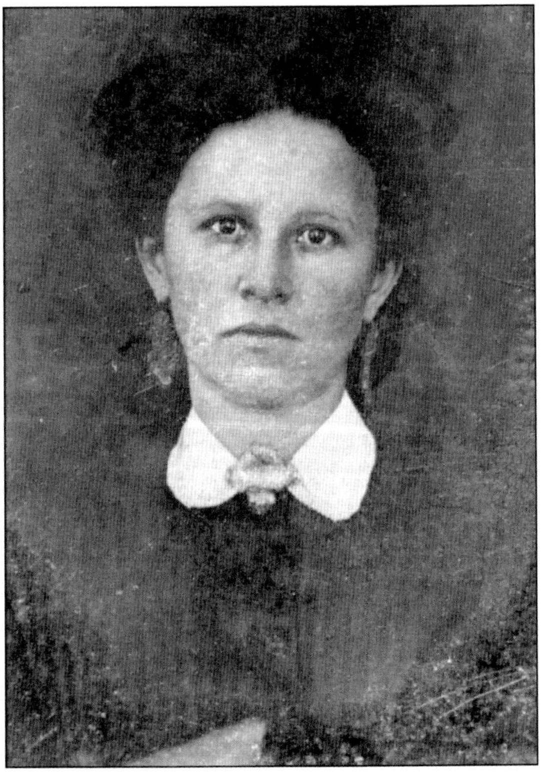

AMANDA CARPENTER HAYNES. She was Raleigh Haynes's first wife and the mother of their eight children; she died in 1892 at the age of 41. This photograph, showing a youthful Amanda, was found behind a mantelpiece in the Hayneses' old house in Cliffside when it was torn down in the early 1970s. (Courtesy Grover Haynes Jr.)

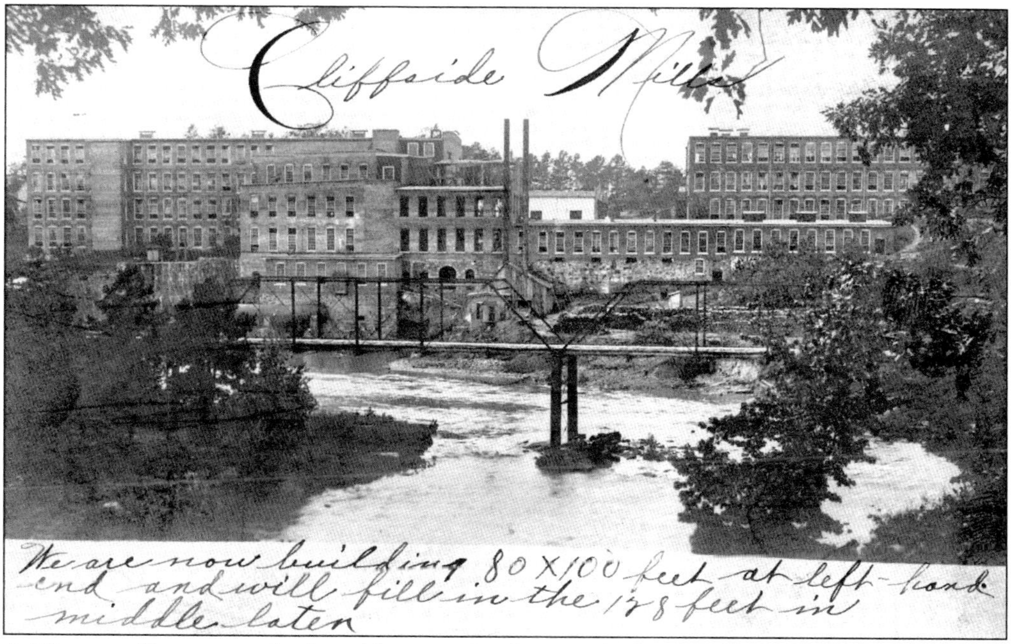

A WORK IN PROGRESS. As this old postcard indicates, the huge mill was built in stages. Some of its features are puzzling compared to the mill as it was known years later, in particular the twin smokestacks and the apparent separation of the two buildings on the right (there seems to be a path from one to the other). Whose fine hand proudly titled the card "Cliffside Mills?" (Courtesy Hazel Haynes Bridges.)

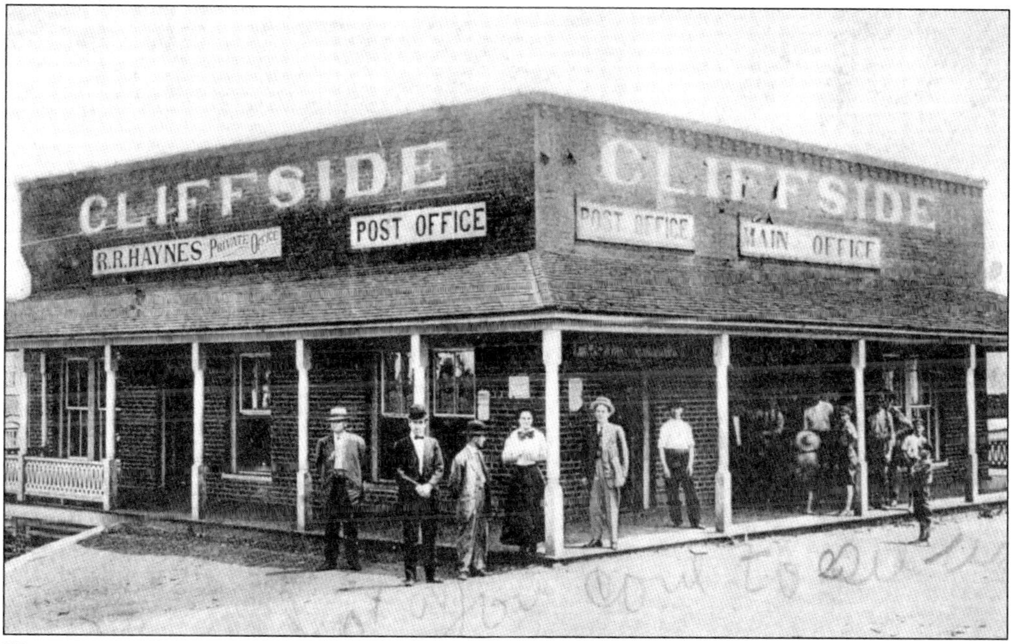

HEADQUARTERS. Aside from the mill itself, this was the heart of the Cliffside Mills operation around 1908. Proudly advertising the town's name and announcing R. R. Haynes's private office, it also housed the second post office in Cliffside's short history. This little brick building was enlarged and renovated several times over the decades. (Courtesy Hazel Haynes Bridges.)

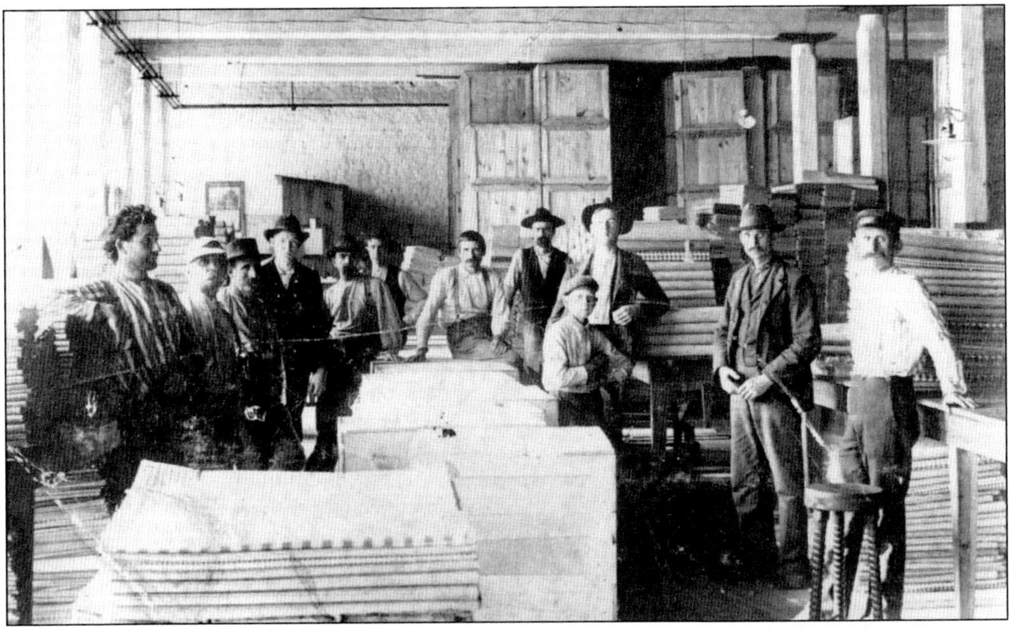

FINISHING ROOM. The packing area at Cliffside is shown in the very early days of its operation. Bolts of gingham and wooden crates were loaded onto boxcars for shipment out to the world. The man at right in the white shirt is Drury Dobbins Fortune (1859–1933), father to Ina Fortune (later Mrs. Grover Haynes) and Vic Fortune, both of whom were life-long Cliffside residents. (Courtesy Hazel Haynes Bridges.)

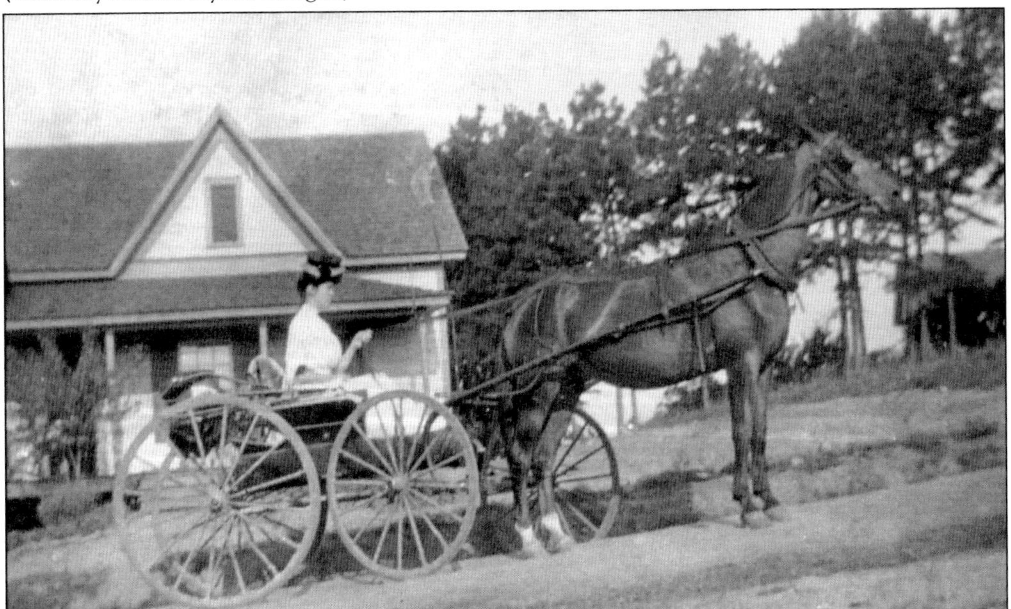

LADY IN A CARRIAGE. She probably rented the rig at Mr. Zeno Hawkins's livery stable at the north end of Church Street. Private horses were not kept at company-owned homes, at least within the town limits. This could have been taken at any of a number of places in town, but the slope of the land looks suspiciously like Cliffside Street. (Courtesy Hazel Haynes Bridges.)

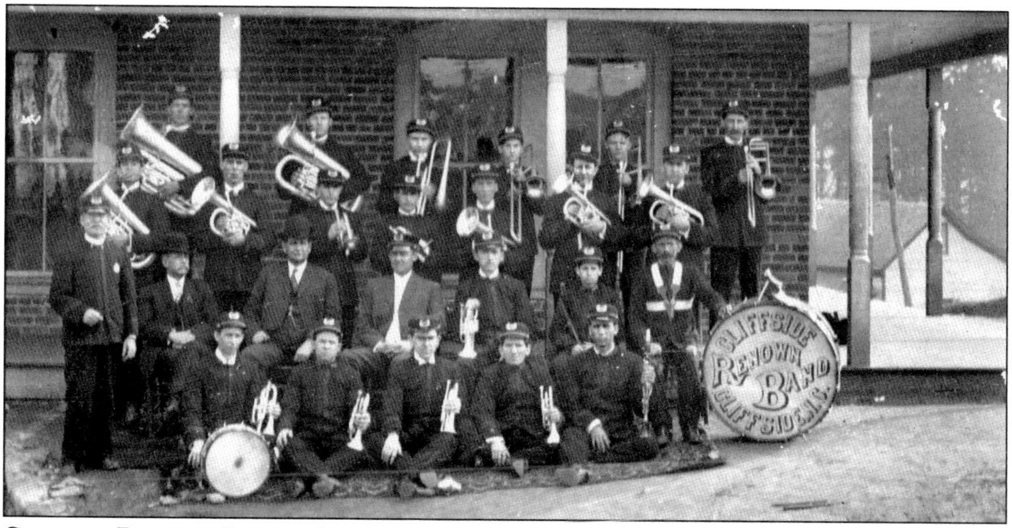

CLIFFSIDE RENOWN BAND. This is the 1908 incarnation of the group. Pictured are, from left to right, (first row) Quinn Womick, Walter Hawkins, Irvin Gregory, Tab Greene, and Rom James; (second row) Prof. Dock Warburton, R. R. Haynes, Lee Packard, Dr. Baxter Haynes, Claude Wilson, Charlie Moore, and Drury D. Fortune; (third row) Silas Bland, Avery Robinson, Frank Haynes, Grover Haynes, T. D. Rudisill, Bill Leicester, and Onslo McBrayer; (fourth row) ? Bland, Landrum Roberts, D. C. Cole, Victor Fortune, "Little Charlie" Haynes, and Asa Hamrick. (Courtesy Hazel Haynes Bridges.)

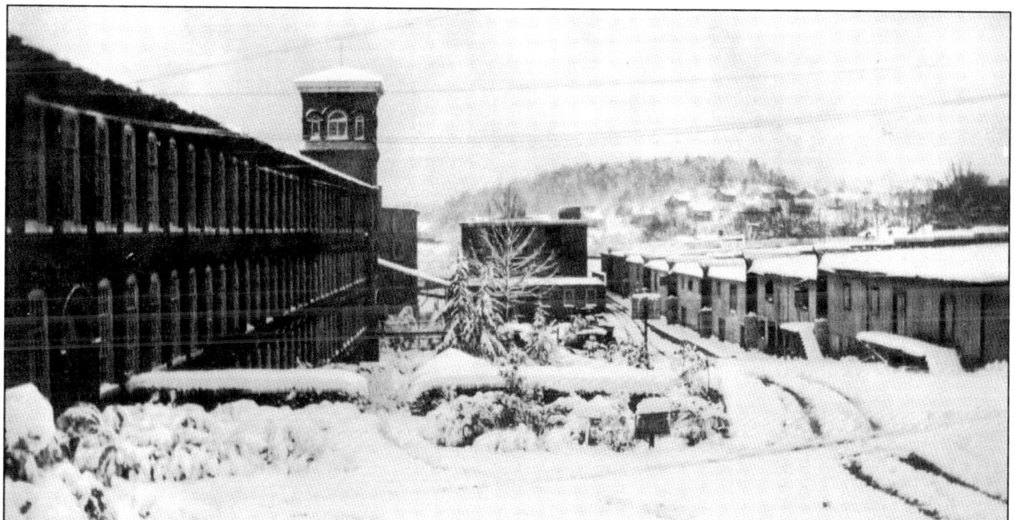

ROUGH WINTER. Every generation was told how much harsher the winters were "way back yonder." Elders spoke of how much deeper the snows were and how the pond would freeze over so that people could actually walk across. This scene in the mid-1920s suggests how hard life was then. (Courtesy Hazel Haynes Bridges.)

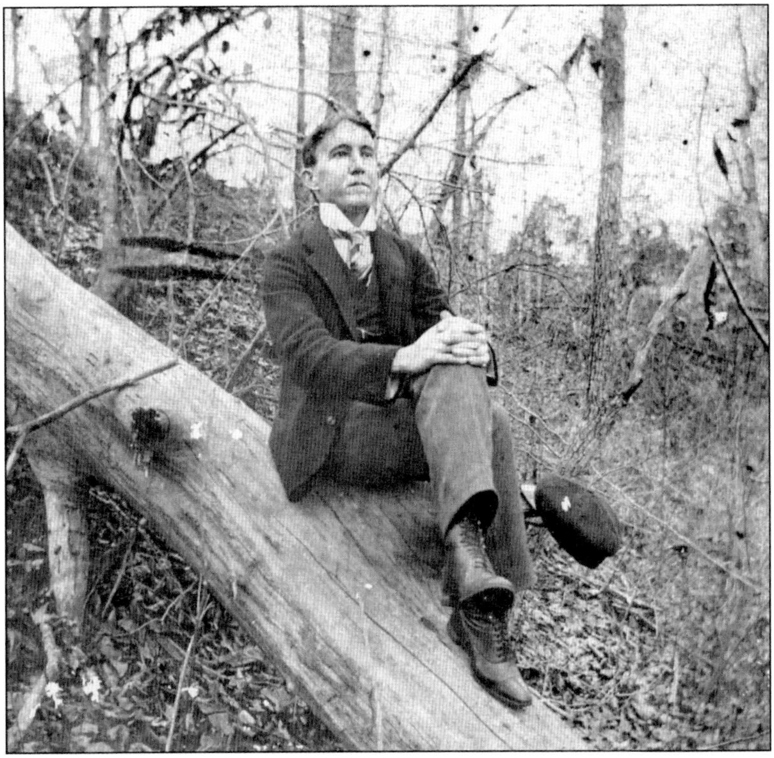

YOUNG CHARLES. At Raleigh Haynes's death, the reins of power passed to his son Charles, shown here about 1897 in his late teens. He may still have been a student at Guilford College in Greensboro. Like his father before him, running the company became his life, which may explain why he did not marry until 1945 when he was 67. (Courtesy Hazel Haynes Bridges.)

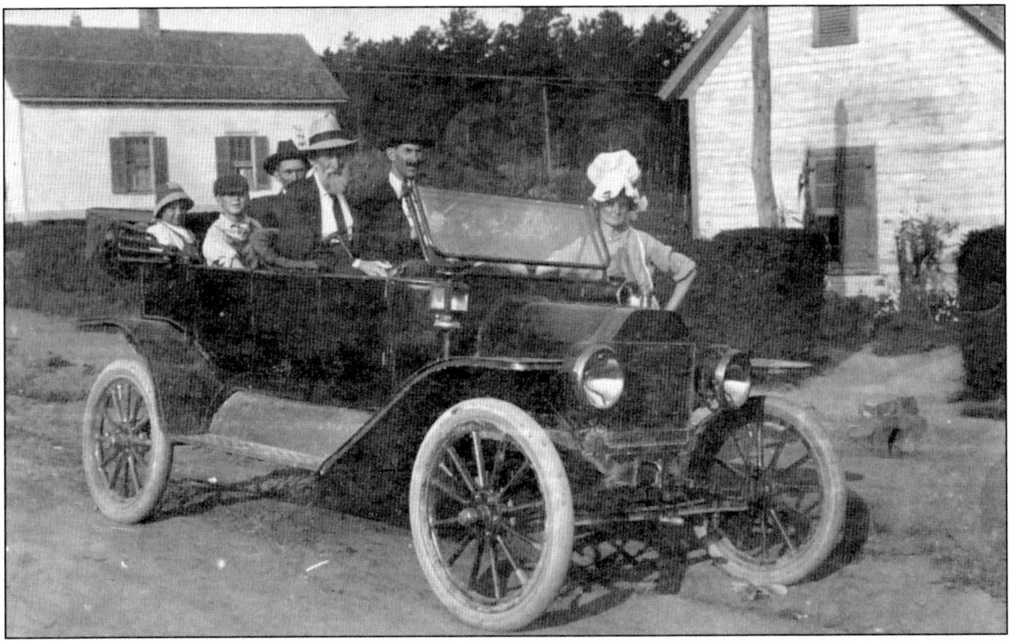

HORSELESS CARRIAGE, 1911. Robert Broadus (R. B.) Watkins is about to drive away with, from left to right, his sons James Craig and Robert Jr., brother Joe, and father, Romulus (in front passenger seat). His wife, Ida Craig Watkins says goodbye. R. B. held a number of positions in town: president of the phone company, magistrate, and member of the school board. Ida was also an active figure. (Courtesy Dena Watkins Chandler.)

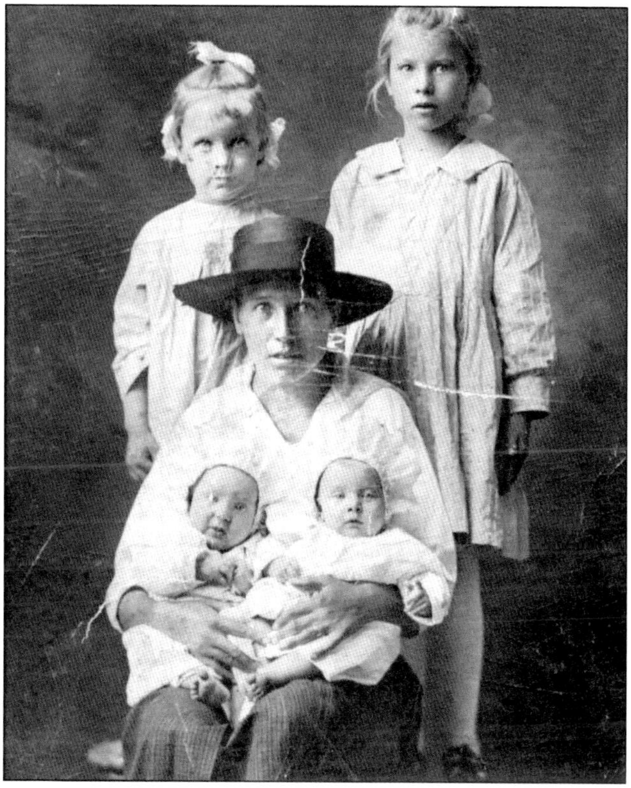

FAMILY IN FOCUS. Bertha Self Greene, wife of Frank Greene, holds their new twins, Willie (a girl) and William, in 1919. Behind are her daughters by a previous marriage, Jewell and Tressie Davis. Jewell later became Mrs. Bill Ingram; Tressie married Arrie Greene. The Greenes had three other daughters: Ruby, Mozelle, and Dorothy. Bertha's first husband vanished before Jewell was born and was declared dead after a seven-year absence. (Courtesy Patsy Ingram Dothard.)

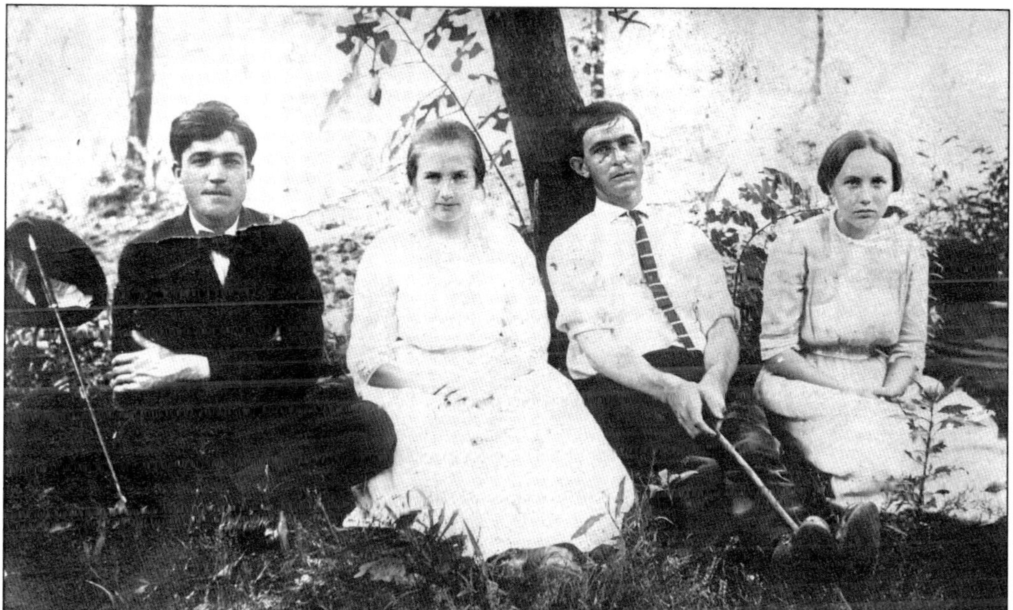

A PLEASANT OUTING. Tom Crow, Cora Mashburn, Cleve Fisher, and India Goode were "keeping company" and enjoying the good weather of a Sunday afternoon about 1914. Had it not been Sunday they would have been busy working in the mill. Could it be that those are golf clubs held by Tom and Cleve? Anything was possible in Cliffside. (Courtesy B. B. Biggerstaff.)

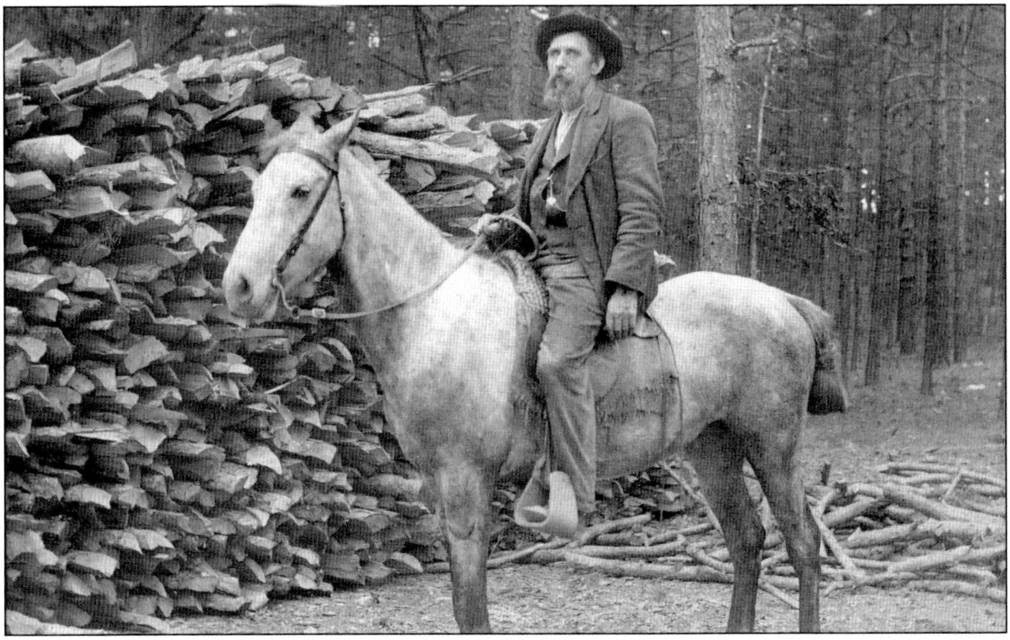

MAN OF ALL SEASONS. One of the pioneers of the area was Joseph Beason (1849–1930). Joe was a horse trader, farmer, and carpenter. He kept a ledger from January 1886 through November 1929, in which he made daily one-line entries for almost 43 years recording the weather and his many activities, which included helping build the streets of Cliffside. (Courtesy Joan Humphries Harris.)

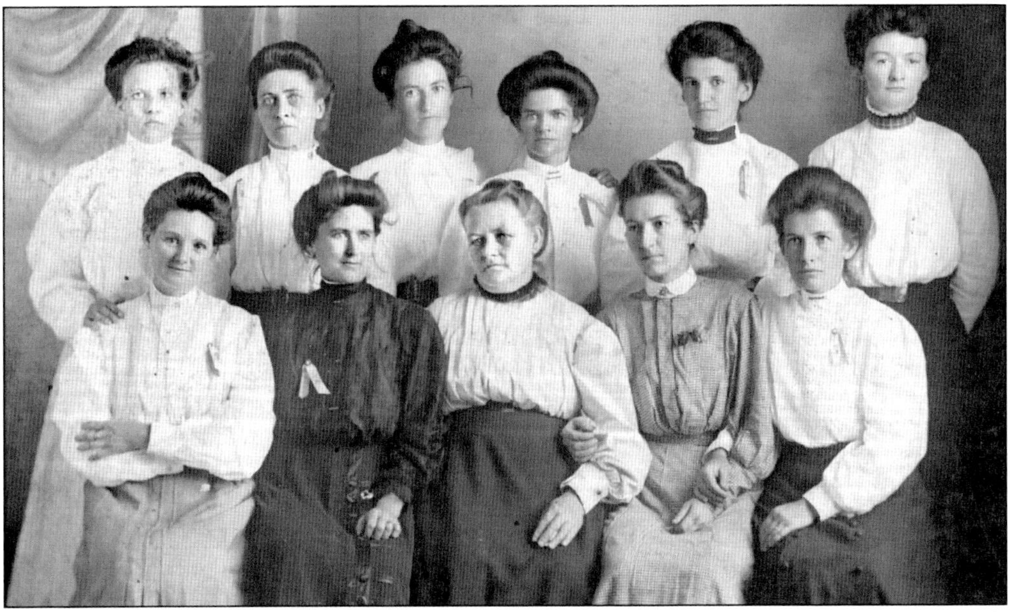

THE CLIFFSIDE "HOME DEPARTMENT" STAFF. The staff did charity work in conjunction with local churches and the company. The group was directed by Ida Craig Watkins, a powerful force in the community until she died at age 91 in 1964. From left to right are (first row) Ida Watkins, ? Bowling, Theodosia Jarrett, ? Harrison, and ? Padgett; (second row) ? Rudisill, ? Lanton, ? Bridges, ? Waters, and two unidentified people. The photograph is dated March 28, 1909. (Courtesy Dena Watkins Chandler.)

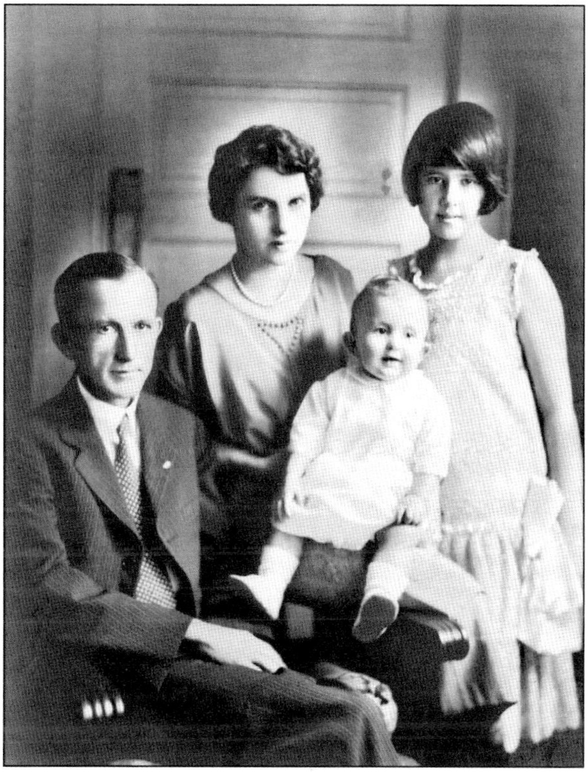

THE GROVER HAYNES FAMILY. R. R. Haynes's youngest son, Grover Cleveland (1884–1950), married Ina Inez Fortune in December 1910. Grover's daughter Hazel was born a year later, and his son Grover Jr. arrived in 1924. Grover was treasurer of Cliffside Mills for several years and supervised construction of the Cliffside Baptist Church in 1924. His several business ventures included a farm supply office and the Hodge Oil Co., which he owned in partnership with his brother Walter. (Courtesy Hazel Haynes Bridges.)

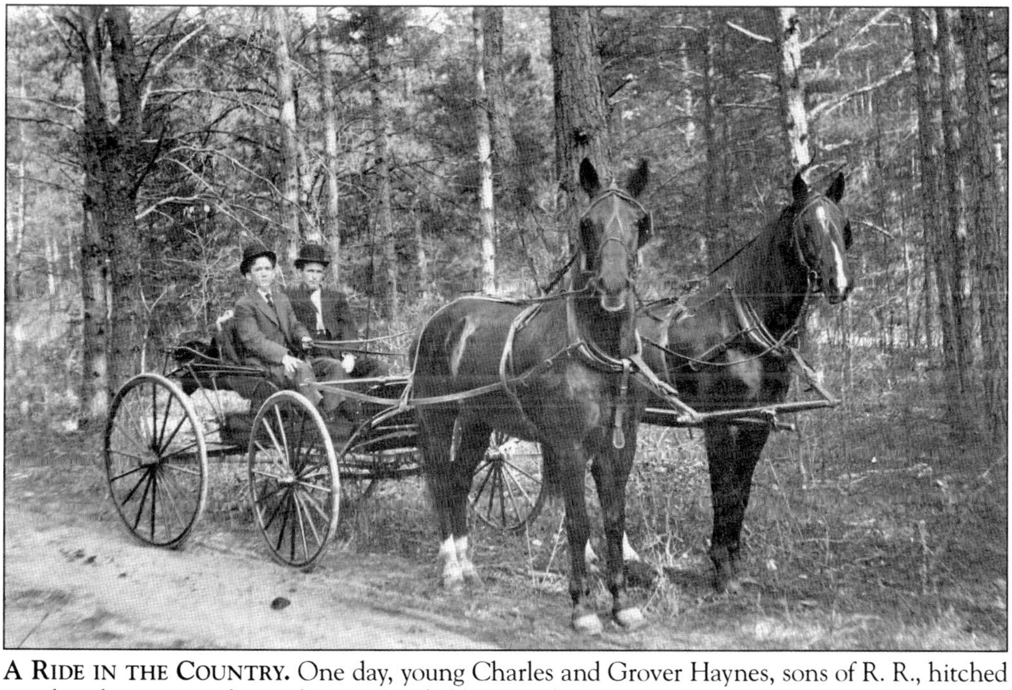

A RIDE IN THE COUNTRY. One day, young Charles and Grover Haynes, sons of R. R., hitched up a handsome team for a ride on a wooded lane. Did someone just happen by and snap this very professional-looking photograph, or had the town photographer been hired for the occasion? Their age suggests this picture was made around 1908. (Courtesy Hazel Haynes Bridges.)

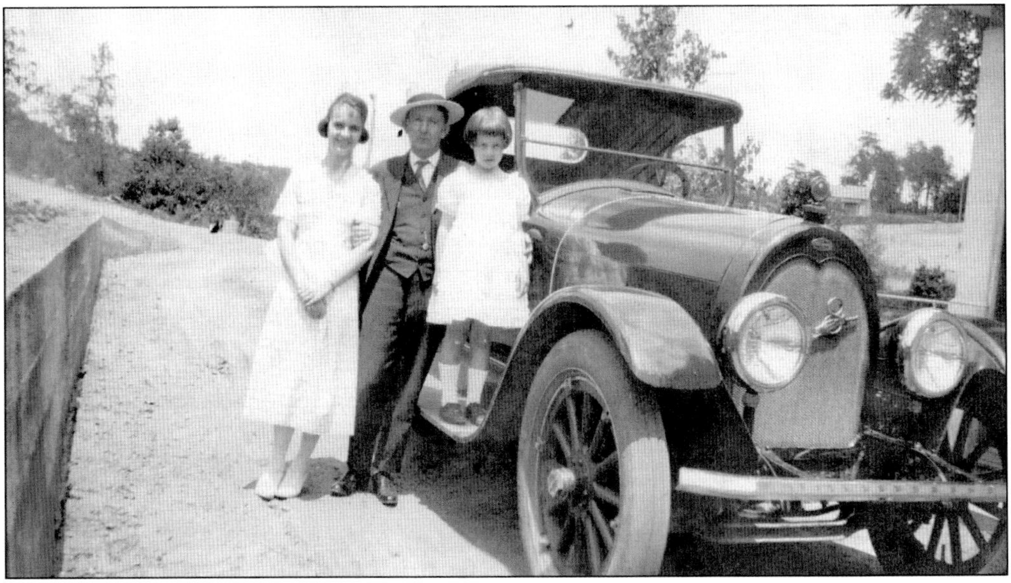

ROADSTER. Charles H. Haynes, president of Cliffside Mills, poses beside his sleek, shiny eight-cylinder Apperson roadster, manufactured in Kokomo, Indiana. The little girl on the running board is his niece, Hazel, daughter of Grover and Ina Haynes. The other girl is Edith Jenkins, another niece, daughter of Z. O. and Florence Jenkins. It was about 1920, several years before any roads around Cliffside were paved. (Courtesy Hazel Haynes Bridges.)

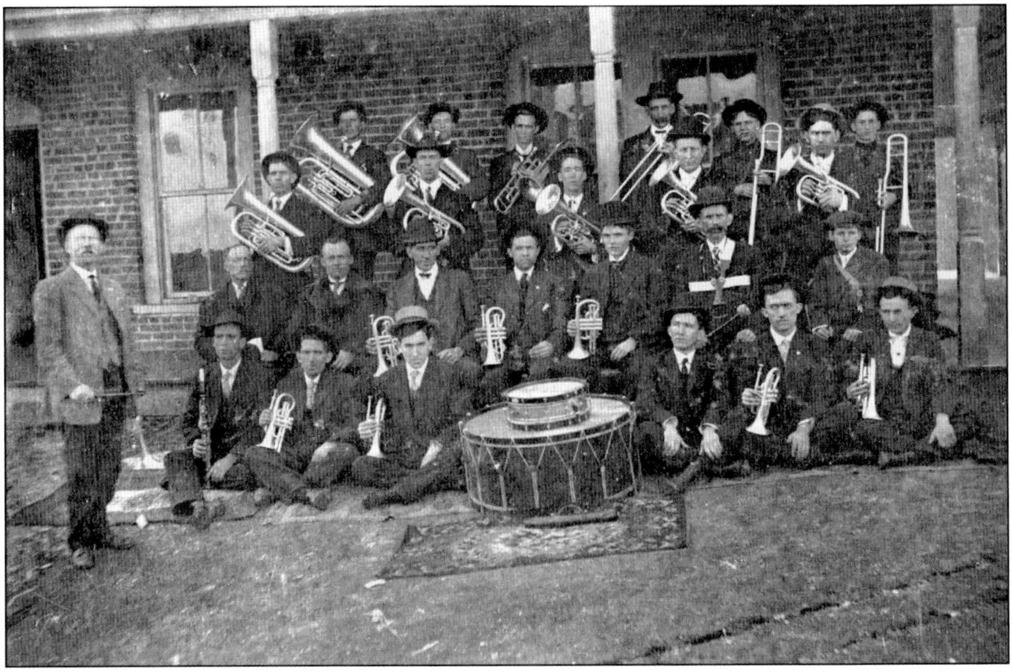

SEVEN CORNETS, FOUR TROMBONES. In another picture of the band, taken around 1910, the members—assembled in the usual place at the mill office—are in street clothes. Raleigh Haynes sits at the left on the second row. In the front row, his son Charles sits to the right of the drums, and another son, Grover, is the last cornet player on the right. (Courtesy Hazel Haynes Bridges.)

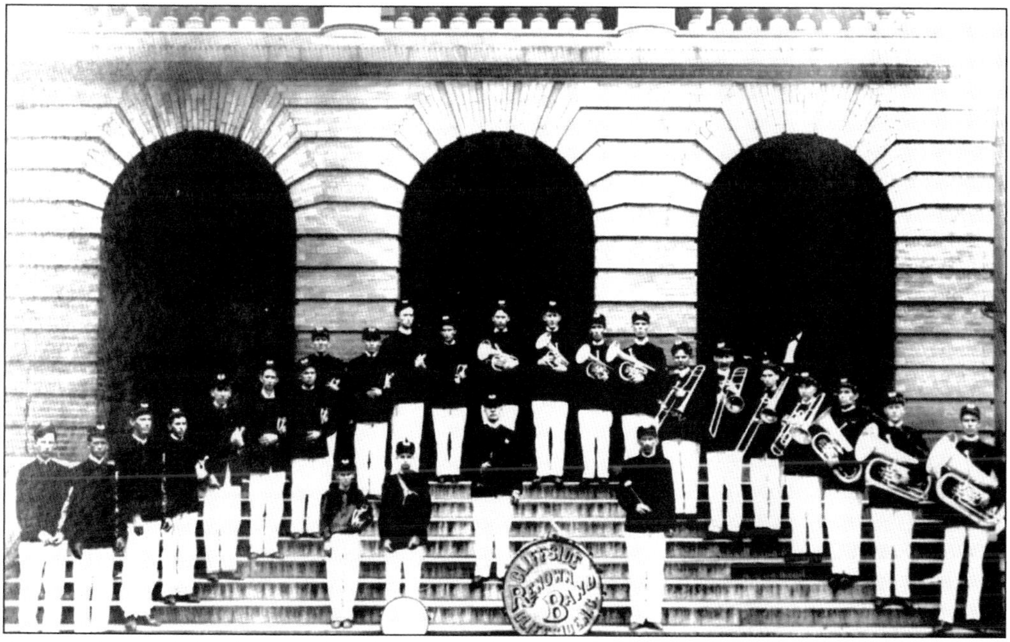

ON THE ROAD. The Renown Band performed at events far from Cliffside, promoting the little town and enhancing its reputation. It often played in competitions in cities like Charlotte, which is probably where this was taken. Mr. Haynes footed the entire bill for the band: the instruments, uniforms, and travel. He probably compensated the musicians as well, above the pay most received as employees of the company. (Courtesy Hazel Haynes Bridges.)

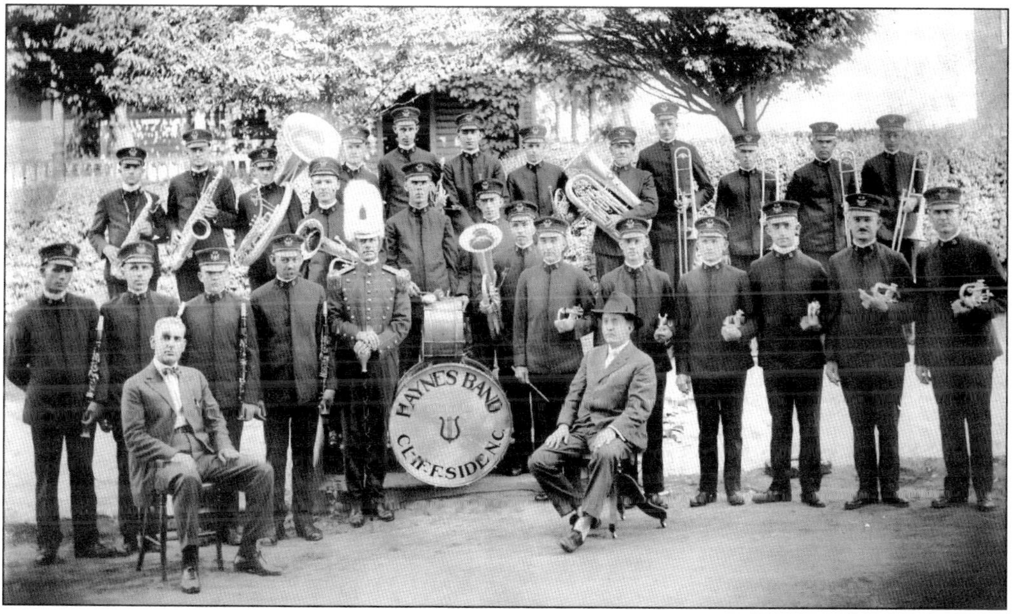

THE NEW BAND. During World War I, the band did not perform. Soon after the war, Charles H. Haynes, now head of the company, revived the organization and called it the Haynes Band. Here, in 1925, Z. O. Jenkins, an executive with the company, sits at left. His brother-in-law, Charles Haynes, sits at right. D. C. Cole (holding the baton) is the conductor. (Courtesy Hazel Haynes Bridges.)

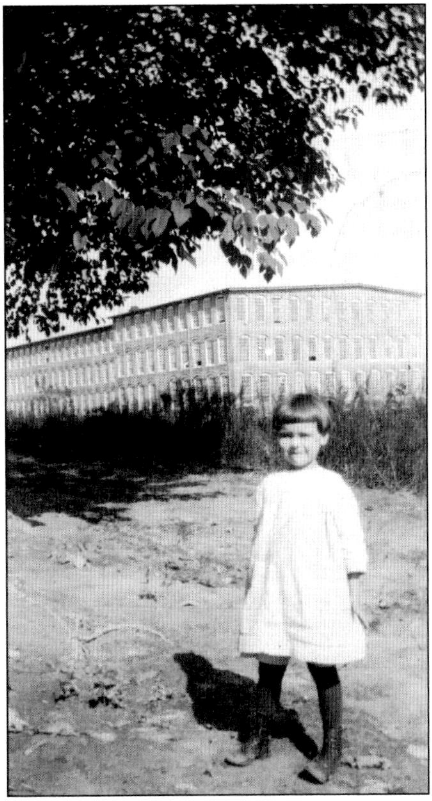

GIRL AT THE MILL. Maude Blanton plays in her yard on South Main Street about 1920. The daughter of Clinton and Orah Blanton, her sisters were Georgia and Lillie Belle (to become Mrs. Robert Hawkins and Mrs. Jim Frye, respectively) and her brother, Lawrence, was a local boxer nicknamed "Cliffside Jack." Maude married Loy Wortman, and they bore a son, Danny. (Courtesy Danny Wortman.)

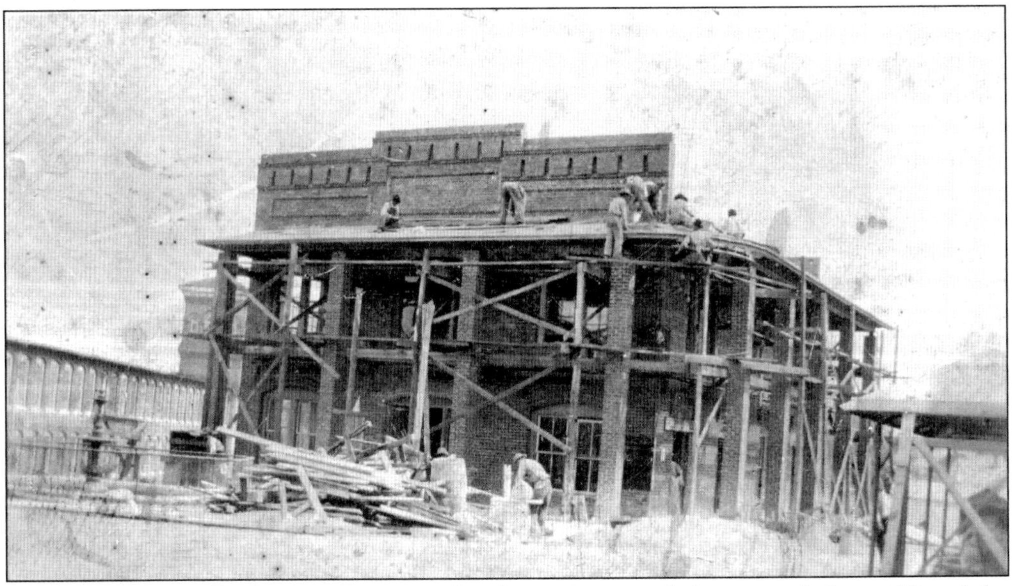

RENOVATION. It is hard to pinpoint exactly when it happened, but around the middle of the second decade of the 20th century, a second story was added to the mill office. In later years, it would be remodeled to close in the front porches with large windows; later the large windows were closed up with a nearly solid brick wall and smaller windows. (Courtesy Carolyn Greene Waters.)

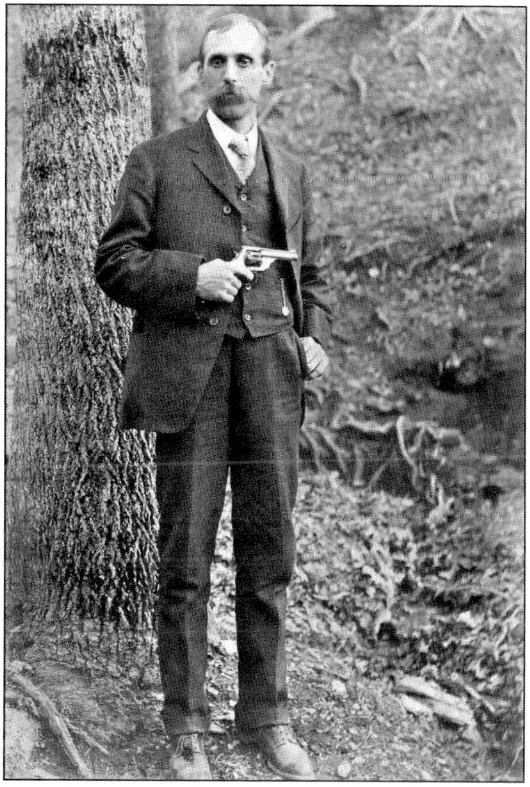

The Photographer. From about 1900 to the 1930s, William Edgar (Will) Hames ran a photography studio in Cliffside. The original location was above the town's first post office building. Later he set up shop in his home on River Street. This self-portrait is only one of his many striking photographs that chronicle the life and times of Cliffside people. Most of Will's glass negatives are said to have been destroyed by fire in the 1940s. (Courtesy Mark Hames.)

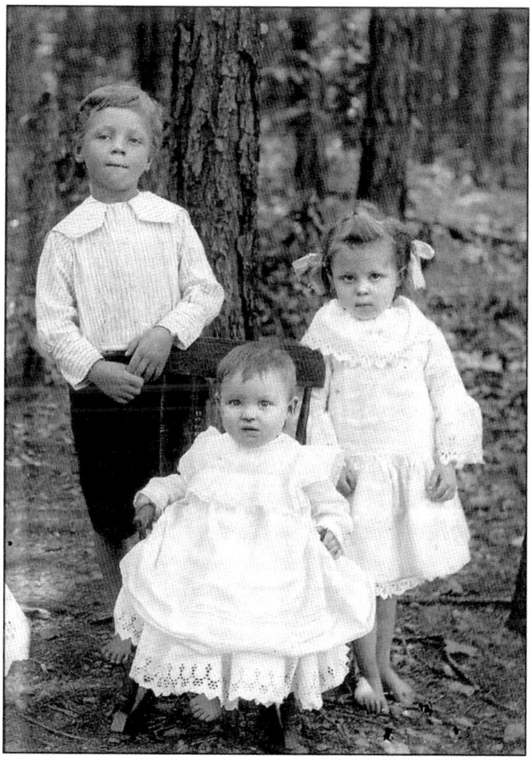

Hames Children. These are Will Hames's children about 1907. From left to right are William Floyd ("Jack"), Zeke, and Elsie. Jack began work in the mill at age 15 and retired in 1965 after 50 years. He ran a taxi business in his spare time. (Courtesy Mark Hames.)

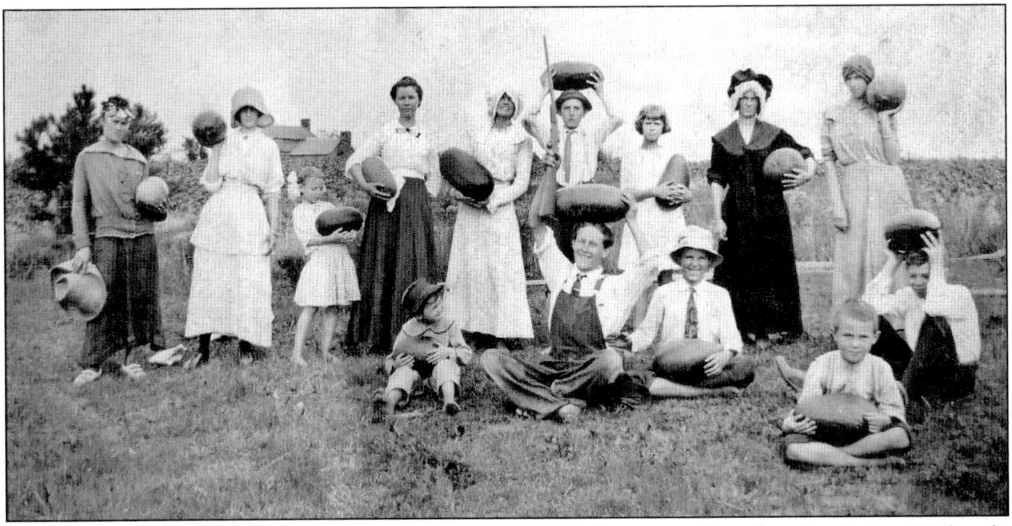

WATERMELON PATCH. Around 1910, relatives of Will Hames gathered at his father Richard's farm on Ferry Road outside of Cliffside. When they returned from picking ripe watermelons, Will set up his camera, had everyone grab a melon, and took this exceptional picture. Little Zeke Hames is seated in the center, and his brother Jack is seated at far right, with the watermelon above his head; both are Will's sons. (Courtesy Mark Hames.)

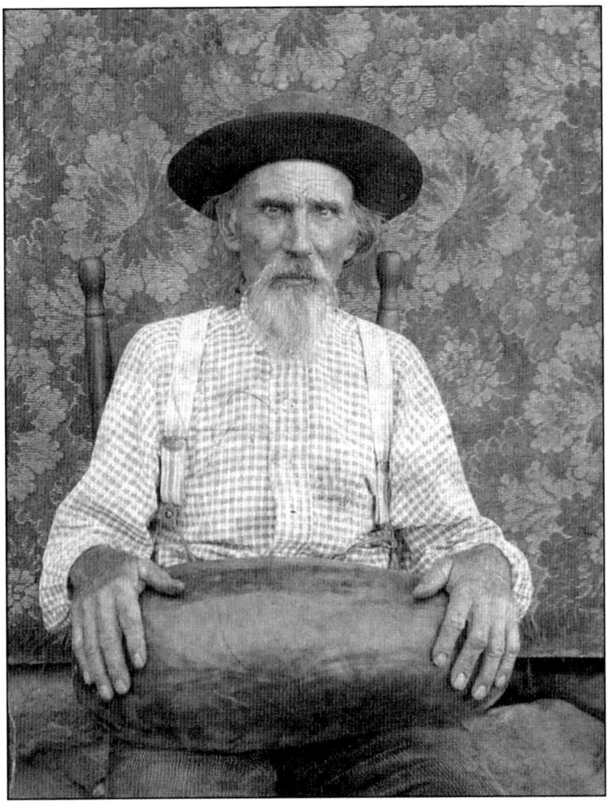

RICHARD HAMES. After the "watermelon shot" in the yard, Will hoisted his big camera and turned to the house to photograph Richard, his father. Will posed the old man in the parlor, with its attractive wallpaper as a background. Almost as an afterthought, Will placed one of the melons on his daddy's lap, which made the photograph all the more striking. (Courtesy Mark Hames.)

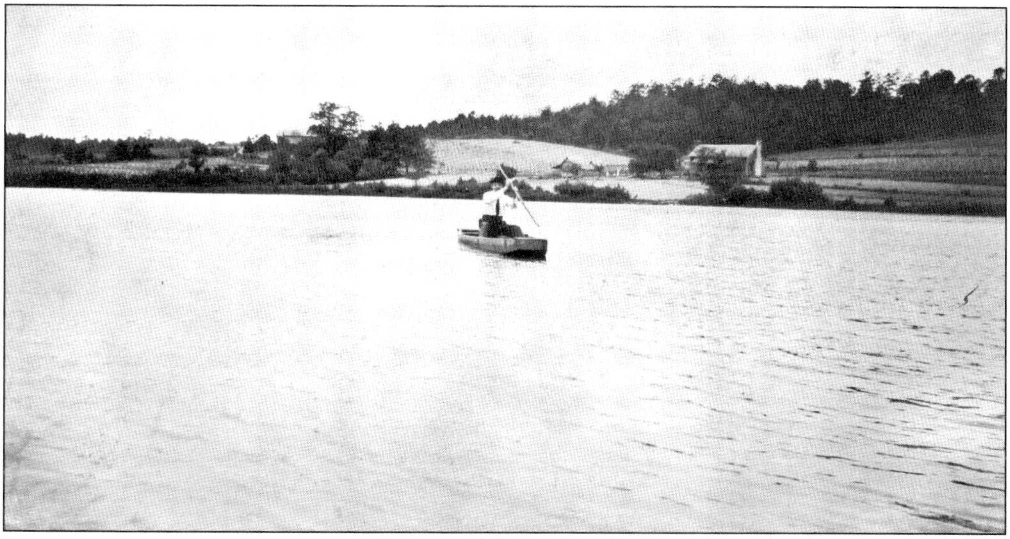

WILL ON THE WATER. One can only imagine how this photograph came about. One day Will was shooting the lovely farms across the river from Cliffside, a vista he had often admired. Sensing the shot lacked a foreground interest, he grabbed a nearby boat and became part of the scene. One can almost hear him barking to his assistant, "OK, Ned, shoot it! Now!" (Courtesy Mark Hames.)

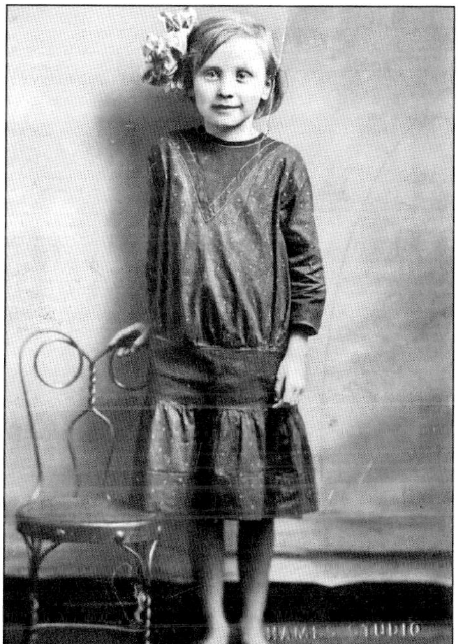

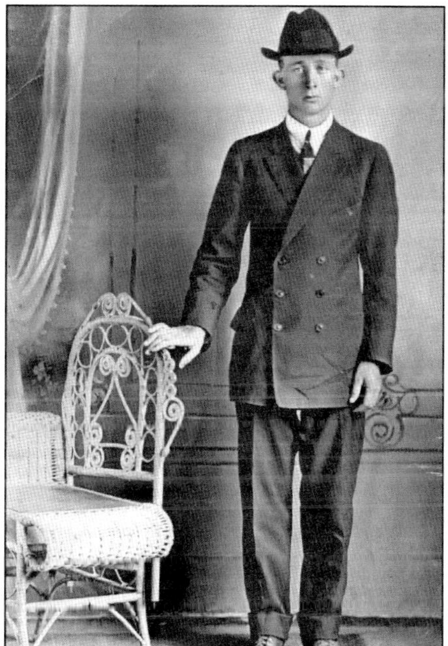

STUDIO WORK. Will Hames's livelihood came from his studio photography, recording portraits of individuals and families in and around Cliffside. At left is Lula Goode at age seven. At age 97, she still remembers the color of the dress she wore that day—two shades of red. At right, James Earnest Atkinson, a doffer in the spinning room, poses in his Sunday best. A doffer removes full bobbins of yarn from machine spindles and replaces them with empty bobbins. (Courtesy Lula Goode Humphries and Joyce Atkinson Hunter.)

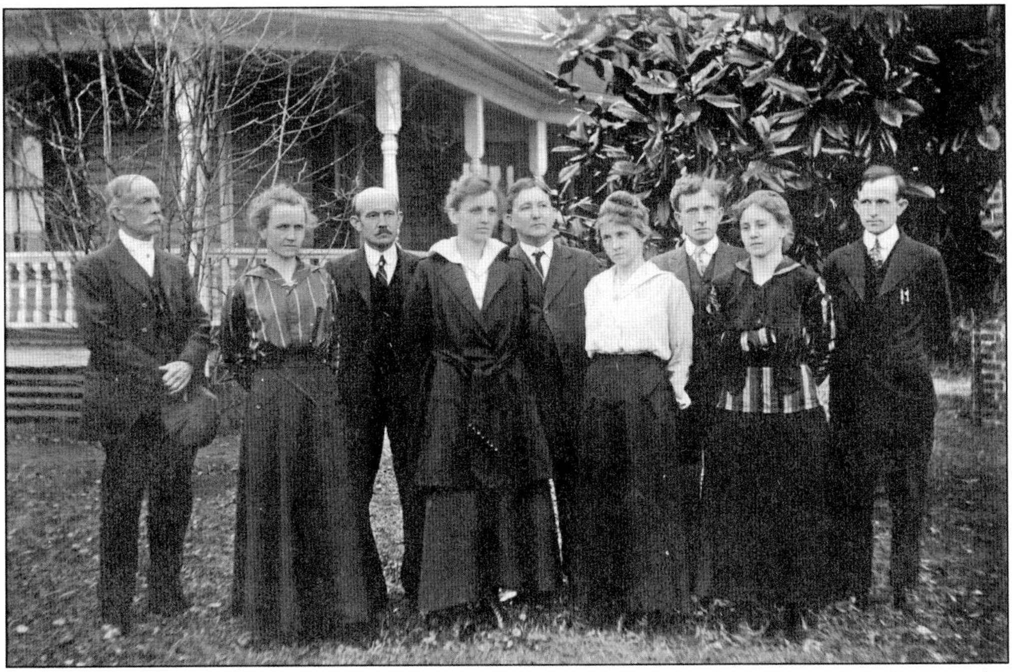

CHRISTMAS DAY, 1916. The sons and daughters of Raleigh Rutherford Haynes join him on the lawn of his big house in Cliffside. From left to right are R. R., Florence (née Jenkins), Robert, Charles, Sara (née Love), Walter, Grover, Eula (née Shull), and Virginia (née Caldwell). This was to be Raleigh's last Christmas. His death a little over a month later left the town in a turmoil of shock and sadness. (Courtesy Hazel Haynes Bridges.)

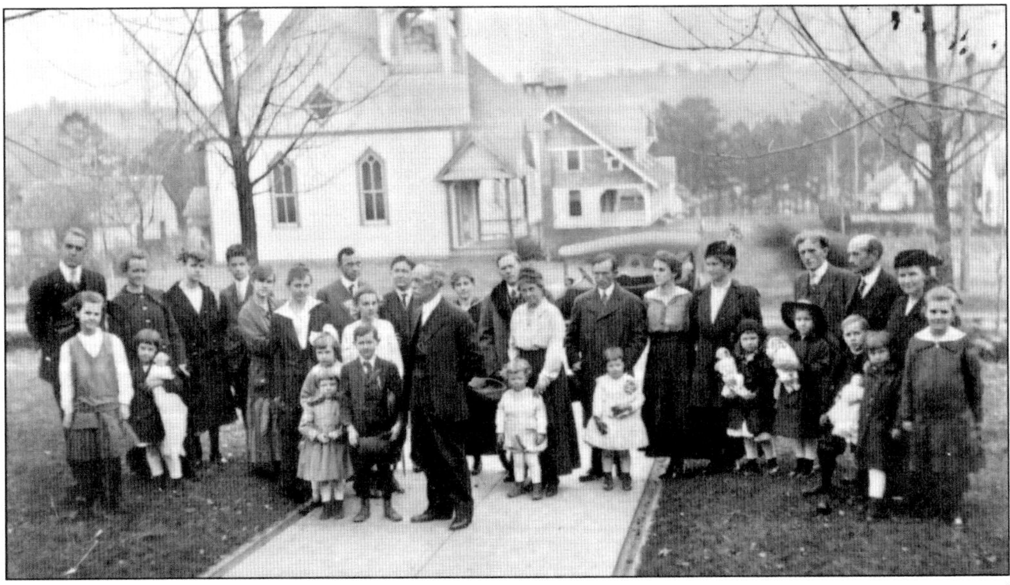

THE LARGER FAMILY. All the children, in-laws, and grandchildren posed as the camera pointed east from the Haynes house toward the old Presbyterian church. R. R., in the center foreground, looks off toward the horizon, as if his thoughts are on some future event. The second little girl to his left, holding the doll, is five-year-old Hazel Haynes, who provided many of the photographs in this book. (Courtesy Jim Haynes.)

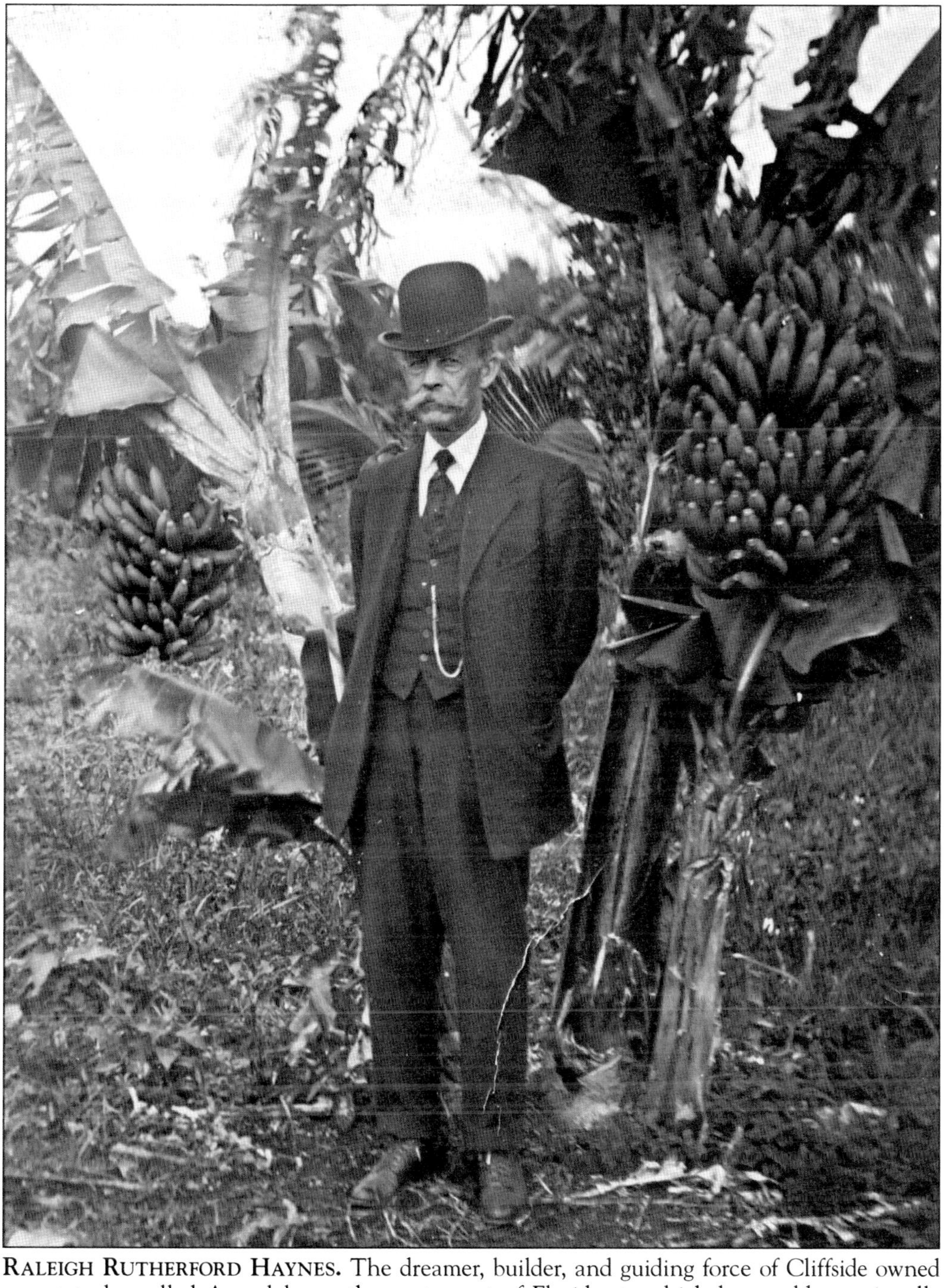

RALEIGH RUTHERFORD HAYNES. The dreamer, builder, and guiding force of Cliffside owned an estate he called Avondale on the west coast of Florida, to which he would occasionally retreat. This picture, taken late in his life beside one of his banana trees, shows a man who, even on holiday, was always ready for business. He fell ill shortly after Christmas 1916 and went to Florida to recuperate. He collapsed and died there on February 6 at the age of 65, and his body was returned by train to a grieving town. The service at the Baptist church and his burial in Cliffside Cemetery was attended by thousands. (Courtesy Myles Haynes Jr.)

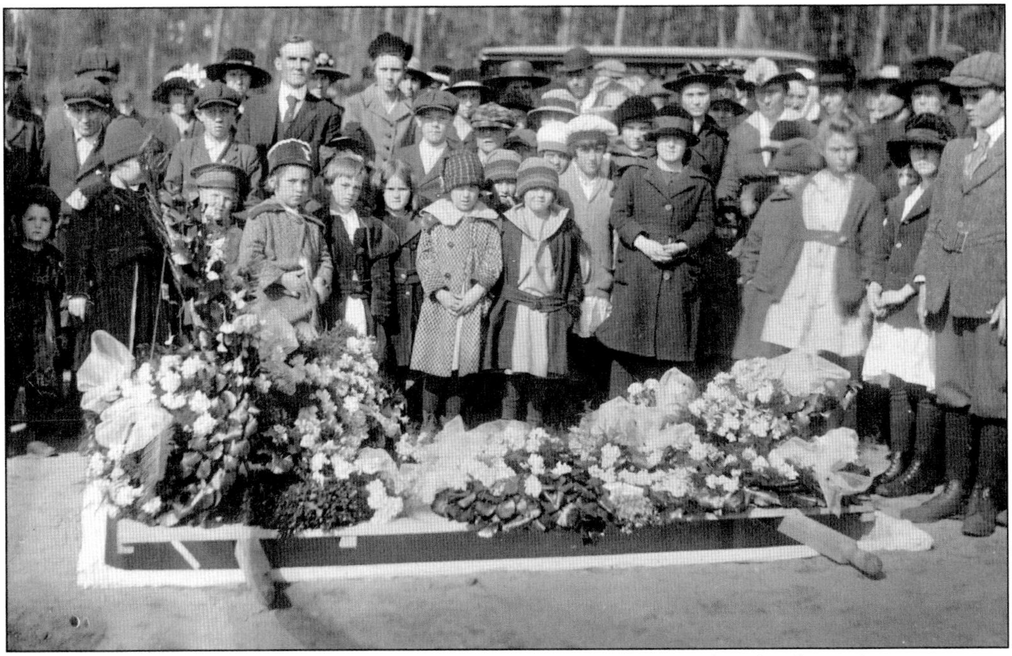

R. R. HAYNES'S BURIAL. The school, located beside the Baptist church where the service was held, let out for the occasion. Many of the children and some adults came to the cemetery before the funeral cortege arrived and stood respectfully at the grave site. The casket would be carried in a black hearse drawn by black horses. (Courtesy Jim Haynes.)

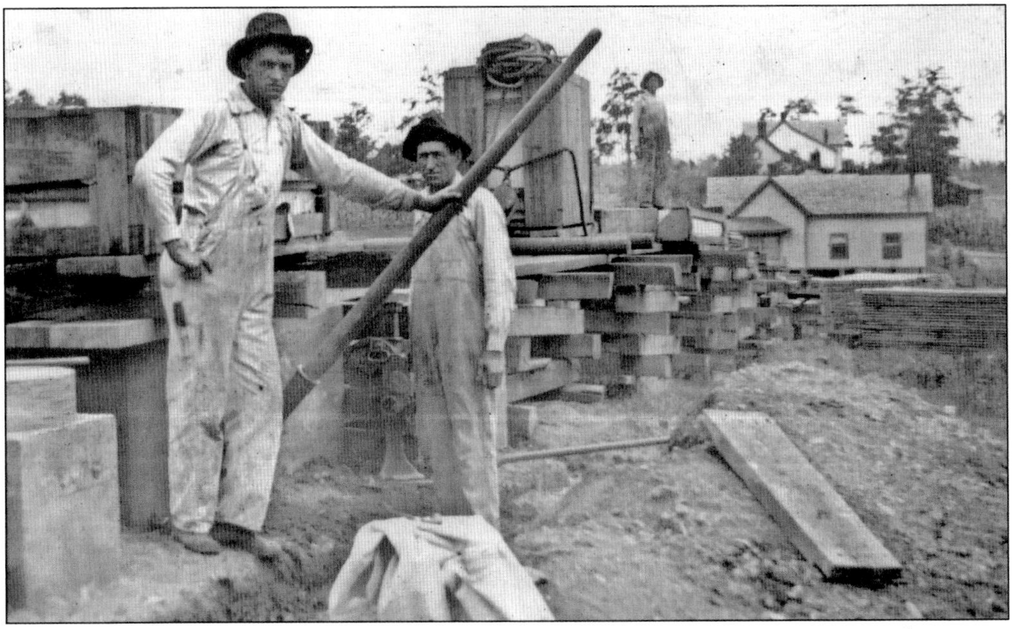

BUILDING THE TOMB. Raleigh Haynes was interred in a temporary grave site until a proper monument could be built. When summer arrived, railroad cars rolled up beside the cemetery. They were loaded with granite and the timbers needed to hoist the stone to its designated place in the graveyard. A work crew spent days creating the tomb for the great man and the remains of his two wives. (Courtesy Jim Ruppe.)

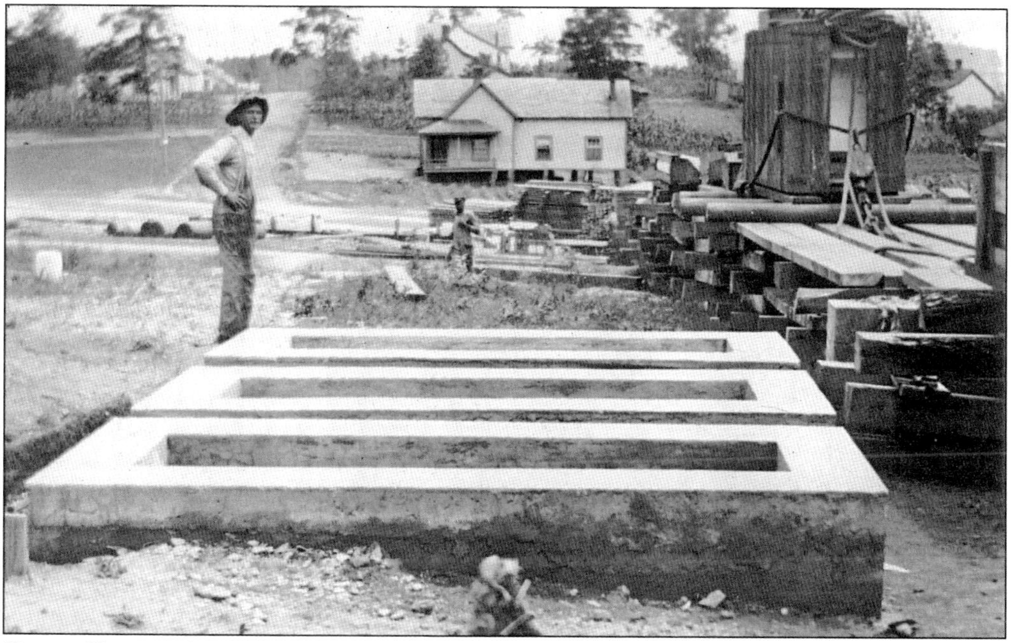

GRAVE VAULTS. Stonemason Press Freeman surveys the work site. The vaults are in place, and the great monument, attached to a block and tackle, has been drawn partway up the ramp on rollers. In the background across the road is the end of Academy Street. Above the crate on the right, the tops of houses on Church Street are visible. (Courtesy Jim Ruppe.)

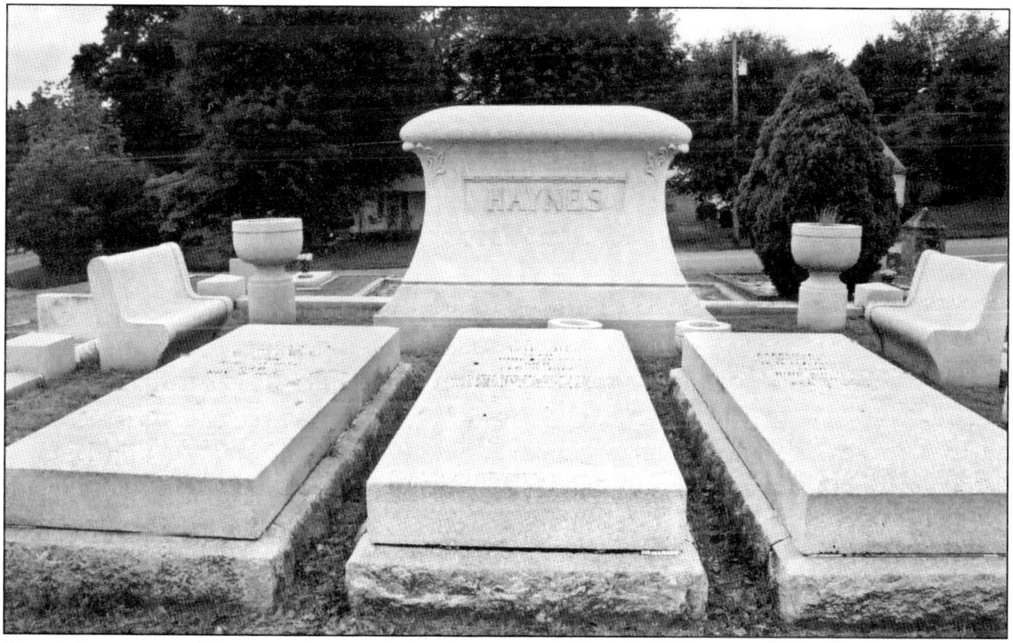

THE MONUMENT TODAY. U.S. senator Clyde R. Hoey said: "In February, 1917, from the soft, southerly, flowery shores of Florida, there came the message that Raleigh Haynes was no more, and that message was like the noise of the falling of a mighty oak in the stillness of the forest. . . . It brought the full realization that his passing would leave a place unfilled in our community life and in the circle of friendship." (Photograph by the author.)

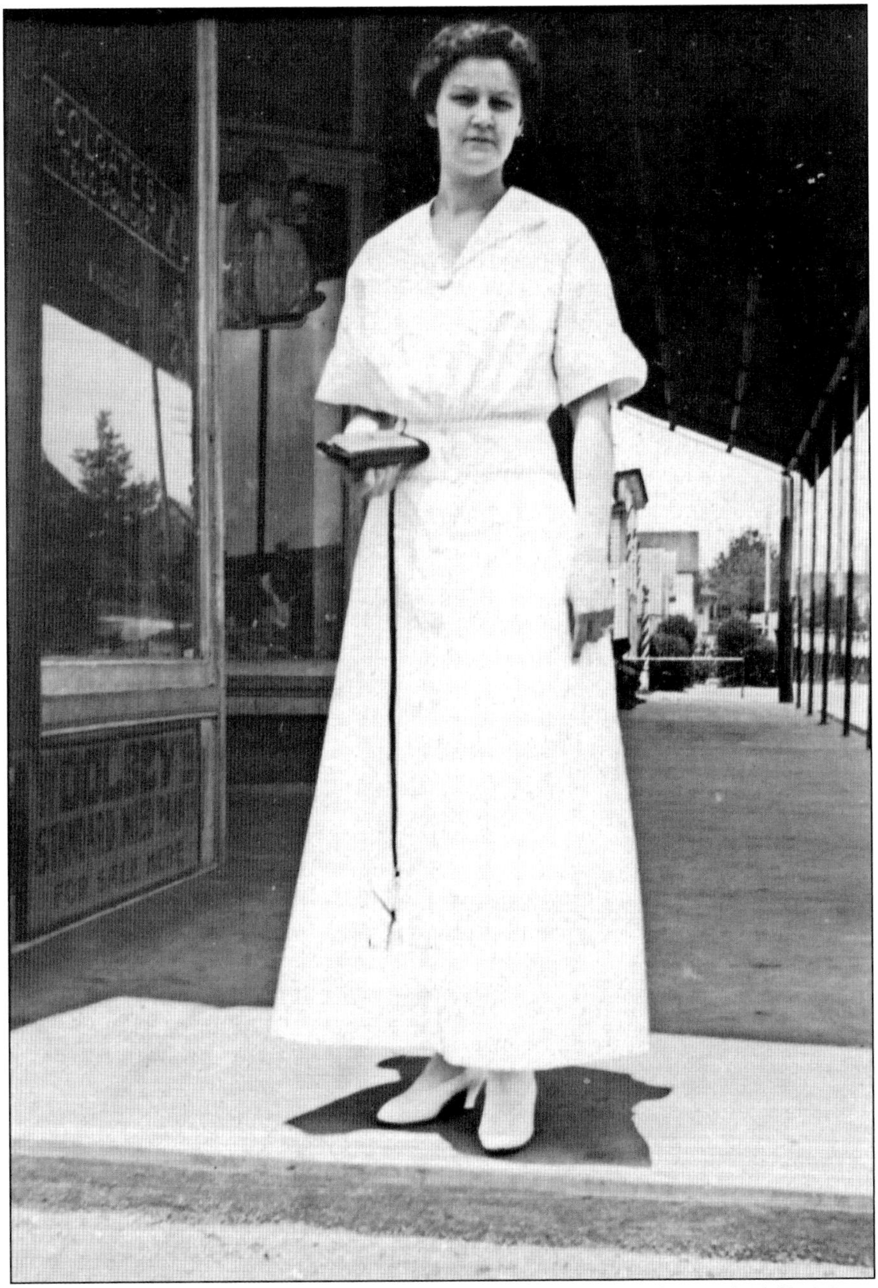

STREET SCENE, C. **1914.** Lela McFarland (1894–1988) is pictured in front of Cliffside's company store, where she worked. The scissors hanging from her waist were used to cut ribbon and fabric. There are signs in the window advertising Colgate Talc Powder and announcing that Woolsey's Standard Mixed Paint is sold here. One of her most fortunate customers was Maurice Hendrick, an up-and-coming executive at Cliffside Mills, for he won her hand in marriage. Their wedding ceremony was held atop Chimney Rock on the evening of July 3, 1917. They appeared the next day in an Independence Day parade. The groom's gift to the bride was a six-cylinder Buick, which they drove to a number of Western North Carolina resorts before returning to their home in Cliffside. (Courtesy Jim Ruppe.)

Two

THE MAMMOTH MILL OF CLIFFSIDE

The plant is equipped with 41,000 spindles and 1,500 looms. Seventy thousand yards of staple and fancy gingham are turned out daily. Nine hundred workers are employed in the plant. . . . The mill uses 7,500 bales of cotton each year.

–*The Charlotte News*, February 1917

Imagine the excitement, the pride, the changes, and the opportunities this great new enterprise provided for the people in this quiet agrarian area. The Industrial Revolution had indeed arrived. It provided jobs and money to people whatever their skills: brick makers, bricklayers, farmers, lumbermen, muleskinners, carpenters, or railroad men. Those without a tradesman's skill could provide food and services to the rest.

That excitement and pride never diminished through all the great years of Cliffside. Those viewing the mill at night, with its lights ablaze and the yellow glow from its hundreds of windows silhouetting the tiny figures inside, felt a strong sense of belonging and of ownership.

The mill and its fortunes were the center of the town's existence, and the company was never "they," it was "we." In the labor strife of 1934, "flying squads" of out-of-town strikers marched on the mill with little success. Cliffside's workers did not have all that much to complain about. For those who were down and out, management and their fellow citizens did all they could to help. They shared food, coal, and clothing. They were never exploited and learned never to exploit each other.

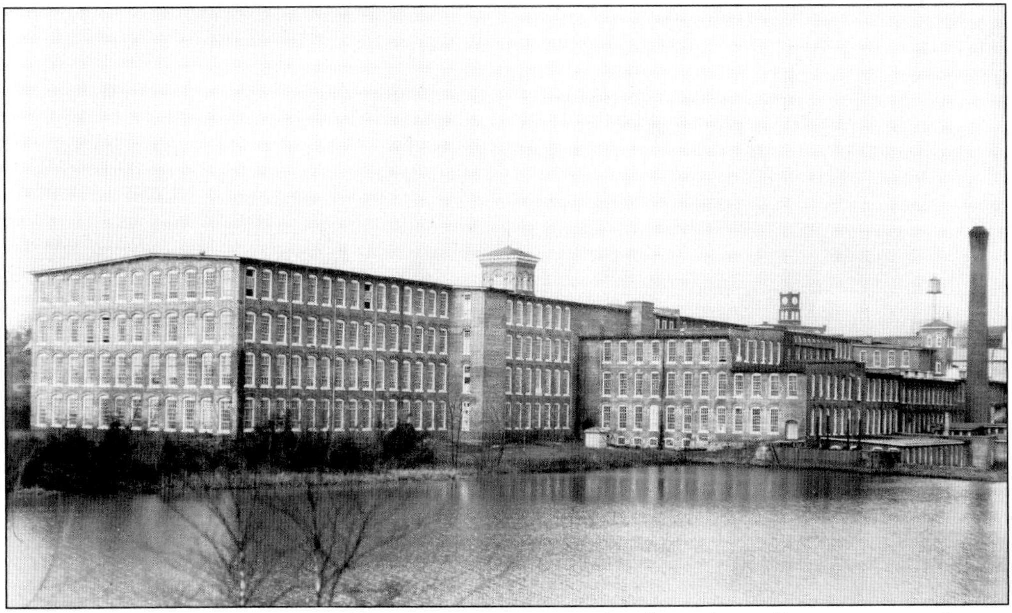

THE BIG MILL IN THE 1920S. There was a constant din from the mill, as spinning frames hummed and thousands of shuttles were smacked back and forth on looms weaving gingham cloth. No one minded the roar and clatter, for it was the welcome rhythm of people at work. Those living close by could feel the mill's vibrations in the floor of their houses. (Courtesy Hazel Haynes Bridges.)

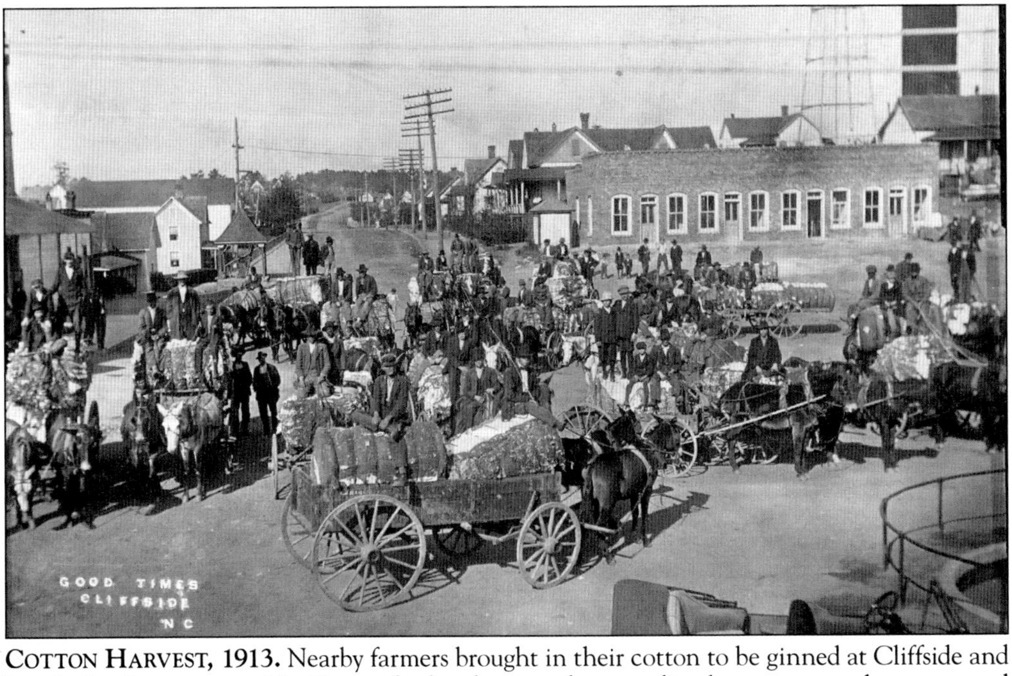

COTTON HARVEST, 1913. Nearby farmers brought in their cotton to be ginned at Cliffside and bought by the company. Mr. Haynes had a photographer standing by to capture the scene, and later made his favorite take—this one—into a postcard. For years, local farmers were the main source of the mill's raw cotton, supplemented by incoming rail shipments from other areas of the South. (Courtesy Hazel Haynes Bridges.)

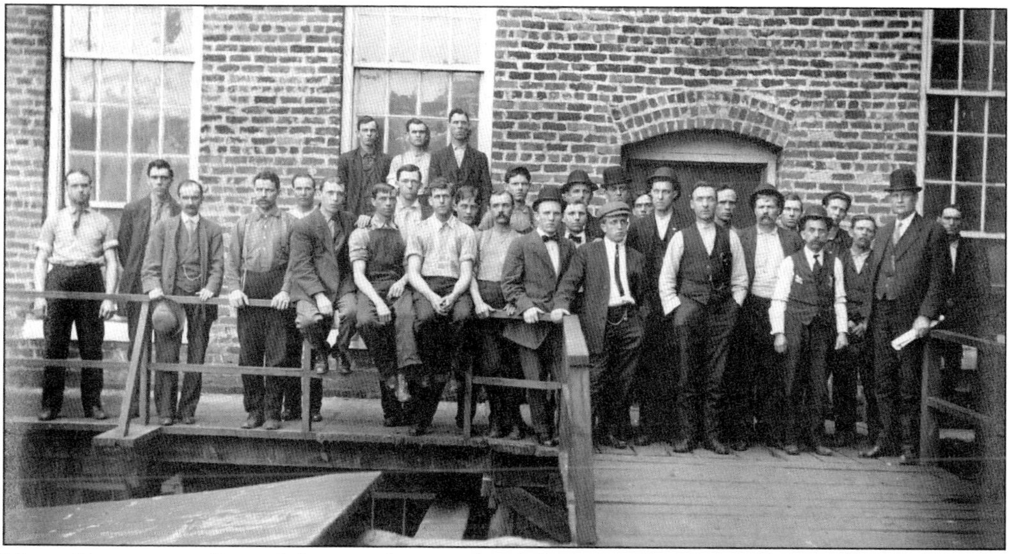

MILL OVERSEERS. From left to right are the following: (first row) Tom Callahan, Millard Watson, unidentified, Grover Padgett, Henry Taylor, Boyce Bridges Sr., unidentified, ? Boling, ? Boling, Lee Hightower, ? Boling, ? Harris, and Lee Packard; (second row) Claude McFarland, two unidentified men, Quince Lemmons, Charlie Lavender, two unidentified men, Tom Jenkins, Quinn Womick, and unidentified; (third row) unidentified, Furman Bland, unidentified, Rom James, and unidentified; (fourth row) unidentified, Tom Dedmond, and Avery Robinson. This photograph dates to c. 1912. (Courtesy Anne Cargill.)

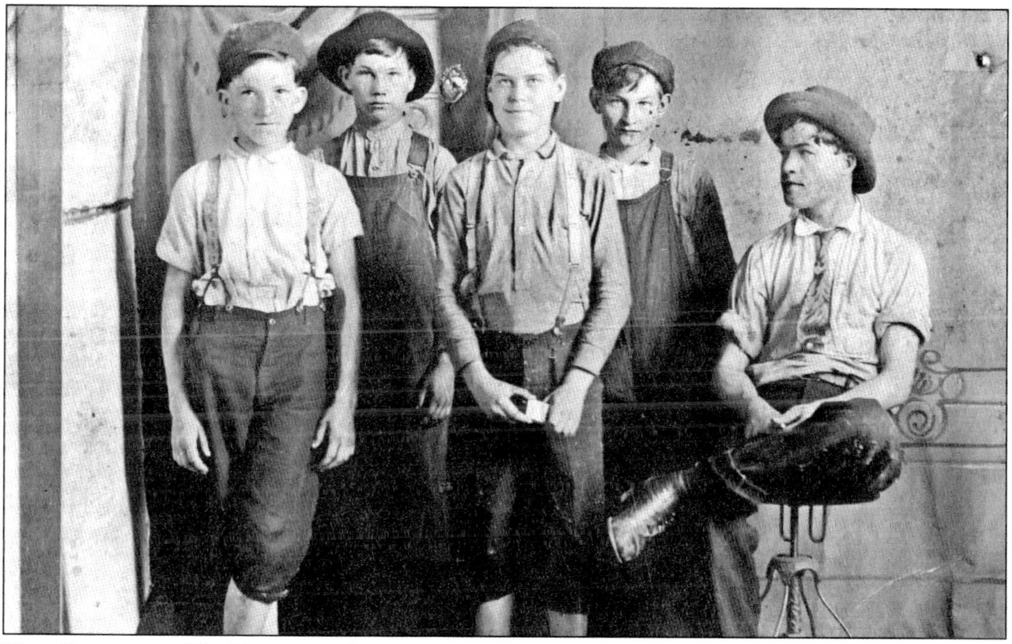

TOM CROW AND HIS DOFFERS. A spinning room group is seen here. The young boys' supervisor was Thomas Mack Crow, seated on the right and wearing a tie, hat, and shoes. None of the boys in the photograph have been positively identified. In those days, it was common for boys as young as nine to work in the mill, but the company strongly encouraged them to also attend school. (Courtesy Judson "Bud" Crow.)

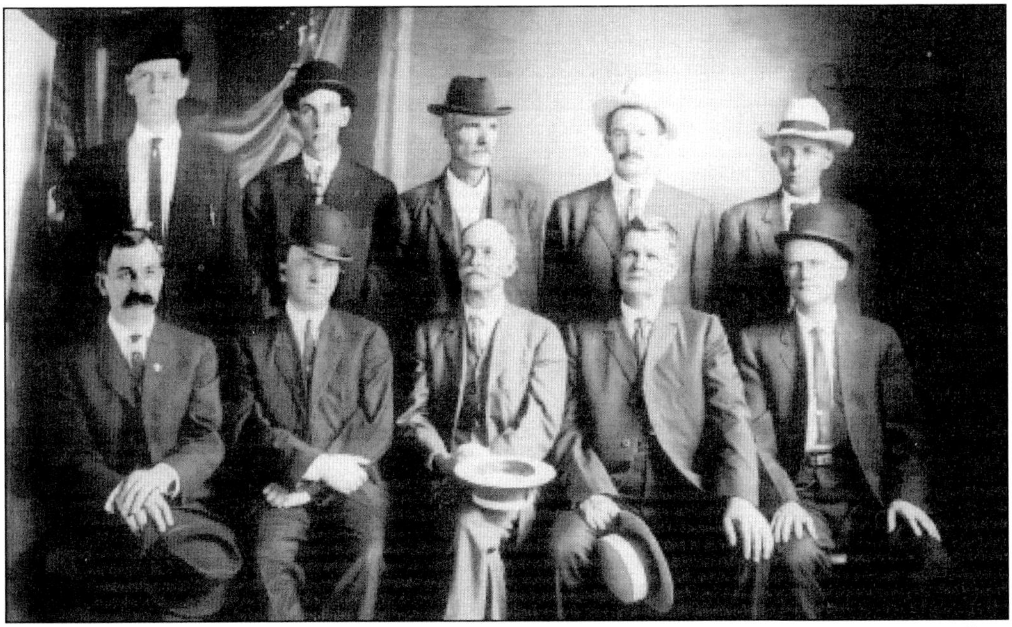

MR. HAYNES'S MEN. This group photograph is from about 1910. From left to right are (first row) Carey Blanton, machine shop; Rucker Bland, spinning room; Raleigh Rutherford Haynes, president and majority owner; William L. Packard, superintendent; and G. W. Tate, card room; (second row) Keesly Collins; Irvin Moore, dye house; Kelly Moore, overseer of grounds, village upkeep, and all construction; Plato C. Hawkins, weave room; and R. L. Wade, slasher room. (Courtesy Gene Shuford.)

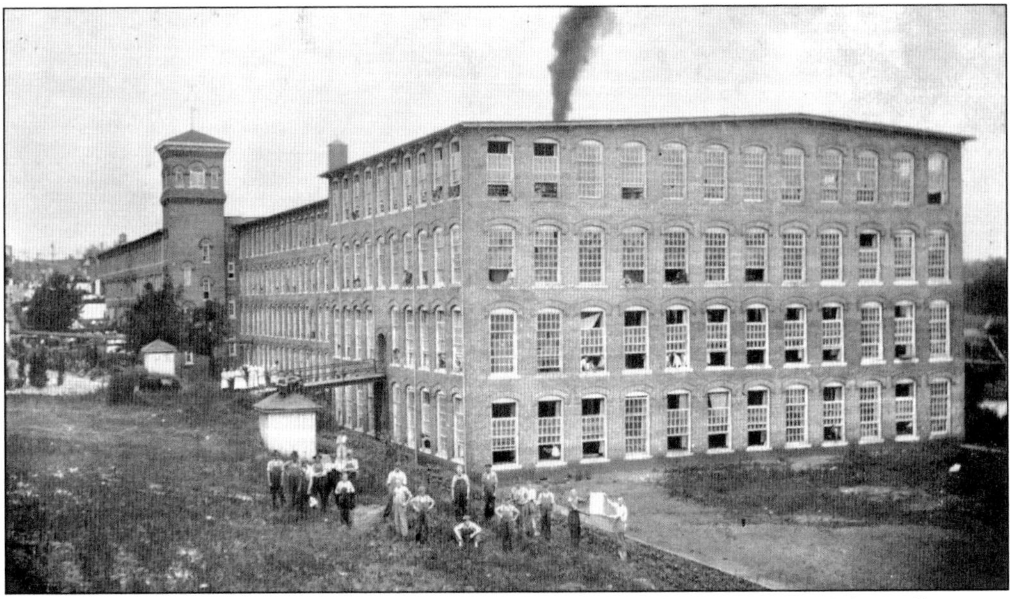

"HELLO FROM CLIFFSIDE." The southwest end of the manufacturing area of the mill is seen prior to construction of the finishing plant later in the 1920s. Note the two optimists on the right holding up a tiny sign to a camera about a hundred yards away. Maybe it says "Hello from Cliffside." The small white buildings contain hoses and firefighting gear. (Courtesy Hazel Haynes Bridges.)

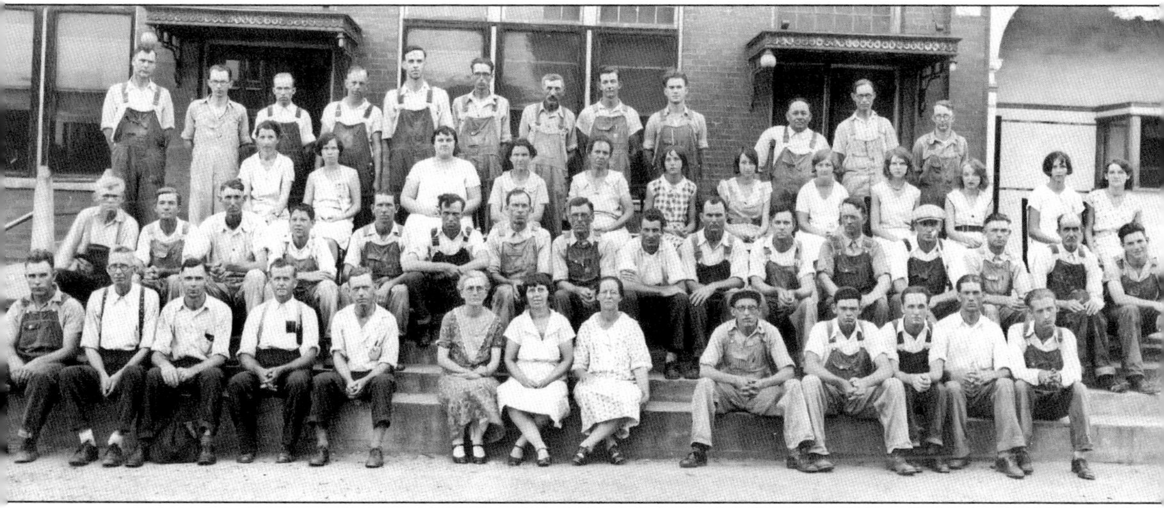

WEAVING, 1931. They were supervisors, weavers, loom-fixers, smash hands, filling boys, and sweepers, all assembled on the steps of the Memorial Building. From left to right are as follows: (first row) Tom Owensby, Quinn Womick, Clarence Watkins, Boyce Bridges, Robert Edward Prewitt Sr., unidentified, Mrs. Sid White, Carl Scruggs, Claude Jonas, Ishel Parris, Dwight Winn, and Dargin Harris; (second row) unidentified, Tom Crow, "Fat" Hardin, ? Hardin, unidentified, Broadus Cash, John Atkinson, Dick Scruggs, Horace White, Jess Stallings, Clyde Hardin, Cling Ellis, P. D. Causby, ? Jonas, unidentified, and Bill Ingram; (third row) two unidentified workers, Bess Hunt, four unidentified workers, Mrs. Tom Thrift, Ocie Lee Thrift, Janie Thrift, and two unidentified workers; (fourth row) Charlie Keeter, unidentified, ? Lancaster, Dargin Tate, Elija Harris, Clayton Scruggs, unidentified, Howard Packard, C. A. "Red" Hamrick, two unidentified workers, and Worth Womick. Just inside the building to the left was the town's library. At right was the movie theater, which in a few years would get a brand new front. (Courtesy Don Bailey.)

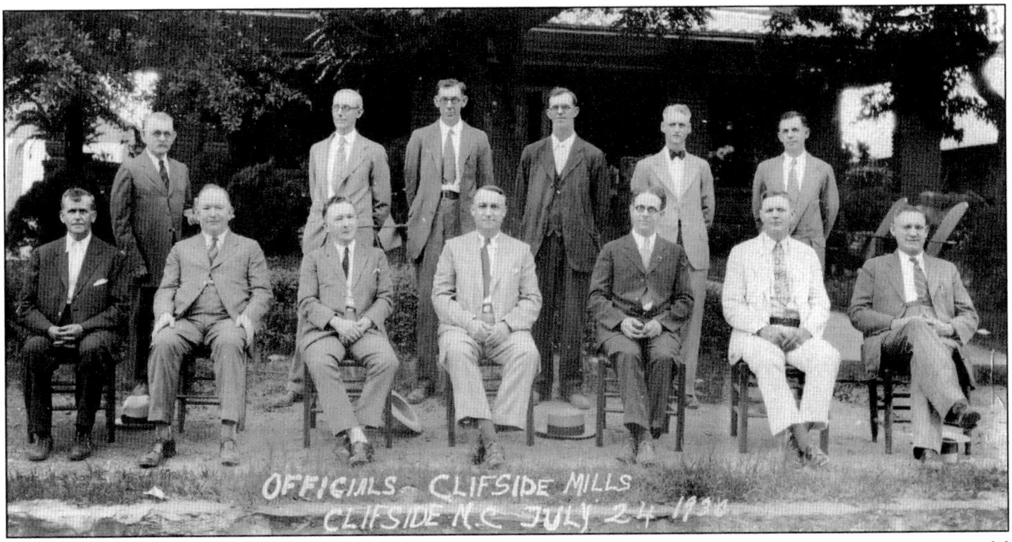

UPPER MANAGEMENT, 1930. Sometimes after formal meetings at the mill office, managers would be photographed in front of the general manager's house, adjacent to the square in Cliffside. From left to right are (first row) Boyce Bridges (weaving), Plato Hawkins (superintendent), Charles H. Haynes (president), Maurice Hendrick (general manager), George Shuford (office manager), Ed Carpenter (engineer), and unidentified; (second row) Carey Blanton (mechanic), D. C. Colvin (office), Irvin Moore (outside), Crawford Carpenter (outside), Ed Prince (dying-finishing), and Austin Roberson (slashing). (Courtesy Mack Hendrick.)

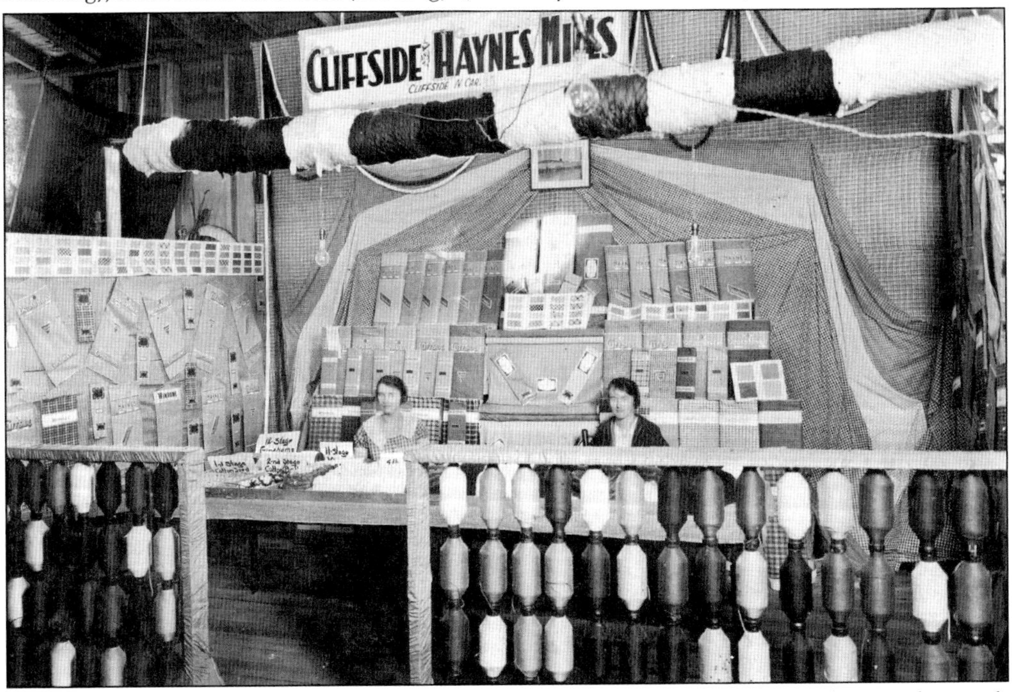

AT THE FAIR. In 1924, Cliffside and Haynes Mill (owned by the same company) teamed up with a booth in the Exhibit Hall at the Cleveland County Fair in Shelby, where they demonstrated the various stages of the cloth-making process. On the walls are assorted styles of gingham with labels like Cliffside, Haynes, Winsome, Roselle, Rompaway, and Broad River. (Courtesy Jane Winn.)

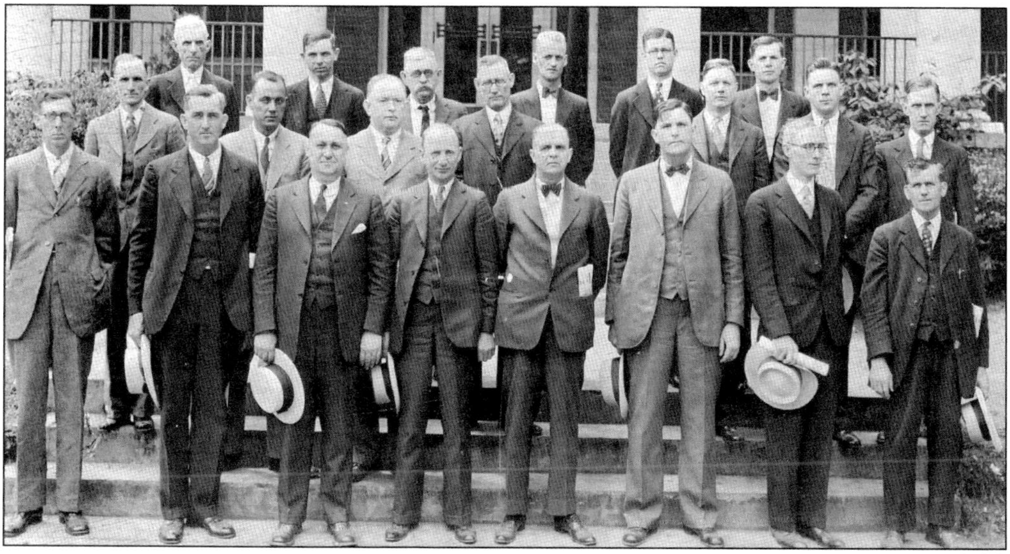

DEPARTMENT HEADS, 1930S. Occasionally the Cliffside supervisory staff would meet in Greensboro, where Cone Mills was headquartered. From left to right are (first row) Irvin Moore, Tom Biggerstaff, Maurice Hendrick, Jim Frye, R. L. Wade, Dave Hawkins, D. C. Colvin, and Boyce Bridges Sr.; (second row) George Silvers, Jim Goode, Plato Hawkins, Locke Thompson, Grady Rollins, Gene Laughridge, and Willie Winn; (third row) John Watkins, Ed Carpenter, Carey Blanton, Ed Prince, Charles Metcalf, and Austin Roberson. (Courtesy Anne Cargill.)

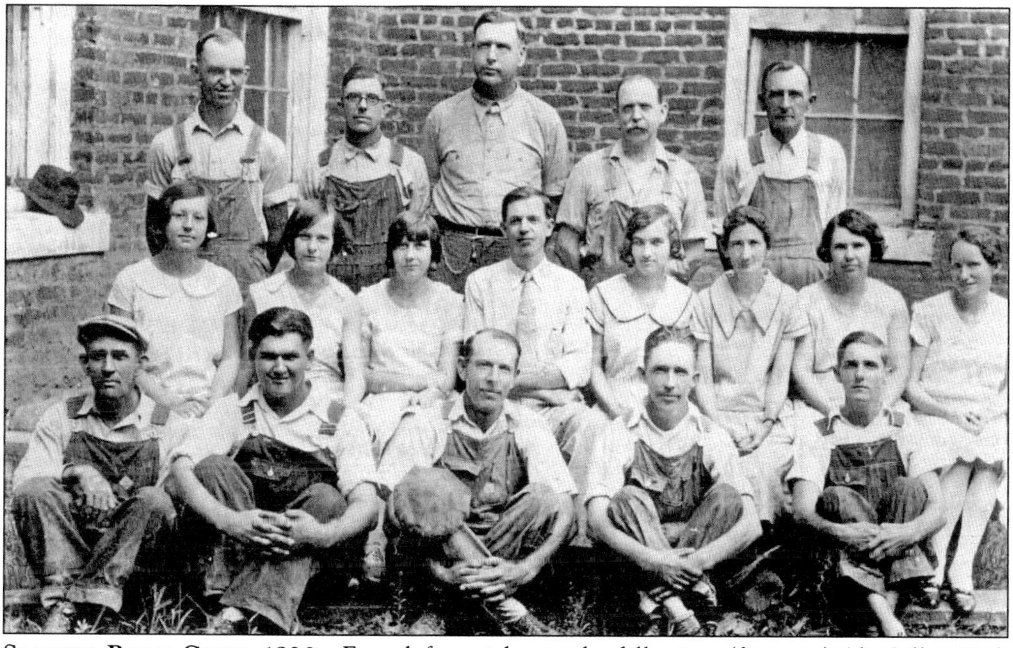

SLASHER ROOM CREW, 1930S. From left to right are the following: (first row) Abe Jolley, Pink Honeycutt, Arthur Rhymer, Earl Brooks, and Wesley McMurray; (second row) Mae Stephens Scruggs, Selma Price Davis, Gladys Stephens Kirby, Austin T. Roberson (overseer), Mabel Harrill, Lovinia Campbell, Sue Hames Waters, and Clara Atkinson; (third row) Jim Callahan, Oliver Stephens, Claude Scruggs, Will Hames, and Jim Packard. Will Hames was the town photographer in earlier days. (Courtesy Ben Humphries.)

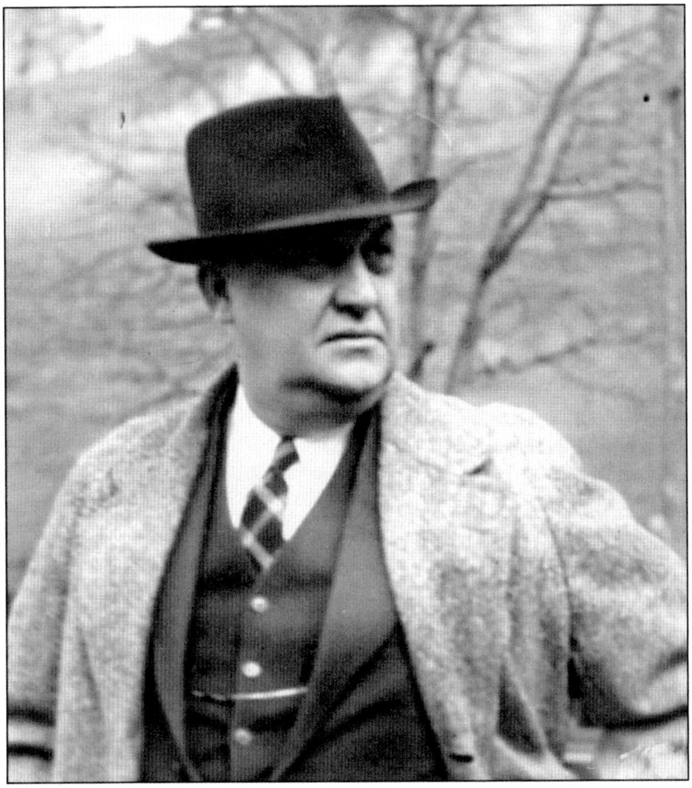

MAURICE HENDRICK (1886–1957). A Shelby native and graduate of North Carolina State College, Maurice was 24 when he began at the mill in 1910. He worked at various jobs and, at the end of World War I, became the first superintendent of the Haynes Mill at Avondale. In 1921, he assumed the same role at Cliffside and progressed to general manager, then president. He retired in 1951. (Courtesy Mack Hendrick.)

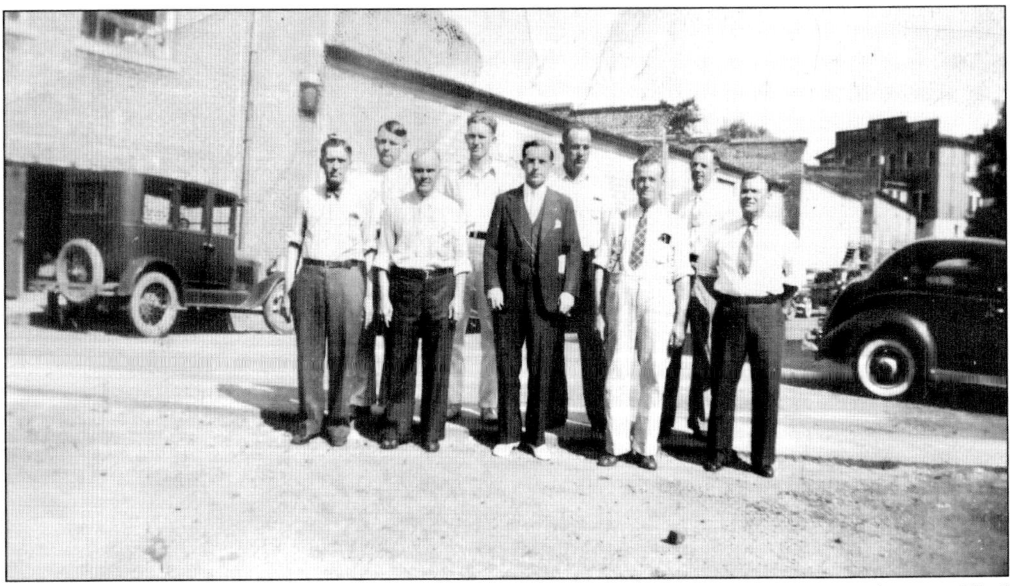

SUPERVISORS, LATE 1930S. The white-walled buildings behind the men are warehouses filled with hundreds of bales of cotton waiting to be processed and made into cloth. From left to right are as follows: (first row) J. P. "Jake" Hill (spinning), John Talbert (assistant supervisor), E. T. Combs (superintendent), Boyce Bridges Sr. (weaving), and Fred Swing (finishing); (second row) Dudley Brown (carding), James Tinkler (dying/bleaching), Jim Goode (machine shop/mechanical), and Austin Roberson (slashing). (Courtesy Hazel Haynes Bridges.)

BOYCE BRIDGES SR. His full name was Doctor Samuel Boyce Bridges, although he was not a doctor. Boyce was born in Burnt Chimney (now Forest City) in 1882. He and his wife, Retter Daves Bridges, a Caroleen girl, moved to Cliffside in 1904. He worked 40 years in the mill, mostly in the weave room. Their children were Robert, Ruby, Mabel, Paul, Inez, Wytle, and Boyce Jr. (Courtesy Hazel Haynes Bridges.)

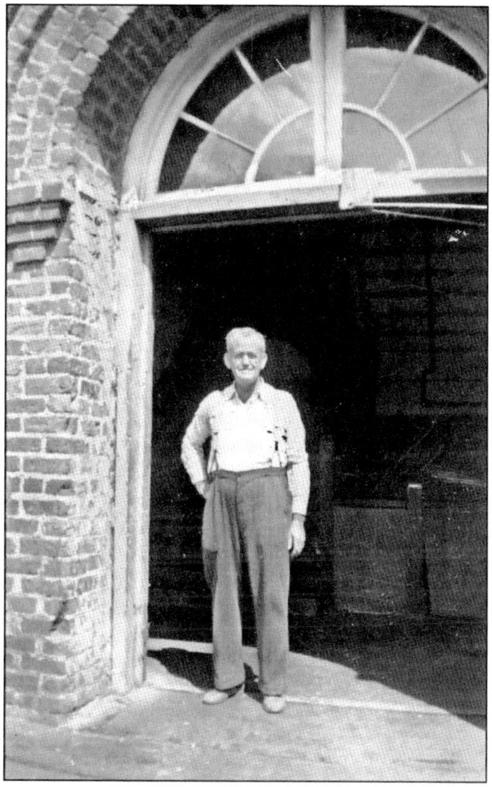

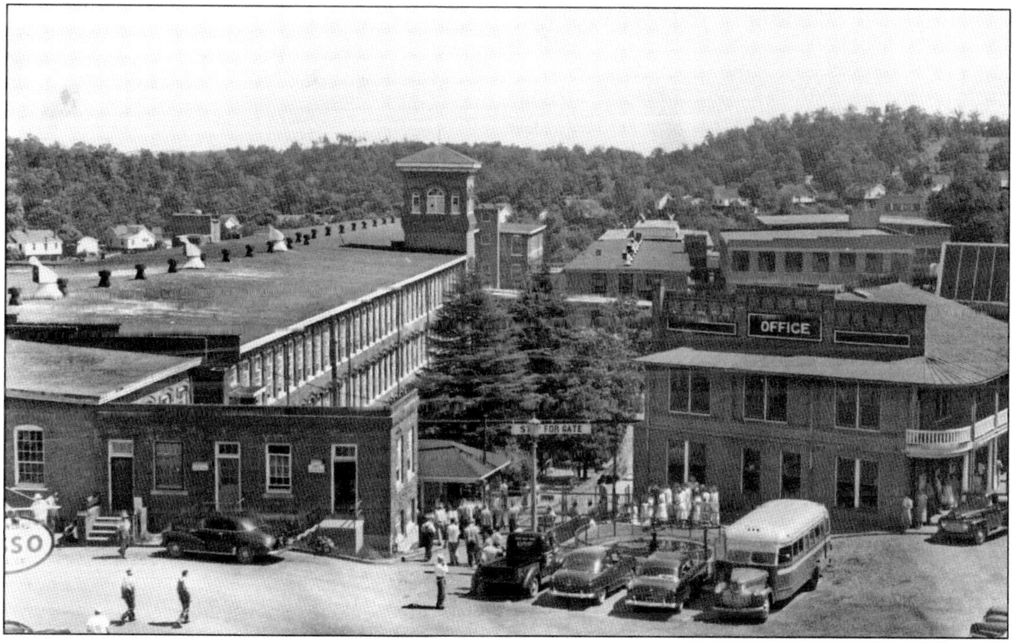

THROUGH THESE PORTALS. The main entrance to the mill is where employees would file in for the day shift at 7 a.m., the second shift at 3 p.m., and the third shift at 11 p.m. Those working in departments where the air was thick with drifting fiber would leave the mill with their hair and clothing spotted with bits of cotton, hence the name "lint heads." (Courtesy Sam Davis.)

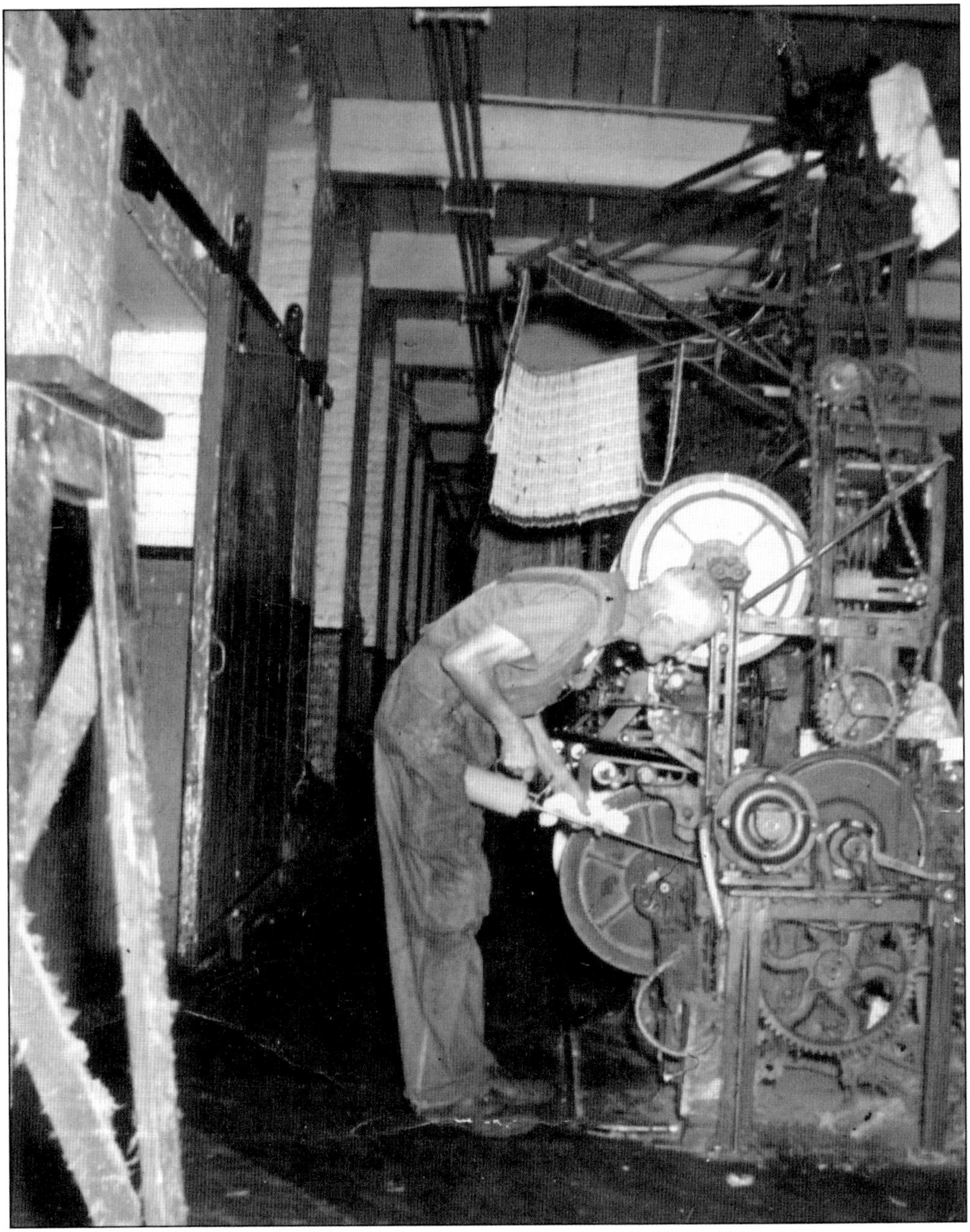

JAMES BOSS SCRUGGS. This was Scruggs's last night on the job in 1953. He was retiring at 66, probably after having worked at Cliffside for 50 years or more. Despite the deafening noise and the dust and lint they breathed, many were able to stay in the mill to a much older age. The Jacquard loom he is oiling may be older than Boss. Jacquards were an example of early automation. The white nearly square object above him is the edge of a stack of punch cards. They were strung together forming a loop that the loom "read" to produce intricate patterns and text on towels, such as "U.S. Navy" or "Statler Hotel." During World War II, a large portion of Cliffside's output was for the military. Navy towels were dark blue letters on white cotton; army towels were khaki with no lettering. (Courtesy Ruby Bailey.)

Three

Downtown

It is noon in the village. Factory whistles are blowing. People are scurrying across busy corners and especially is the "village center" swarmed with traffic. The village folk are hurrying to dinner, for to them it is always "dinner.". . . they pass bits of conversation about the evening plans of entertainment—and so to work. And the village lazes into the afternoon.

–F. C. Thompson, May 1934

Changing time was Cliffside's rush hour, a vital time for the stores and shops. Second-shift workers came to town early to conduct their business and do their shopping, and many first-shift hands, getting out at three, would linger awhile to do the same.

Shortly after noon, the hands would begin to arrive. They would sit on any available shady surface: the dock in front of the hardware store, car fenders and running boards, the Memorial Building steps, or the fence rail around the fish pond. They would visit, gossip, enjoy a smoke, cut up, act the fool, and tell jokes and lies. From the laughter and the banter, it could be surmised this was the happiest part of their day. They would see what was playing at the show, check out the new merchandise in Jackson's window, look through the magazines in the drug store, have a prescription filled, get a haircut, and maybe buy themselves a "dope" (soft drink). Changing time was their town meeting, daily paper, fraternity, and support group. This interaction and bonding of these wonderful people formed the heart and soul of Cliffside.

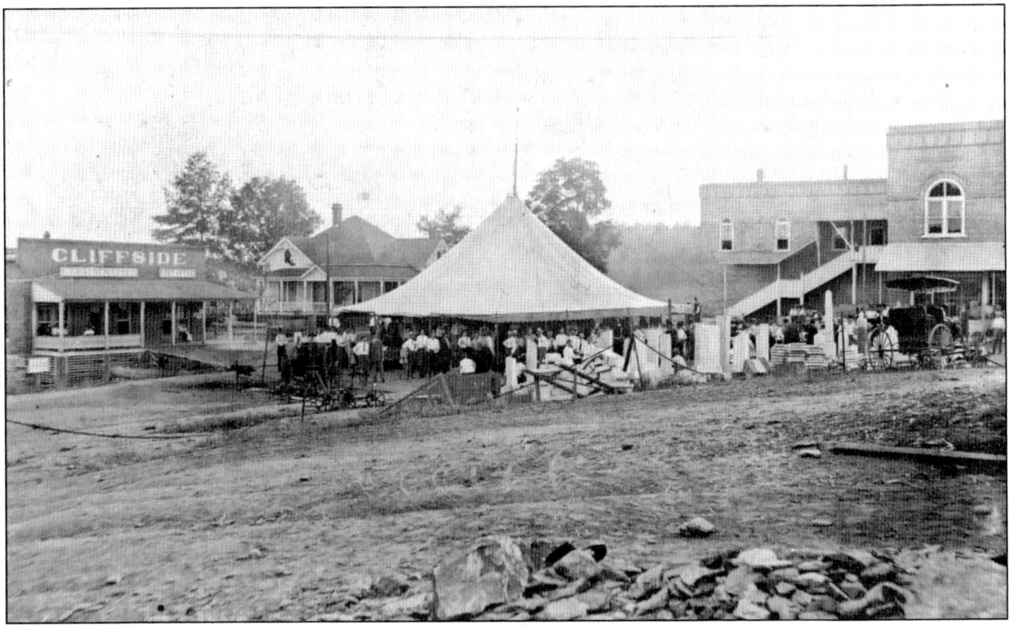

Revival Tent. When automobiles were rare, the square was used for a number of things—concerts, parades, and, in this case perhaps, a revival. The year is uncertain, but it was after 1909, when the store building at right was erected. The general manager's house can be seen beyond the tent. An interesting feature is the headstones and blocks of marble lined up along the side of the tent. (Courtesy Hazel Haynes Bridges.)

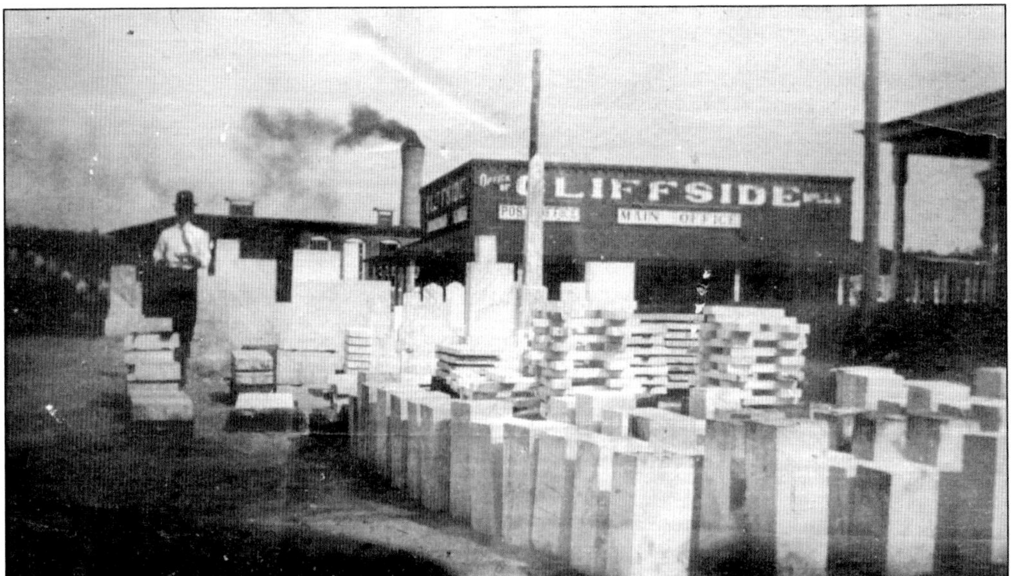

Marble Mystery. This is another angle from the same day. In the street between the general manager's house at right and the store building are more stacks and rows of stones. If these are gravestones, why are there so many, and why in the center of town? Was there a plan afoot to build a community building using some of this material, a plan possibly thwarted by Mr. Haynes's death? (Courtesy Hazel Haynes Bridges.)

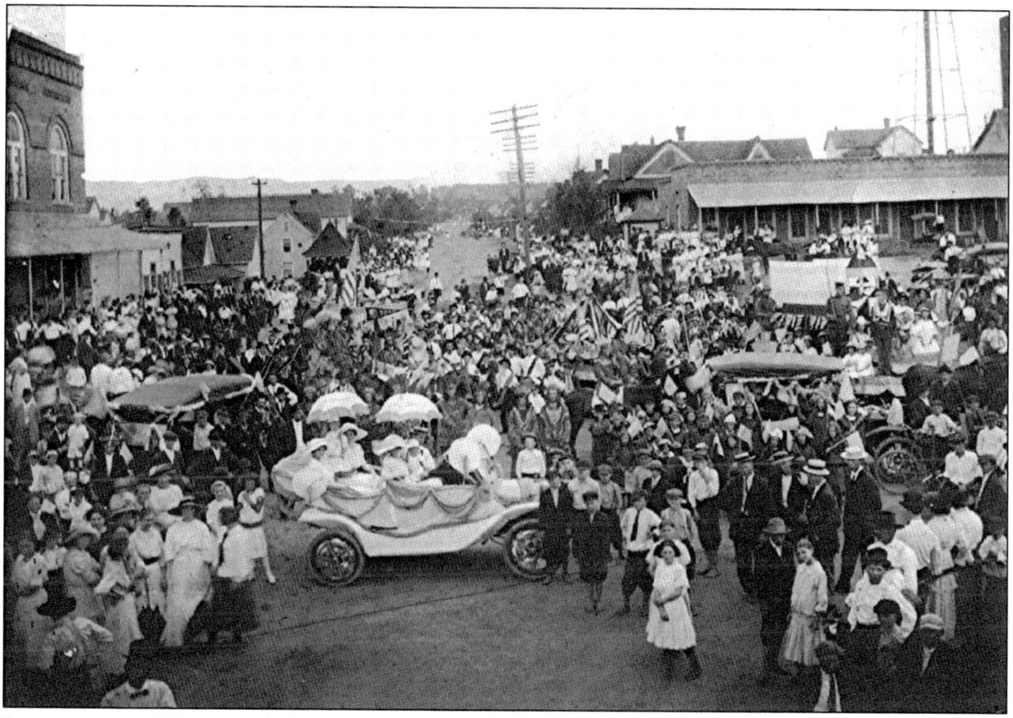

JULY 4, 1914. The parade had just ended. Celebrants still lined the route far up North Main. There were decorated autos and buggies, and in the center of the throng, under the American flag, is the float of the Improved Order of Red Men, whose members are dressed like Native Americans. It was quite a crowd and a very big day for the proud people of Cliffside. (Courtesy Mary Quinn Womick Prewitt.)

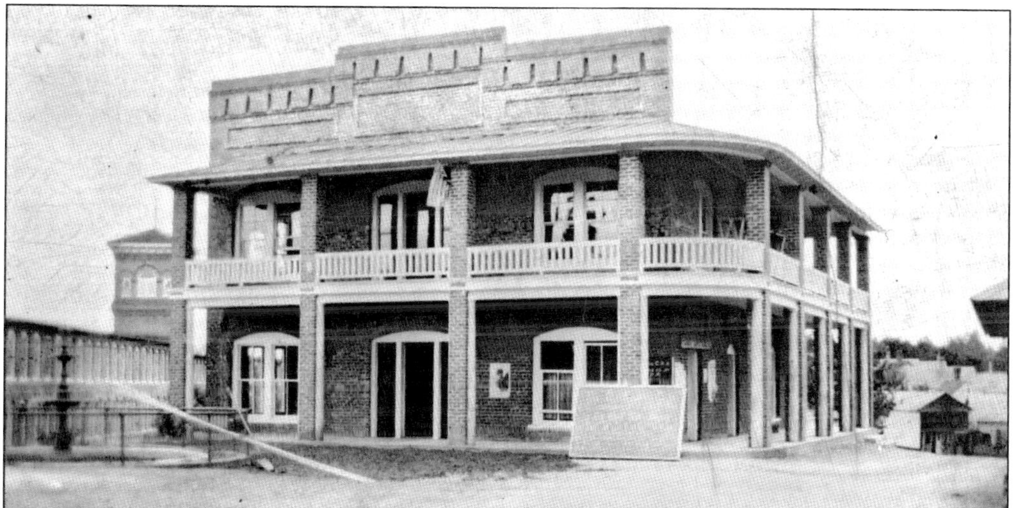

SKYSCRAPER. The little office building's renovation to a two-story colossus is nearly complete. Scraps of wood lie about, windows and doors are agape, and a large chalkboard leans on a post with a notice to all. Down South Main Street on the extreme right sits the old engine house, with one of the Cliffside Railroad's old steam engines partly visible. The year of this photograph is unknown. (Courtesy Hazel Haynes Bridges.)

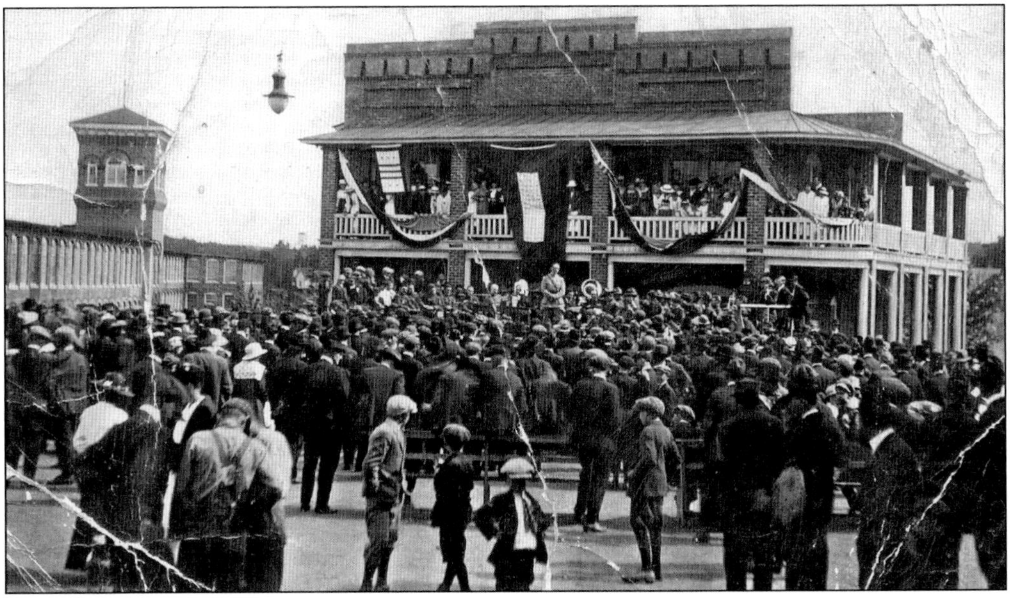

CONCERT. John Phillip Sousa once came to Cliffside, but no one knows when and no account of the event has surfaced. This may be the day. Shown is a military band, but the man standing is not Sousa. He may be Barron P. Caldwell (1882–1952), who after serving in the World War in France, was appointed superintendent of Cliffside School. Caldwell was the husband of Raleigh Haynes's daughter Virginia. (Courtesy Don Bailey.)

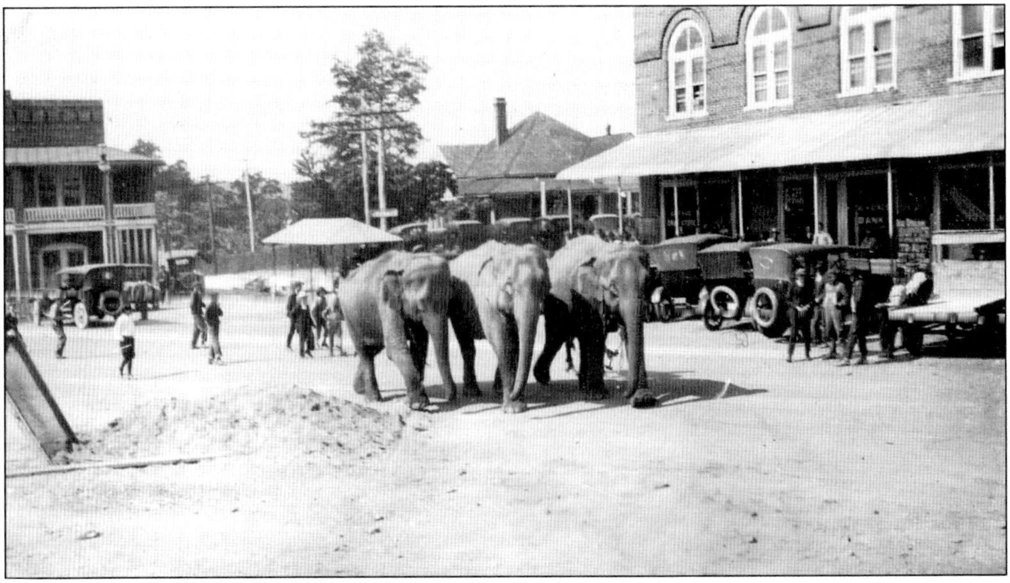

PACHYDERMS. "I remember those rascals," said Lula Goode Humphries. A circus was in Cliffside around 1913, when she was five or six. She was scared to death; she had only seen cats and dogs, nothing like an elephant. "One reached over into the fish pond with its trunk and got a drink of water. All the kids thought that was really something." (Courtesy Hazel Haynes Bridges.)

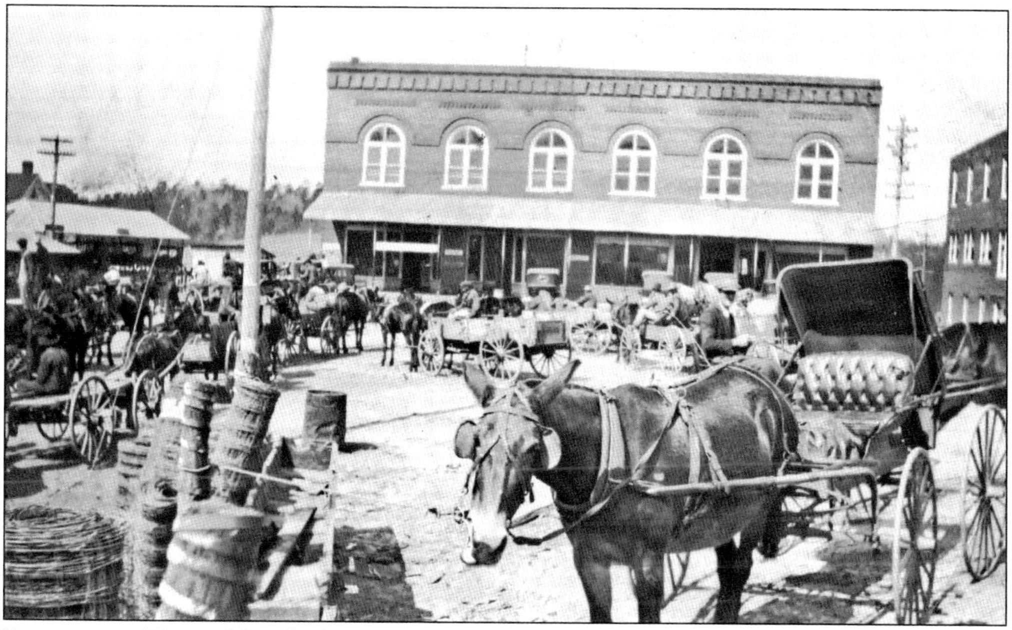

FARMERS IN TOWN. Usually farmers would come to town individually for their supplies or to bring the yield of their crops. But once a year in the spring, the company's tenant farmers all came on one day to get their fertilizer and seed to begin planting. Here they wait to get in line. Note the rolls of wire fencing in the foreground. This picture was taken about 1920. (Courtesy Hazel Haynes Bridges.)

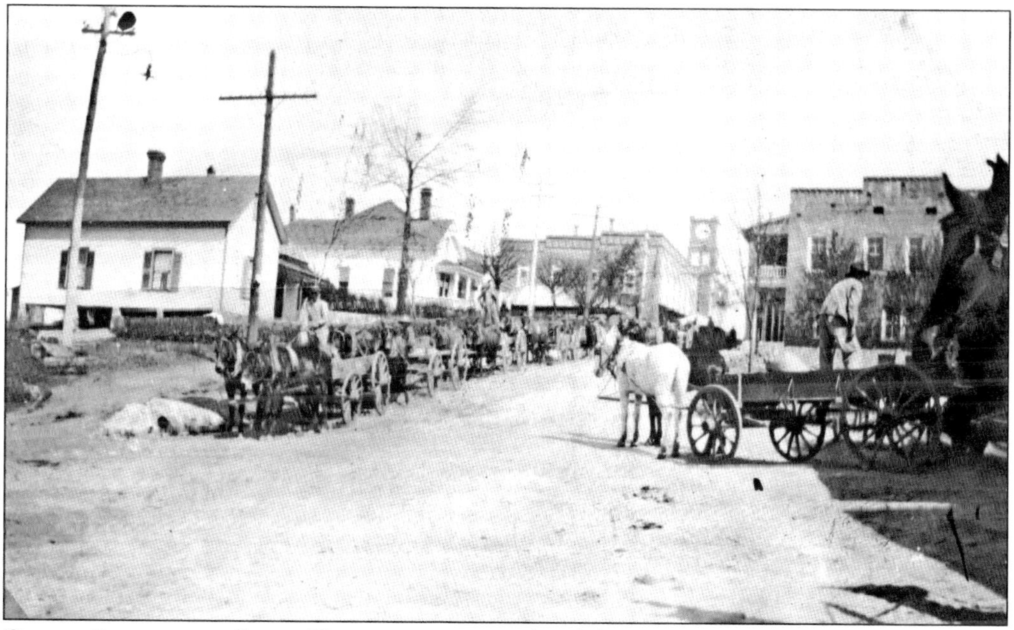

OTHER END OF THE LINE. This is a reverse angle of the photograph above. The wagons are lined down South Main Street, the drivers patiently waiting their turn to pick up the seed, fertilizer, and "sody" (nitrate of soda) they will need to start a new cotton crop. It is likely the company provided these essentials at no cost for a share of the farmers' profits. (Courtesy Hazel Haynes Bridges.)

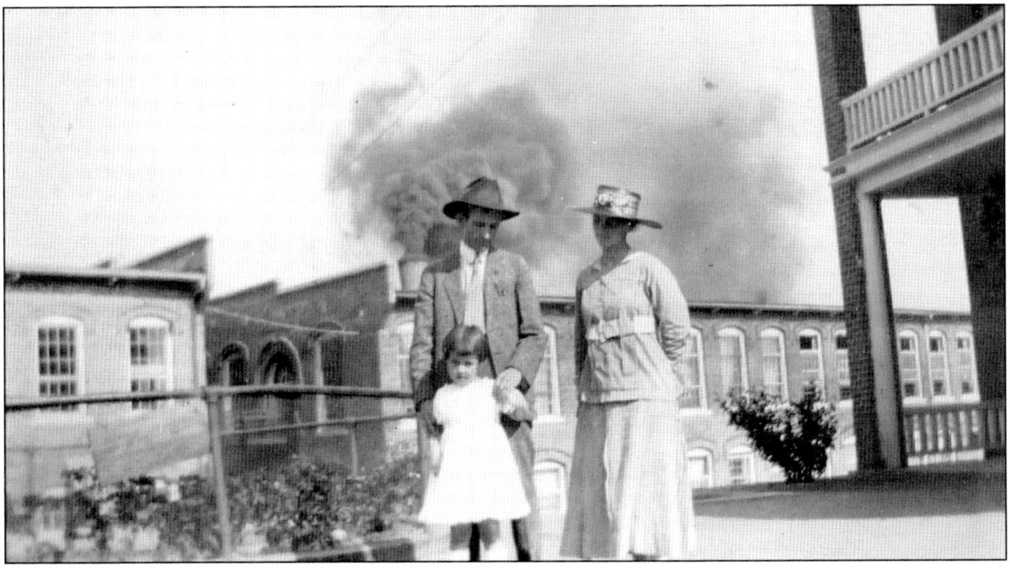

A Place to Pose. It was rare that a photographer would turn down a shot of someone at the town fountain, especially if the mill's smokestack was belching a big black cloud in the background. This is Grover and Ina Haynes and their daughter, Hazel, c. 1919. Years later, Ina would write a biography of R. R. Haynes, her father-in-law. (Courtesy Hazel Haynes Bridges.)

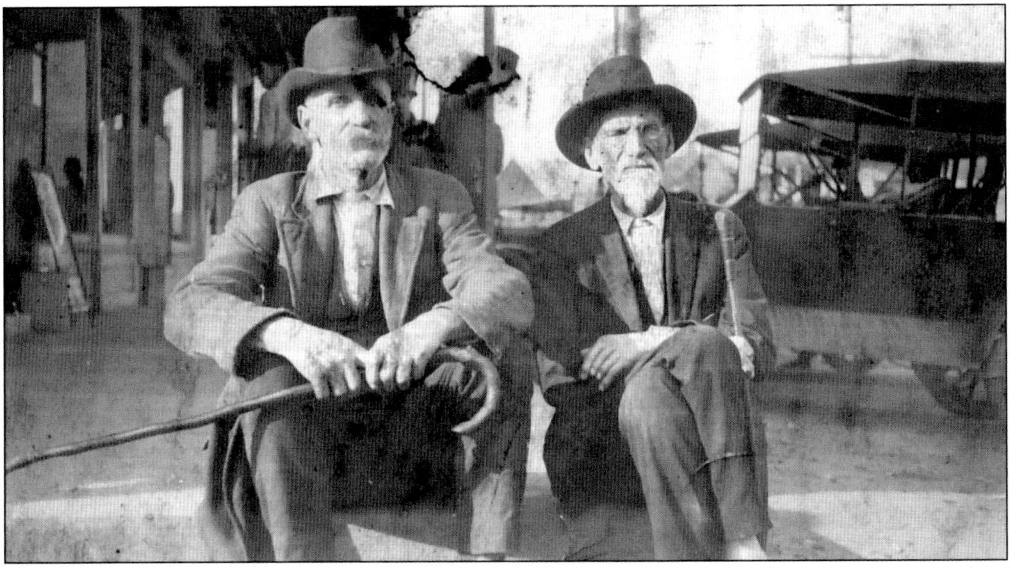

Buddies. Holding their walking canes, these old-timers are taking the sun at the end of Cliffside's store building around 1918. The man at left is thought to be John C. McCraw (1845–1923). The other man may be John's older brother Chesley. Both were Civil War veterans. In the 1950s and 1960s, one of John's grandsons, Carl G. McCraw, was president of First Union National Bank. (Courtesy Carolyn Green Waters.)

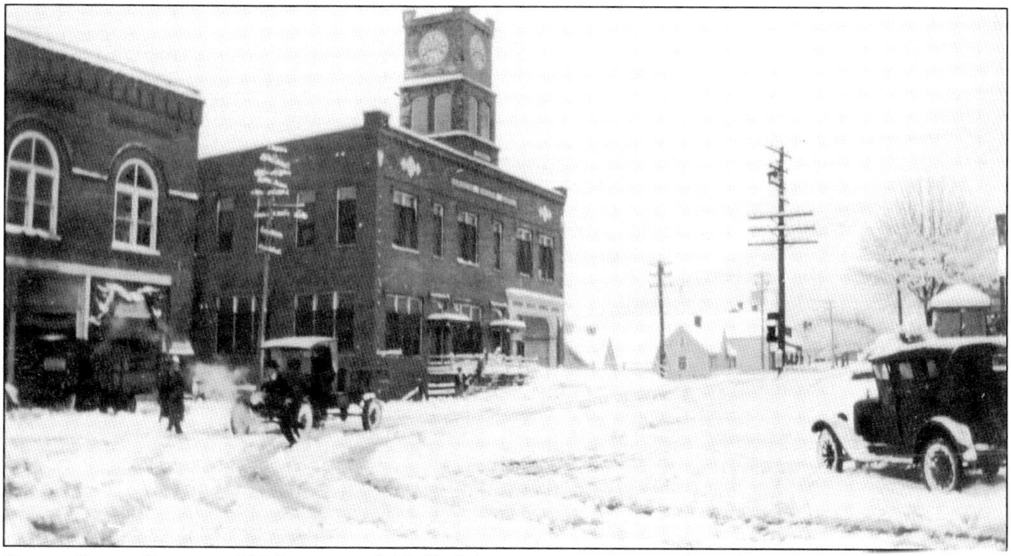

SNOW FALL. Prior to 1926, none of Cliffside's streets were paved, and any attempt to clear the snow turned them into a sloppy mess. Most folks walked to work anyway, and those few who did own cars would leave them at home. But some risked the hazards of bad weather, usually ending up being towed out of the mire by a team of company mules. (Courtesy Hazel Haynes Bridges.)

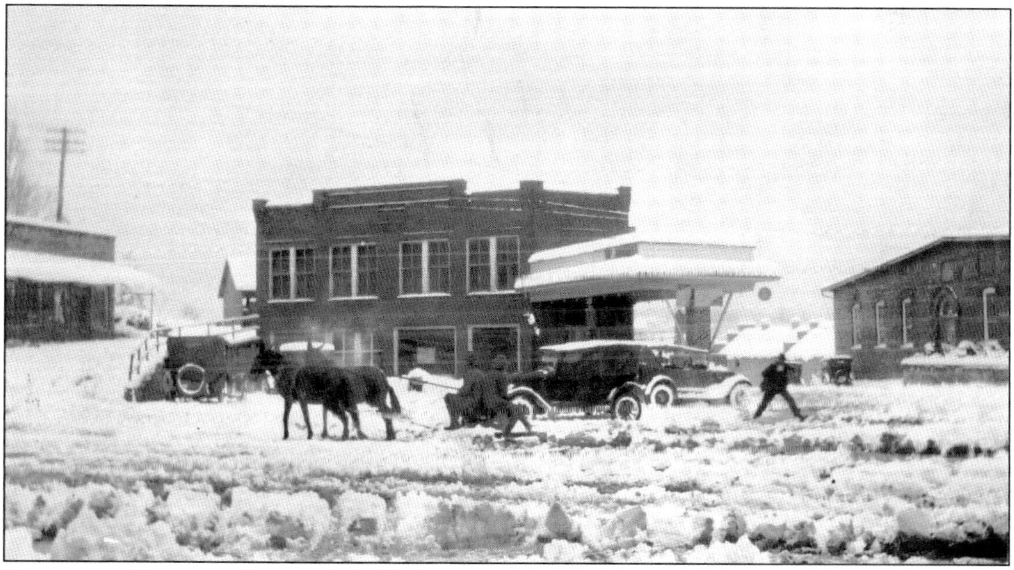

SLEDDING, CLIFFSIDE STYLE. A 1923 photograph of the east side of the square shows a canopy over the gas pumps at the garage. By the time of this picture, the building at the right, previously a funeral parlor, had been turned into a hardware store. The man driving the mule-drawn sled may be the grandfather of Frances McMurray Houser, Fred L. Byers, who often took teachers to school in snowy weather. (Courtesy Hazel Haynes Bridges.)

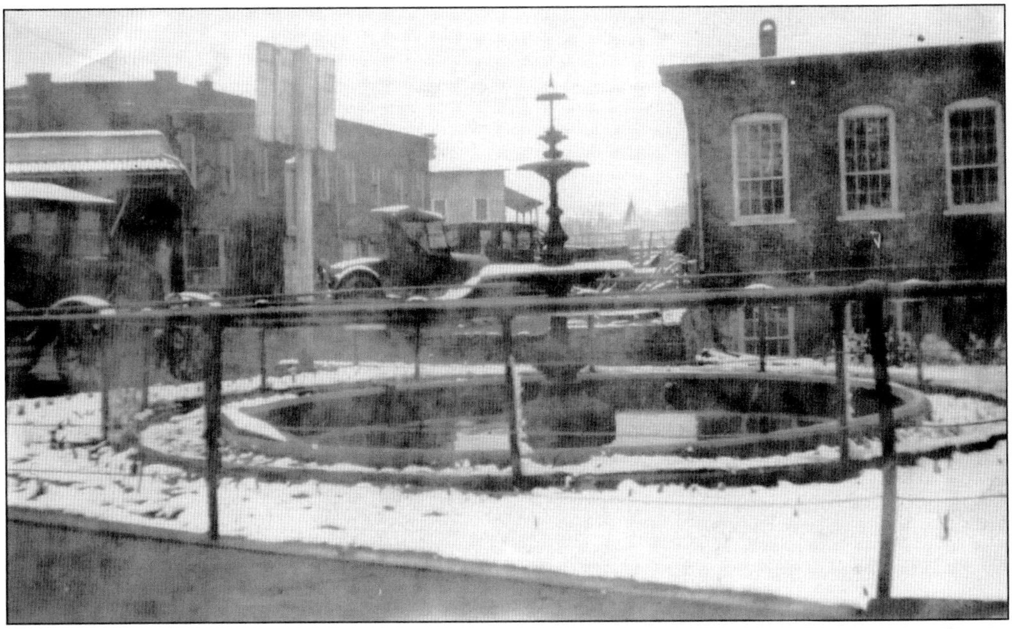

WHITEOUT. This shot across the town fountain shows a building no one seems to remember or can identify, the one beyond the cars with the sloping roof on what appears to be a second-story porch. The spire of the Cliffside Methodist Church in the distance can be seen to the right of the fountain. Icy weather never seemed to bother the goldfish in the little pond. (Courtesy Hazel Haynes Bridges.)

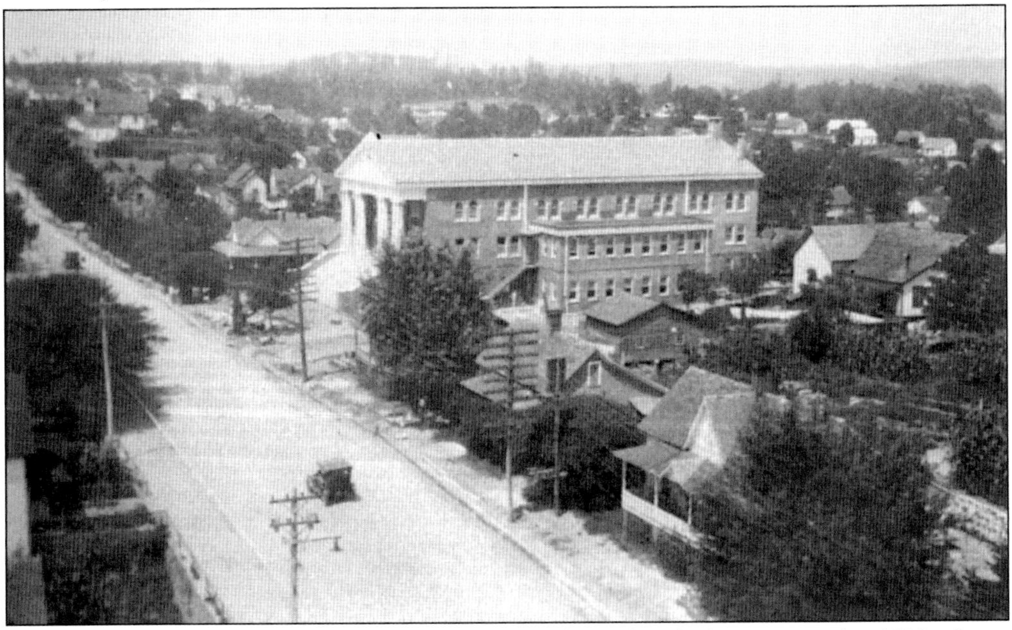

GRAND VIEW OF NORTH MAIN STREET. A view from the clock tower in the 1920s shows Cliffside toward the northeast. The massive building in the center is the Baptist church; the clearing just above its roof is the cemetery. Every available space around the homes is filled with flowers, gardens, and other evidence of contented lives. A mere 30 years before, none of this existed. (Courtesy Hazel Haynes Bridges.)

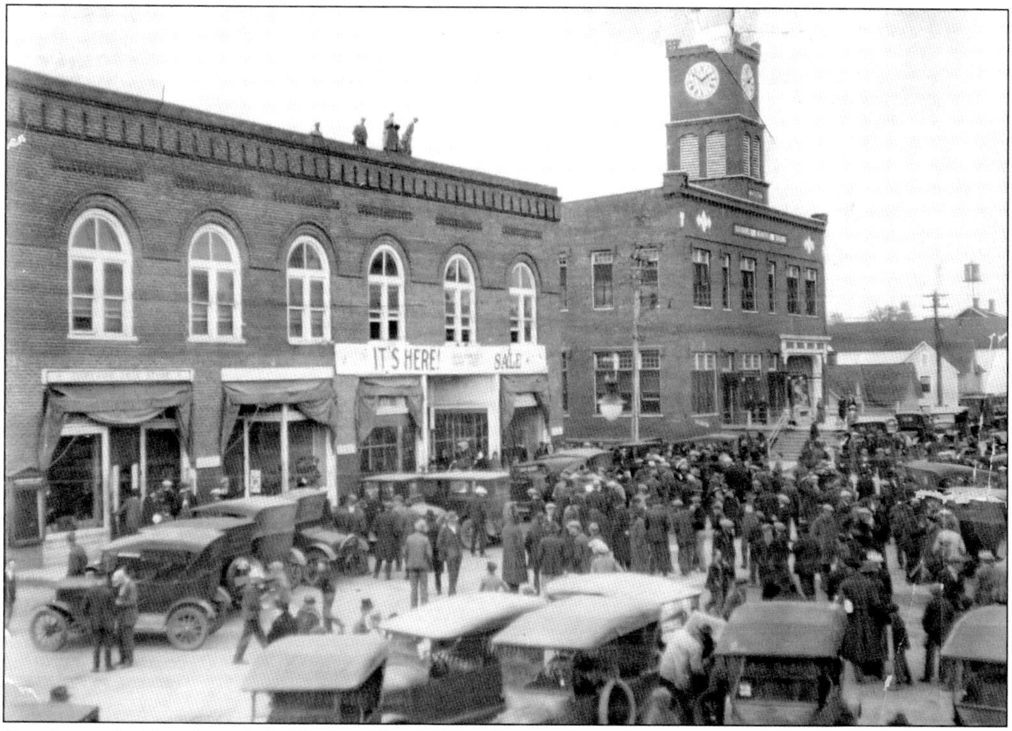

BIG SALE. In October 1927, the art of merchandising was alive and well in Cliffside, as this milling crowd of excited shoppers would affirm. In those days, the Cliffside Mills Department Store was billed as Rutherford County's largest. On the first day of the great sale, manager John G. Roach estimated there were over 500 waiting for the doors to open. (Courtesy Hazel Haynes Bridges.)

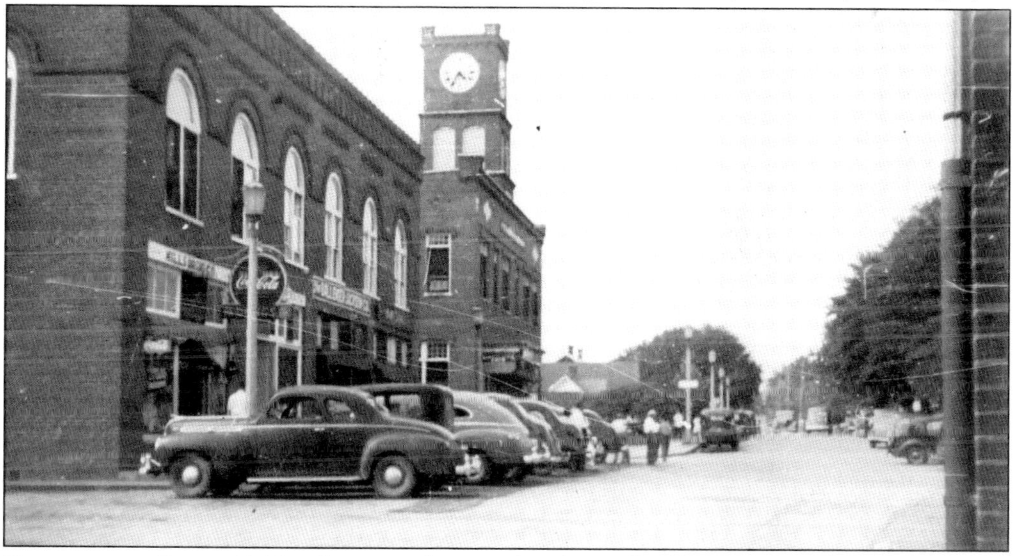

DOWNTOWN, LATE 1940S. Stepping from under the mill office portico after checking the mailbox and saying hello to Spud Crawford or Elvin Price in the post office, one faced north to see Cliffside's pride, the clock tower, rising above the Memorial Building. Up North Main Street are the dry cleaners, the Baptist church, and, at the top of the rise, the old Haynes home. (Courtesy Grover Haynes Jr.)

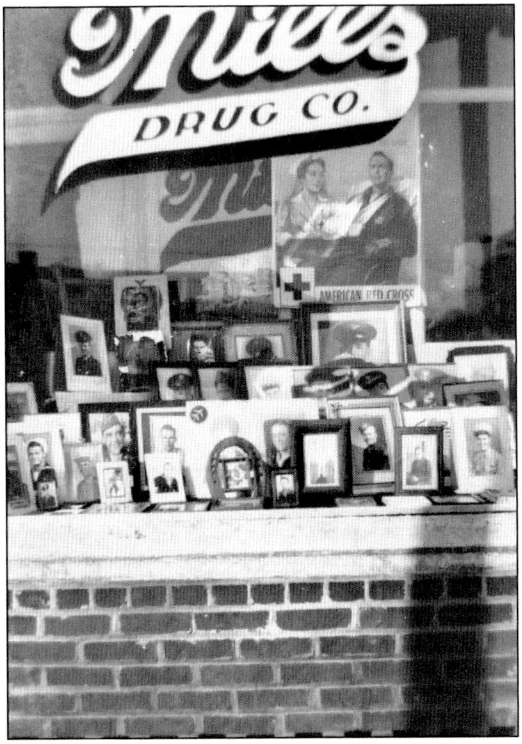

STOREFRONT TRIBUTE. In World War II, at least 366 men and women from the immediate Cliffside area went into the services. Their names were added to a large plaque mounted outside the post office. Here, pictures of many of them have been displayed in the drug store window, reminding all passersby of the sacrifice these brave soldiers and sailors were making. (Courtesy Frances McMurray Houser.)

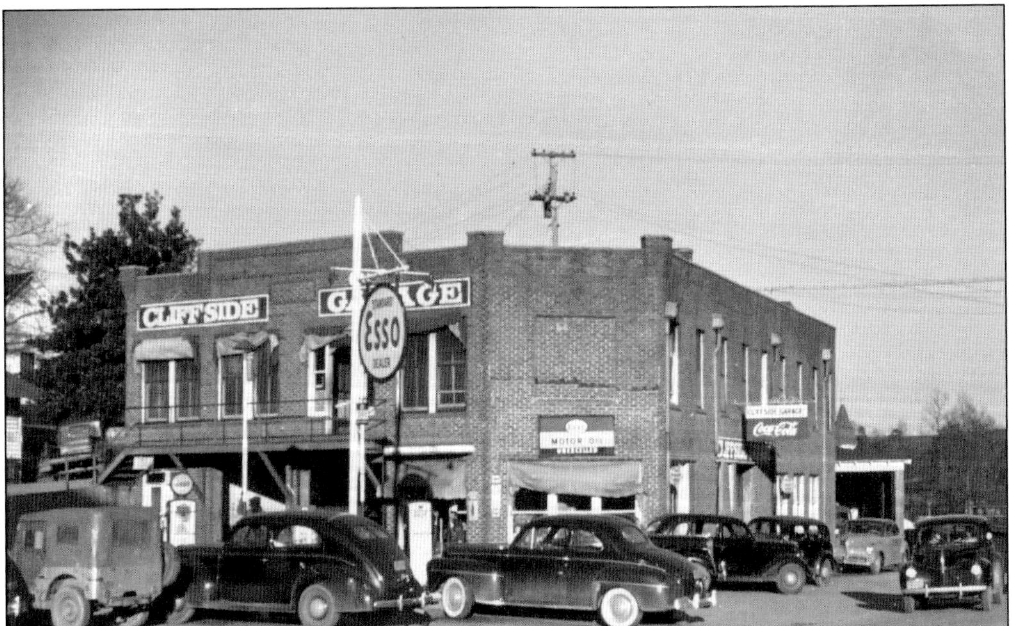

A DOLLAR'S WORTH, PLEASE. Inside the curve at the square was the Cliffside Garage building, housing a garage service station on the ground level, where Esso regular was 15¢ a gallon, and a café upstairs that served cheeseburgers all the way. You could get gas at either place. Out front, much too close to the roadway, four cars could be parked, inviting vehicles trying to navigate the curve to grind off their taillights. (Courtesy Hazel Haynes Bridges.)

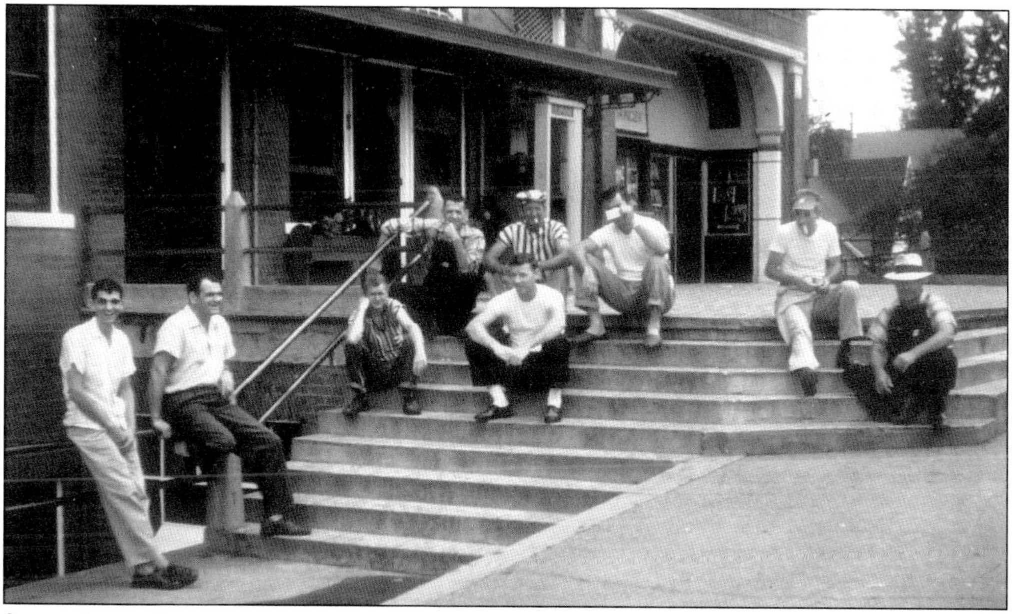

SHININ' THE RAILS. A favorite pastime was to lean or sit on the Memorial Building rails or steps and converse with your friends. This was called "shinin' the rails." Someone said there was no better forum for discussing politics, religion, or your supervisor. From left to right are the following: (first row) Gartha Harris, Ambres White, Jimmy Pearson, Billy Rollins, and Eartell Sarratt; (second row) Ambrose Brackett, Dewitt Rollins, Robert Waters, and Frank Greene. (Courtesy Charles "Red" Humphries.)

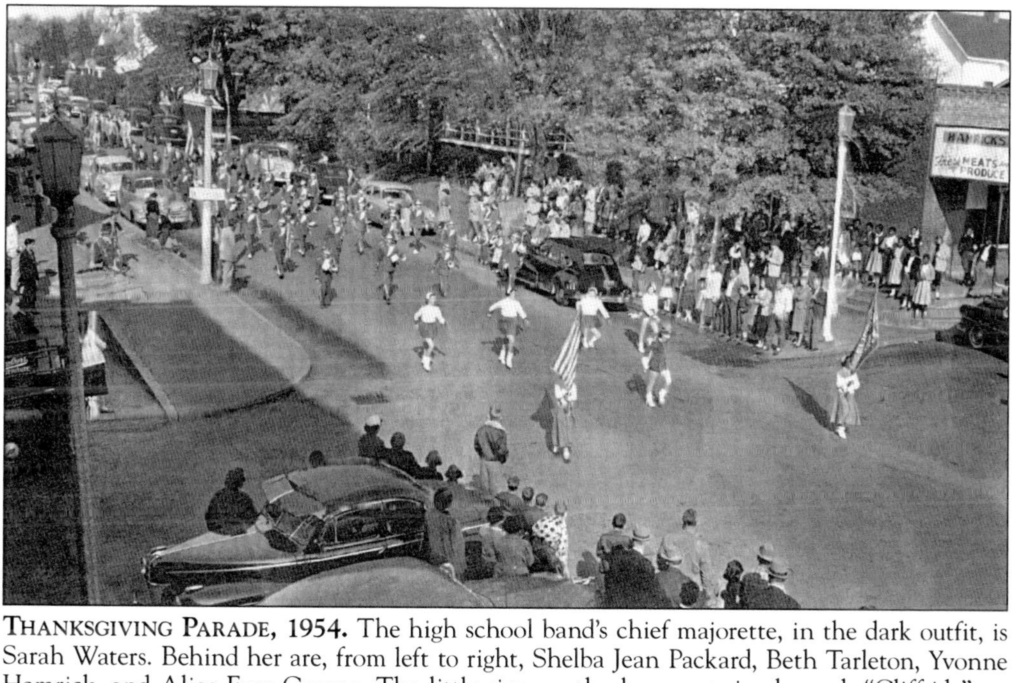

THANKSGIVING PARADE, 1954. The high school band's chief majorette, in the dark outfit, is Sarah Waters. Behind her are, from left to right, Shelba Jean Packard, Beth Tarleton, Yvonne Hamrick, and Alice Faye Greene. The little sign on the lamppost simply reads "Cliffside" on both sides. The town limits were defined by the thickness of a lamppost. (Photograph by Roy Lee Harris; courtesy Phillip White.)

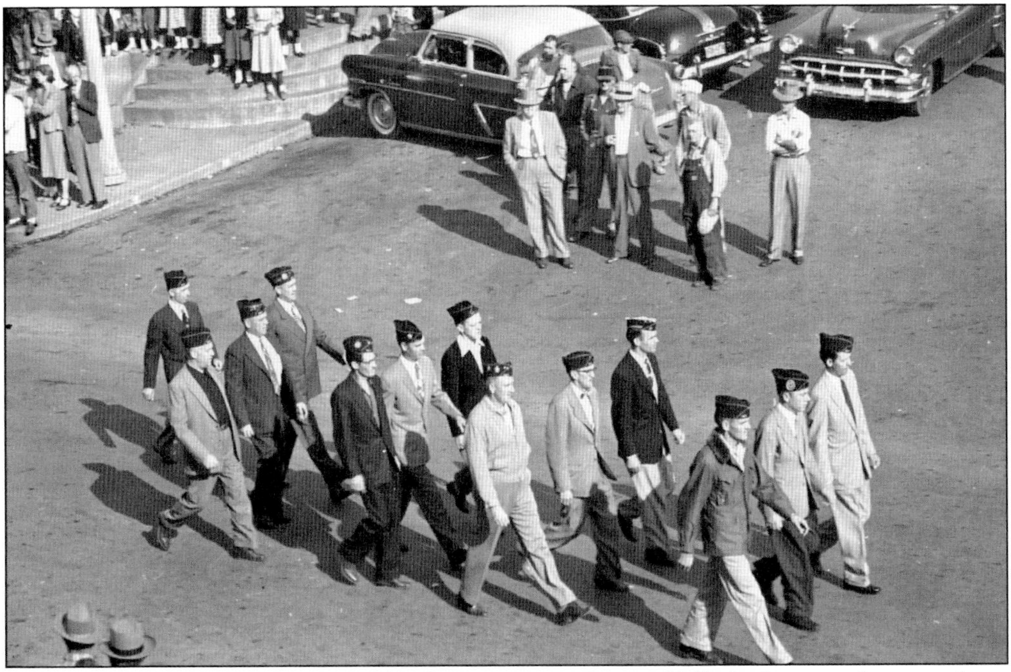

VETERANS PARADE, FEBRUARY 1955. A crisp winter day in Cliffside does not deter residents turning out to honor former servicemen. Pictured from left to right are (first row, far right) Ed Scruggs, Carl Jolley, and Earl Johnson; (second row) Broadus Hamrick, Jarvie Hawkins, and Joe Swing; (third row) Aster Harris, Leroy Parris, and Clyde Winn; (fourth row) Paul Bridges, Coyou Greene, and Fred Greene; (fifth row) Gerard Davidson. (Photograph by Roy Lee Harris; courtesy Hazel Haynes Bridges.)

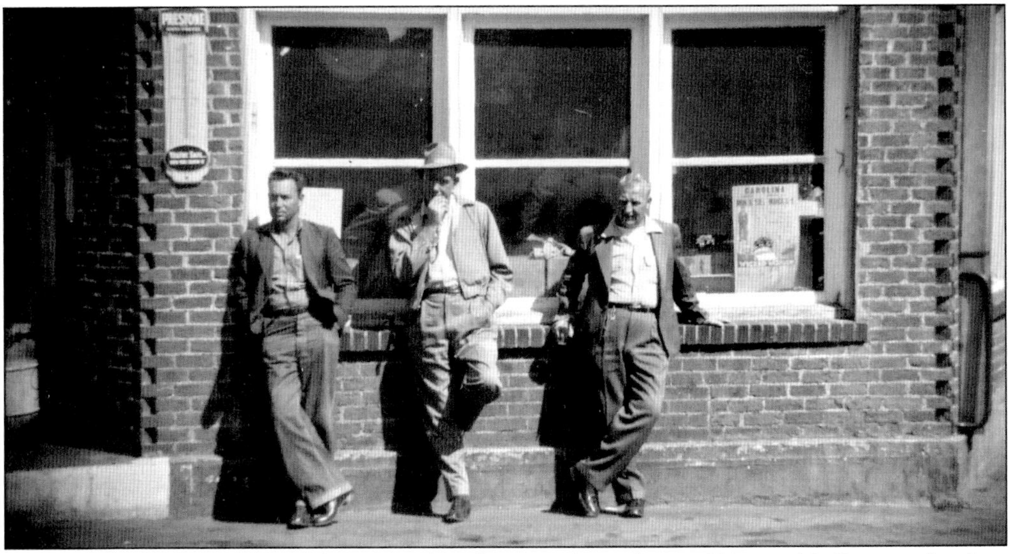

ON DUTY IN CLIFFSIDE. On this December day in 1954, in front of Hamrick's Garage, the duty fell to Joe Beason (left), Albert Bridges (center), and Paul "Whitey" Bridges (right). To be "on duty" in Cliffside was not a responsibility to be taken lightly. It required that two or more men or boys station themselves against a wall and just lean, all the while keeping a sharp eye on things. (Courtesy Madeline Scruggs Hardin.)

Four

LANDMARKS

The first house ever built in Cliffside was moved last week from Main Street to a site on Park Avenue to make room for the new Baptist church. Work on the church will start immediately.

–News item, July 27, 1922

Some of the most memorable Cliffside landmarks were insignificant and never captured on film. They were ordinary places and objects passed by without a second thought, like the well house beside the tracks down on South Main; "the ropes," a place on the river where boys would swing out and drop into the water; the swimming hole up on Hill's Creek at the Roller Mill; or the weathered old weight machine on the sidewalk outside the drug store that, for only a penny, would tell fortunes.

There was the footbridge over the creek to Church Street, whose floorboards would creak as you hurried home in the dark from a scary movie; the monkey ladder on the school playground; the candy-striped revolving poles at Sparks's and Biggerstaff's barber shops; the Toyland in the gloomy basement of Jackson's Department Store at Christmas; the unique concrete lampposts that added a touch of Victorian elegance to downtown; the stone wall around the graveyard; the rusty trash barrel behind your house, which, if it became too full, you would set afire.

Some of the places in these photographs did not exist in our lifetimes, but we revel in their memory all the same.

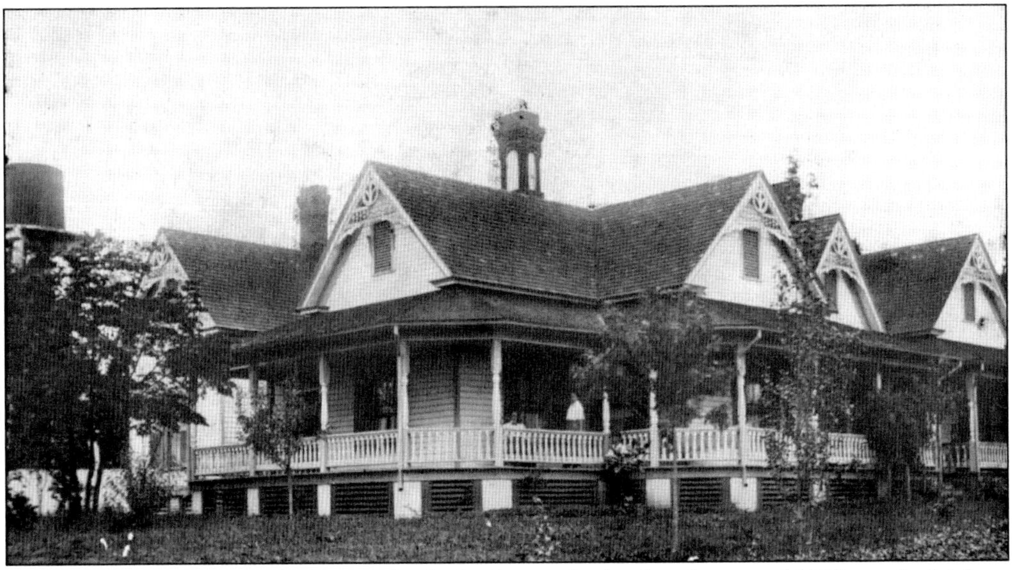

The Haynes House. R. R. Haynes built this house for his family around 1900 on the highest knoll in Cliffside, several blocks north of the center of town. It was the largest and grandest home in the village. After the elder Mr. Haynes died, his son Charles lived here until his own death in 1958. The house was razed in the early 1970s. (Courtesy Hazel Haynes Bridges.)

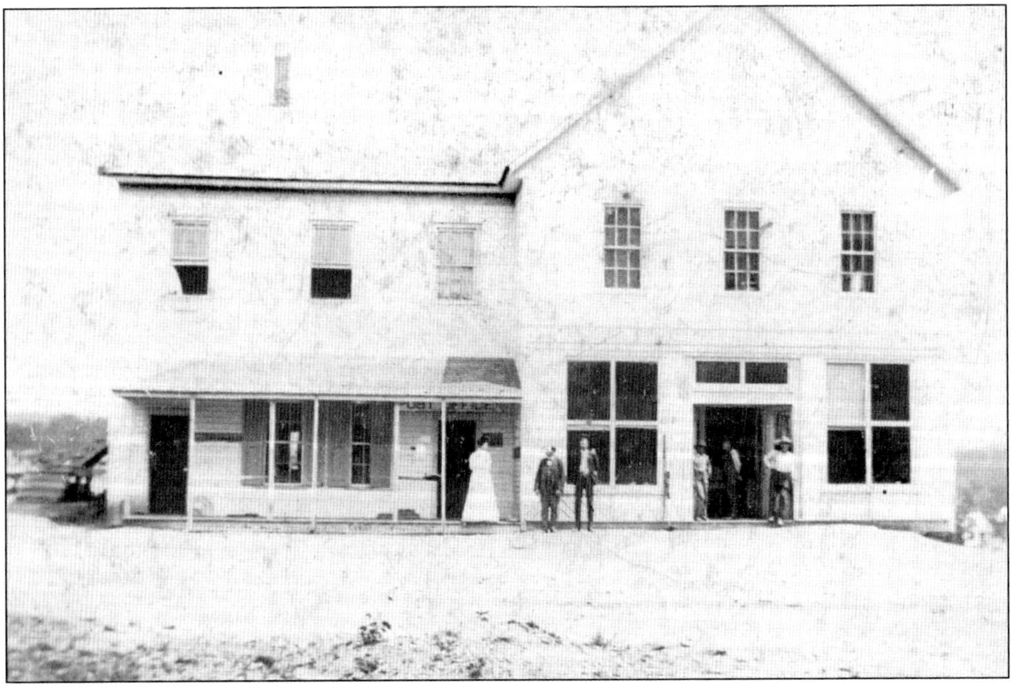

The First Store. This large white structure was built around 1901 on the site where the garage later stood. It housed Cliffside's first post office, a general store, and a meeting hall, among other things. It burned about 1908, prompting the erection of the store building across the street. The site then stood vacant for a few years. (Courtesy Hazel Haynes Bridges.)

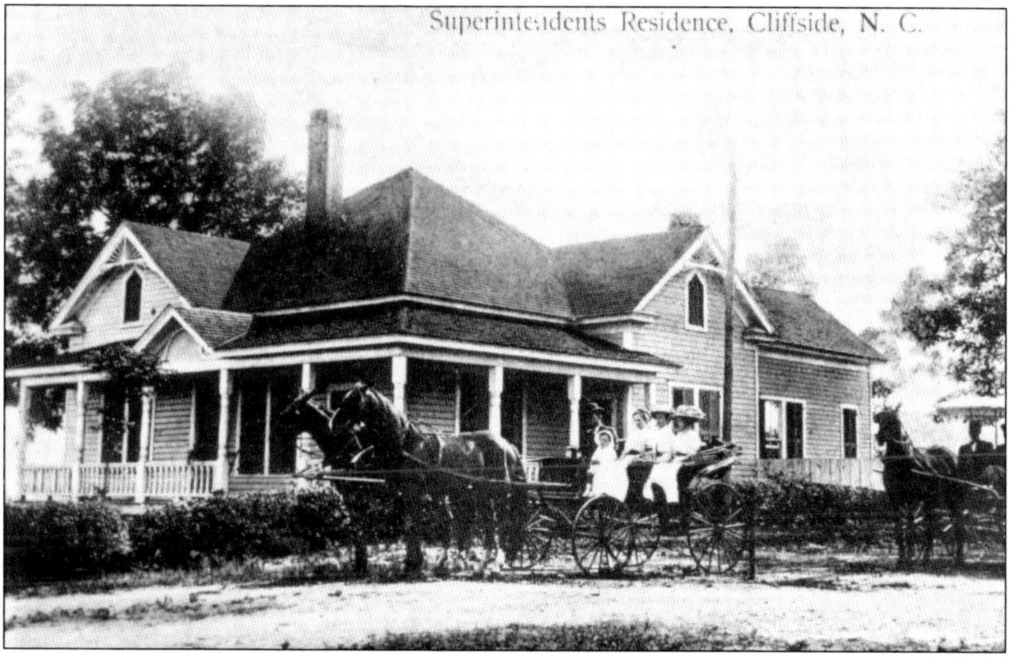

THE SUPERINTENDENT'S HOUSE. At the center of town, across the street from the mill office, stood the residence of the mill's superintendent. Note the weeds growing in the street, indicating a scarcity of automobile traffic. Later this house was replaced by a brick, tiled-roof residence known as the general manager's house, which was demolished in the early 1960s to make way for a parking lot. (Courtesy Hazel Haynes Bridges.)

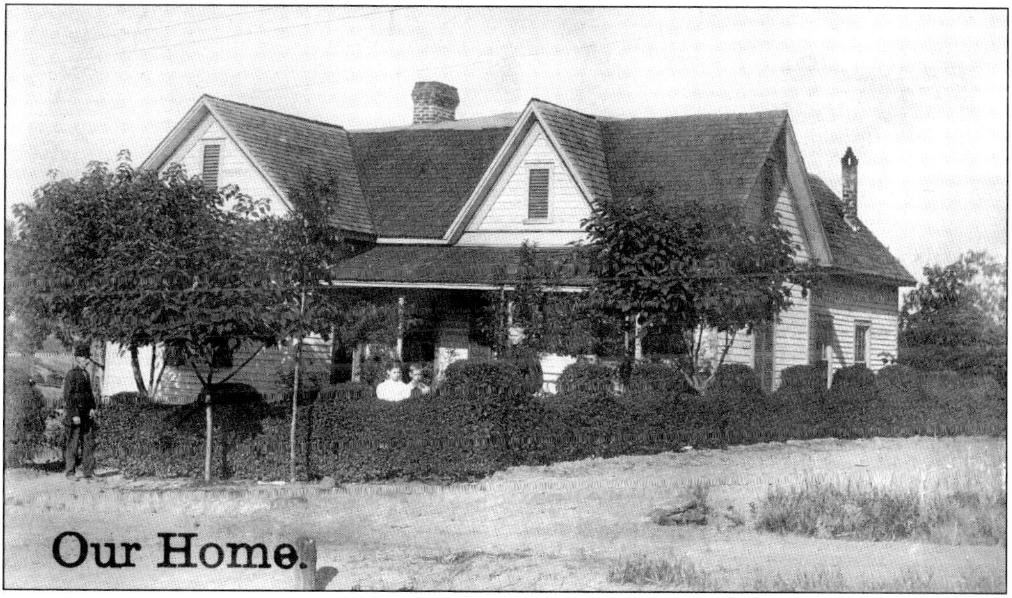

"OUR HOME" POSTCARD. This was 31 North Main Street about 1912, the home of Drury Dobbins Fortune (at left) and his second wife, Johnnie, standing behind the labor-intensive camelback hedge that must have kept Dobb busy. Their twins, Irene and Eugene, stand in the center. Dobb's older children by his first wife included Ina, Victor, and Guy Fortune. West Fifth Street runs beside the house. (Courtesy Hazel Haynes Bridges.)

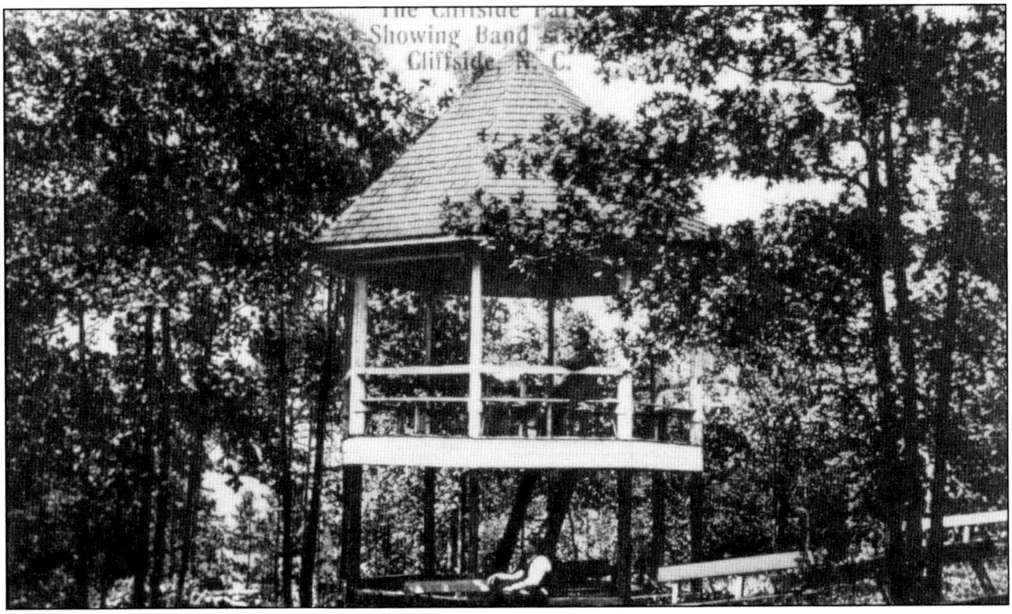

Bandstand. On the west side near the river, there was once a little park where townspeople would come on Sunday afternoons to picnic and listen to Cliffside's band play from this little bandstand. Years afterward, the frame of the bandstand was used to construct a tiny house with a conical-shaped roof. G. C. Fisher and his family once lived there, as did Riley and Helen Dedmond Callahan. (Courtesy Hazel Haynes Bridges.)

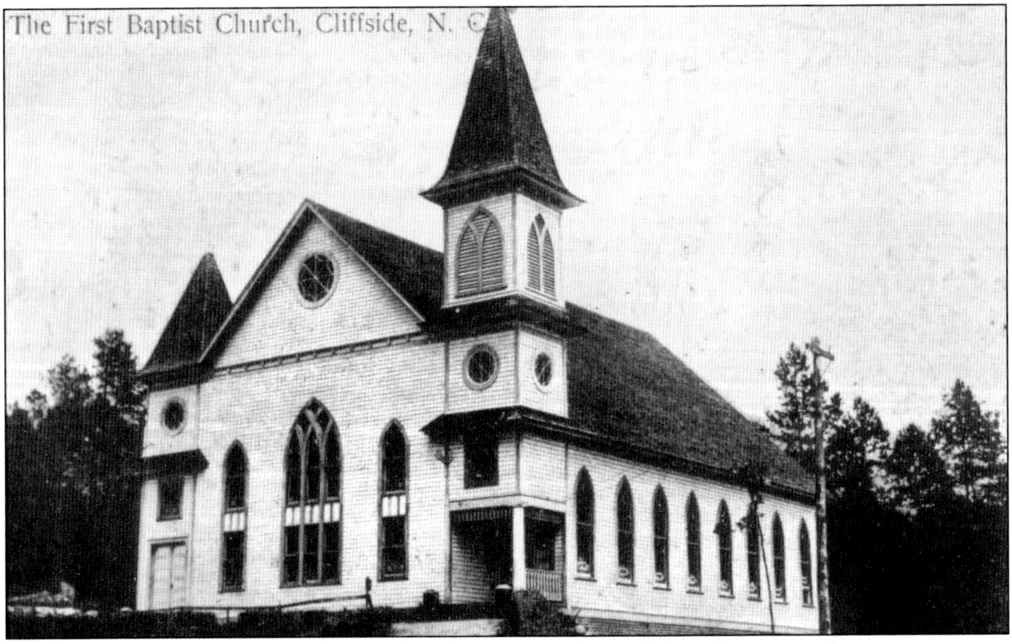

Old Baptist Church. Built on North Main Street and dedicated in 1909, this structure was used as a church until 1924, when a new, more modern church was completed a block from the center of town. The old building then became a gymnasium for basketball and other activities. When a real gym was constructed on the school grounds in the late 1930s, the old church building was razed. (Courtesy Hazel Haynes Bridges.)

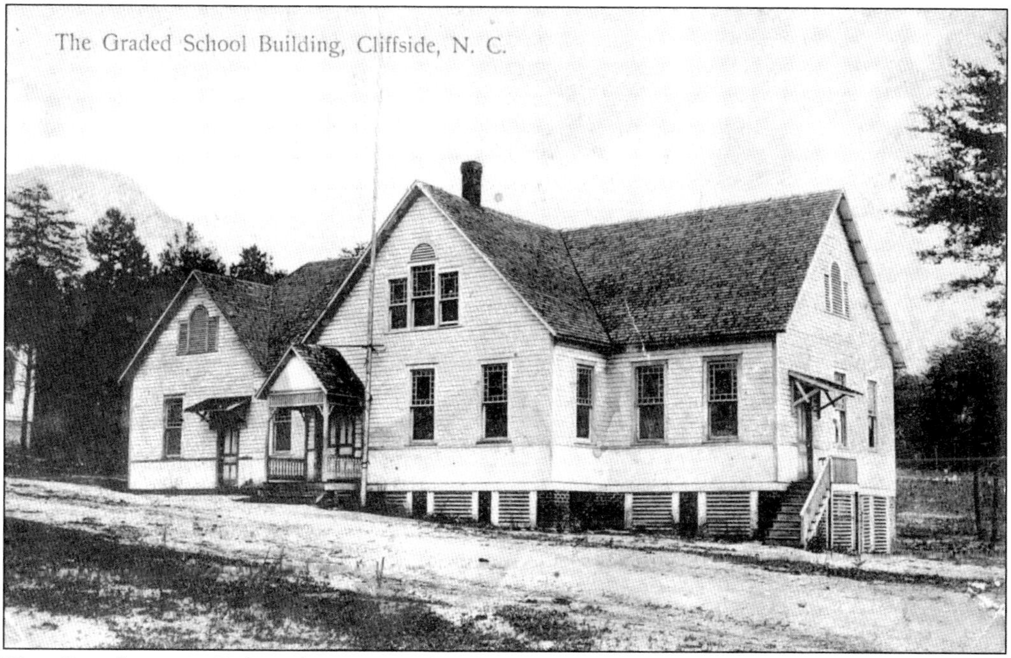

THE OLD SCHOOL. Below the Baptist church was Cliffside's first school building. In 1921, the new school was completed further up the street. Lula Goode Humphries remembers all the students being herded up the hill to the new building. On the way, she held the hand of a first-day student, little Myrtle Greene (Mashburn). Myrtle was still teaching piano when she recently celebrated her 90th birthday. (Courtesy Don Bailey.)

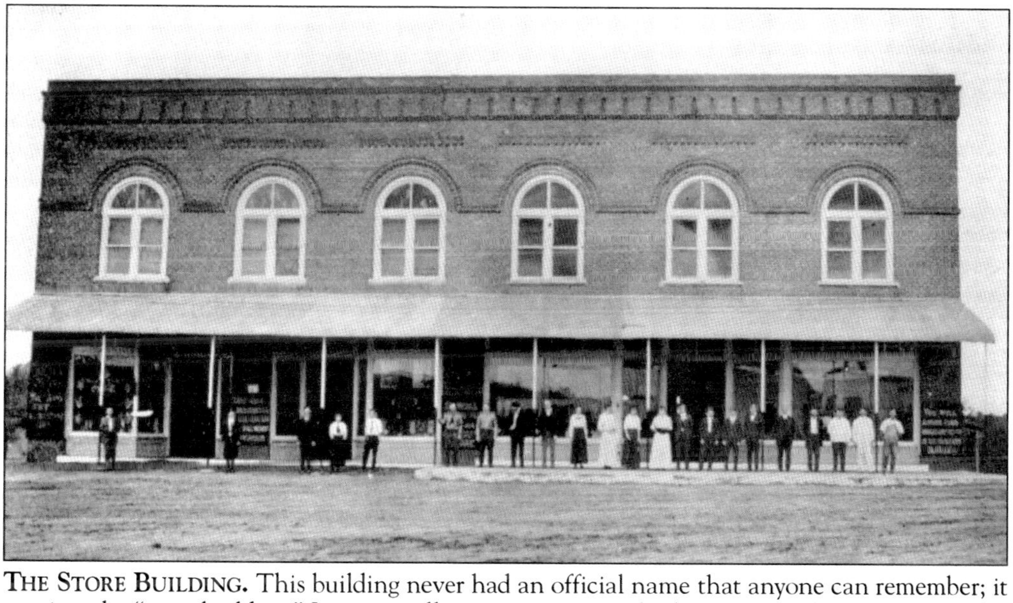

THE STORE BUILDING. This building never had an official name that anyone can remember; it was just the "store building." It was an all-purpose structure built in 1909 to house the Cliffside Mills Store on the ground floor and a town hall and a doctor and dentist's office on the upper floor. The store had three branches on River Street, Fairview, and North Main. (Courtesy Hazel Haynes Bridges.)

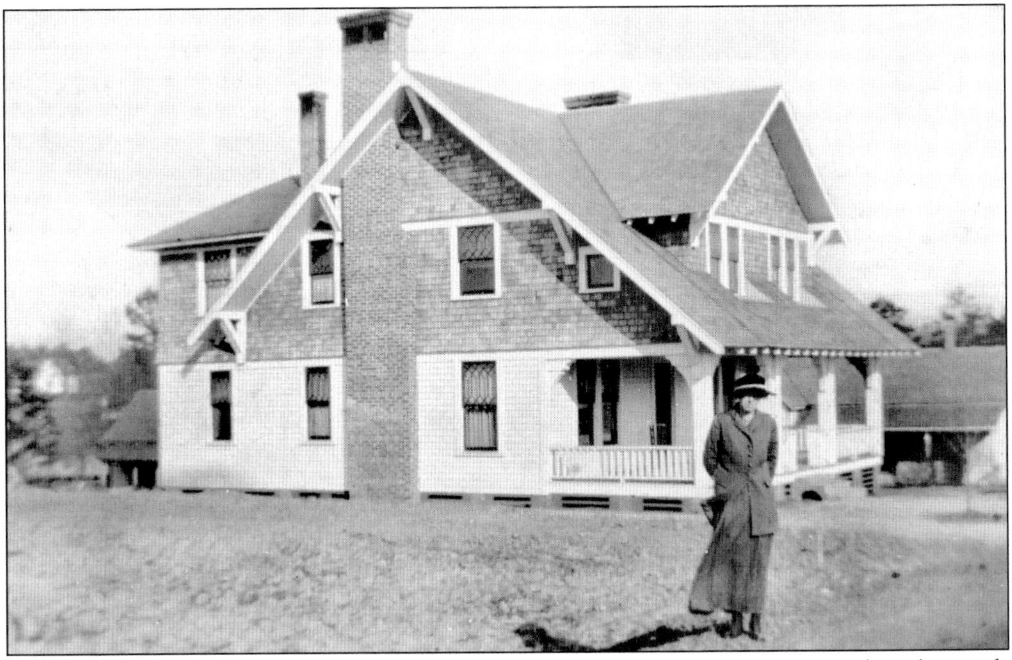

AN UPSCALE HOME. This was one of a few houses of a size and style to accommodate the needs of the more affluent. Others like it were built in Avondale. In the 1930s and early 1940s, this was the home of the Grover Haynes family. Beyond this house was another of equal size that for a time housed Cliffside's teachers. The lady is Blanche Edwards Campbell. (Courtesy Carolyn Greene Waters.)

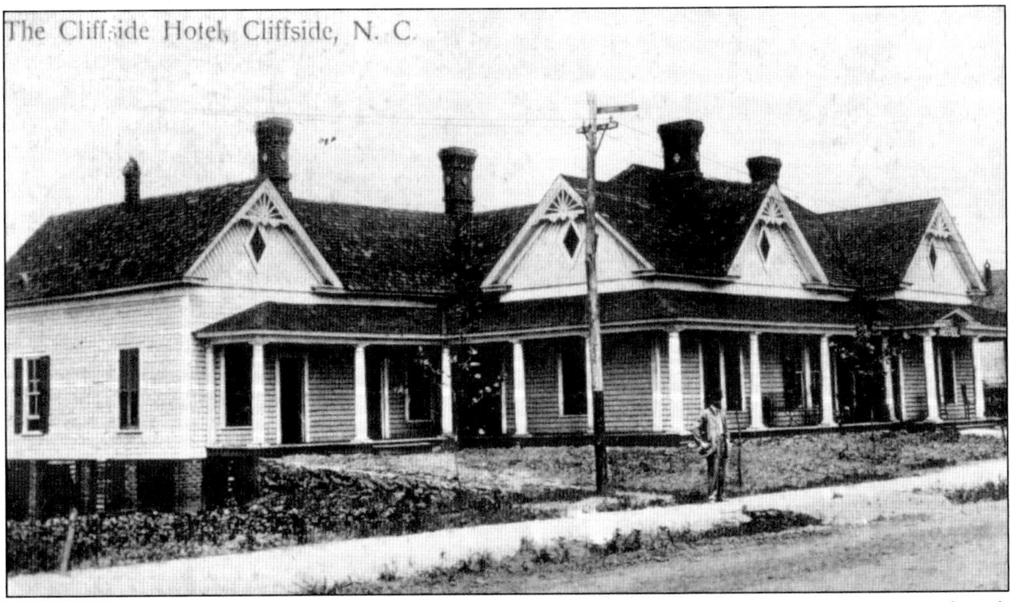

THE CLIFFSIDE HOTEL. Three blocks up North Main from the square was this one-story hotel, not to be confused with upstairs quarters for rent in the Memorial Building. In the late 1930s, this was no longer a hotel but the residence of Mrs. Annie Thompson, widow of one-time finishing room overseer Sidney Locke Thompson, and three of their sons, George, Francis, and Samuel. (Courtesy Hazel Haynes Bridges.)

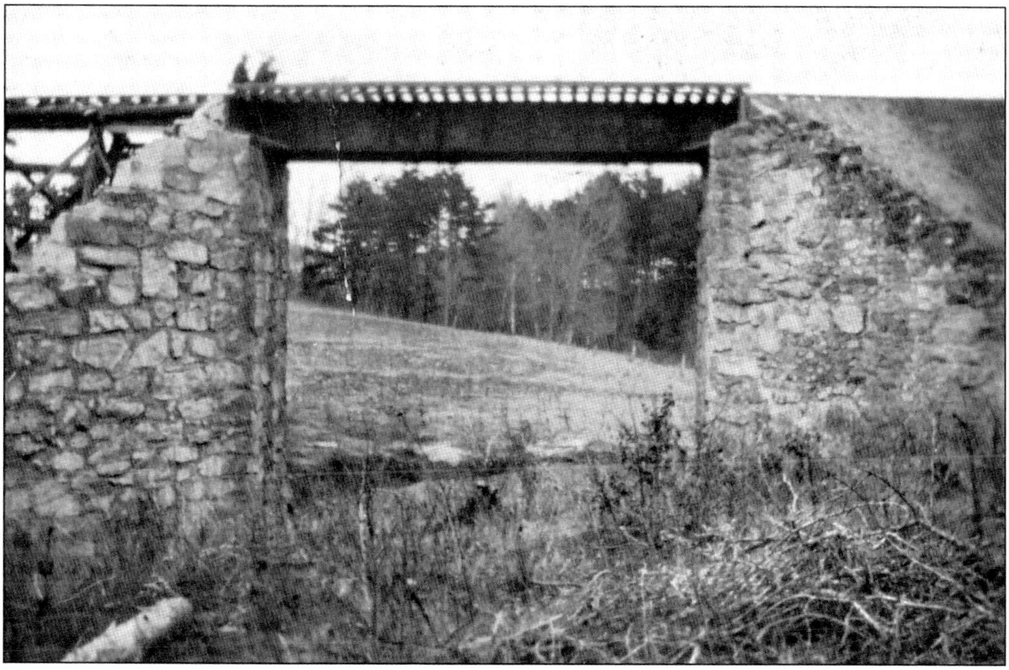

TRESTLE OVER RIDDLE'S CREEK. East of Academy Street, there were once railroad tracks leading toward the Mt. Pleasant area, where Mr. Haynes proposed to build a power generating plant. Those plans were scrapped around 1930, and eventually the tracks were ripped up and salvaged. This old trestle remained. On Sunday afternoons, young daredevils would tempt fate to impress their girlfriends by walking across it. (Courtesy Carolyn Greene Waters.)

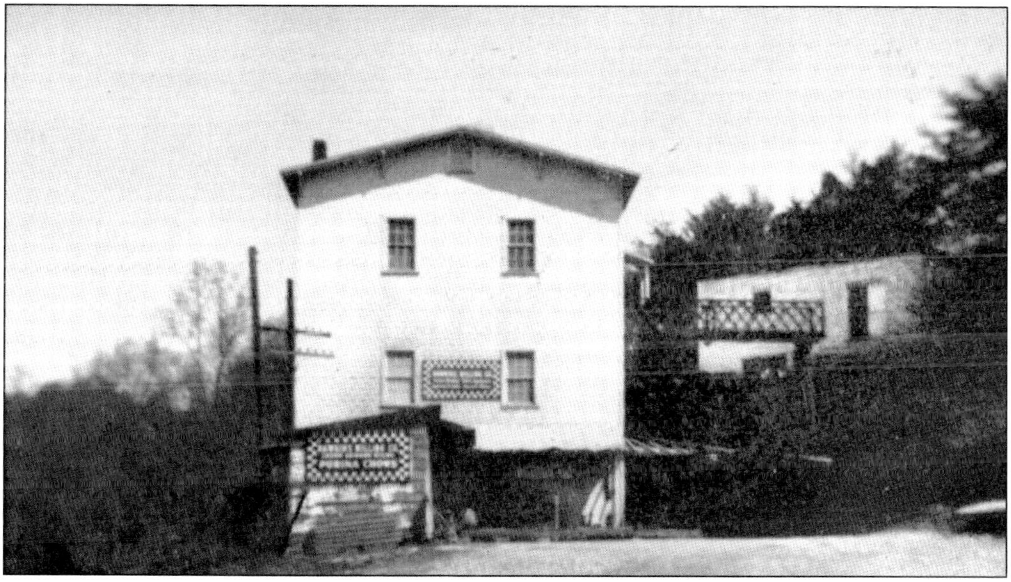

THE ROLLER MILL. About a mile above town was the Farmers' Milling Company. William McKinley Earley was the head miller during its last 30 years. Its brands of flour were popular in the foothills area. The last to operate the facility was Alfred "Buck" Hawkins. One night in 1953, the old mill was struck by lightning and burned to the ground. It was never rebuilt. (Courtesy Hazel Haynes Bridges.)

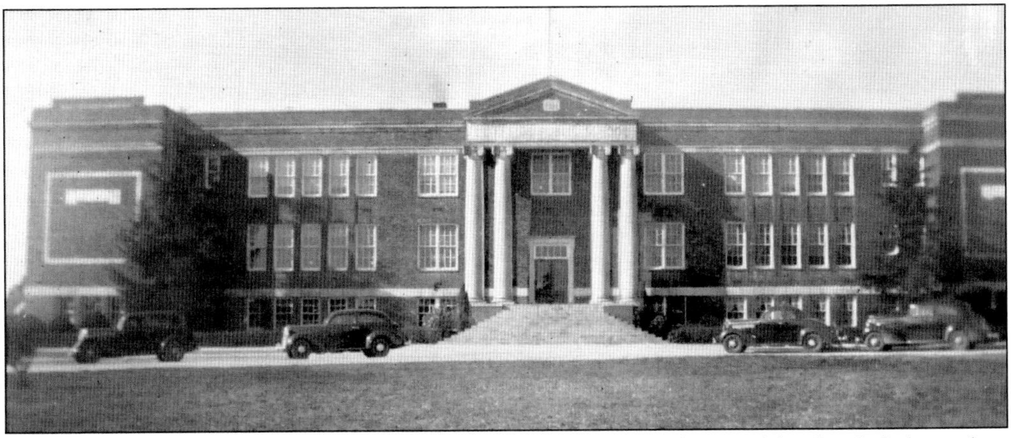

CLIFFSIDE SCHOOL. The area had never seen anything like this model school dedicated in 1922. It was designed by a famous Charlotte architect, Louis H. Asbury, who later designed the Rutherford County Courthouse. Fashioned of two million red bricks and trimmed with blocks of Indiana limestone, it had 24 classrooms, an 800-seat auditorium, and a library, among other things, and cost $250,000, paid for entirely by the company. (From 1938 yearbook.)

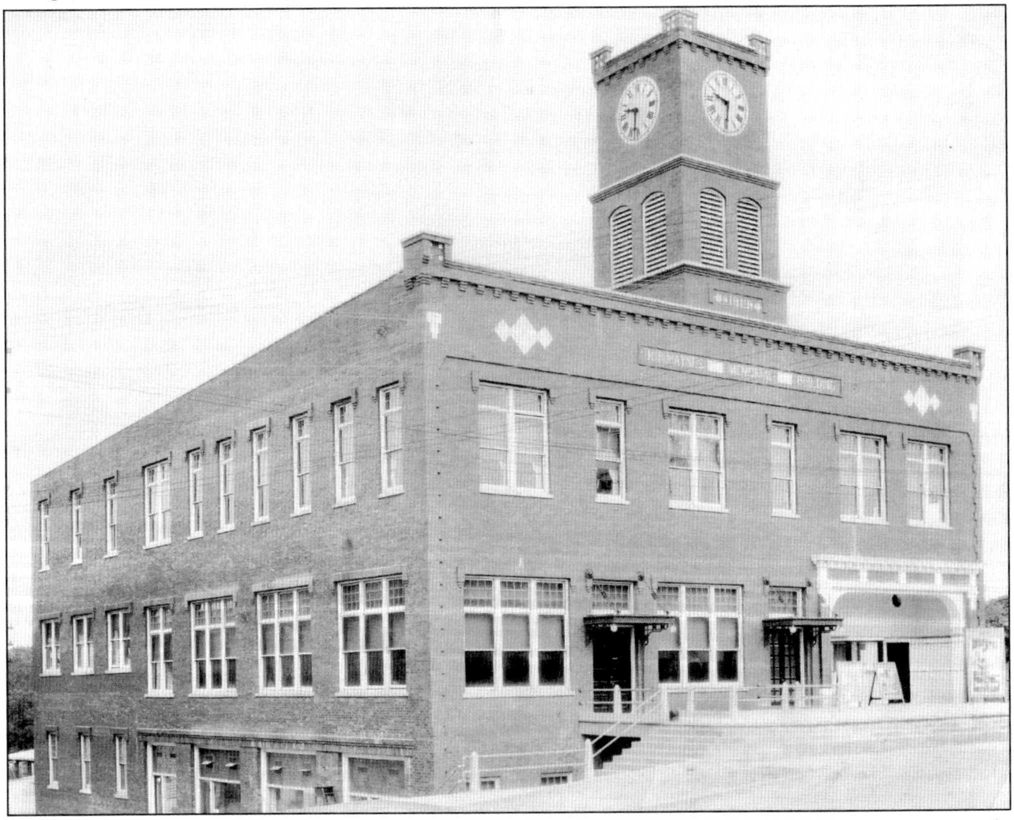

THE R. R. HAYNES MEMORIAL BUILDING. Although other mill owners were known to provide conveniences for their employees, a $100,000 community building like this one was unheard of. For amusement and relaxation it had nearly everything: a library, movie theater, gymnasium, beauty shops, banquet hall, barbershops, baths, and a café. It had been planned by Mr. Haynes and was delayed by his death, but it was completed in 1922. (Courtesy Hazel Haynes Bridges.)

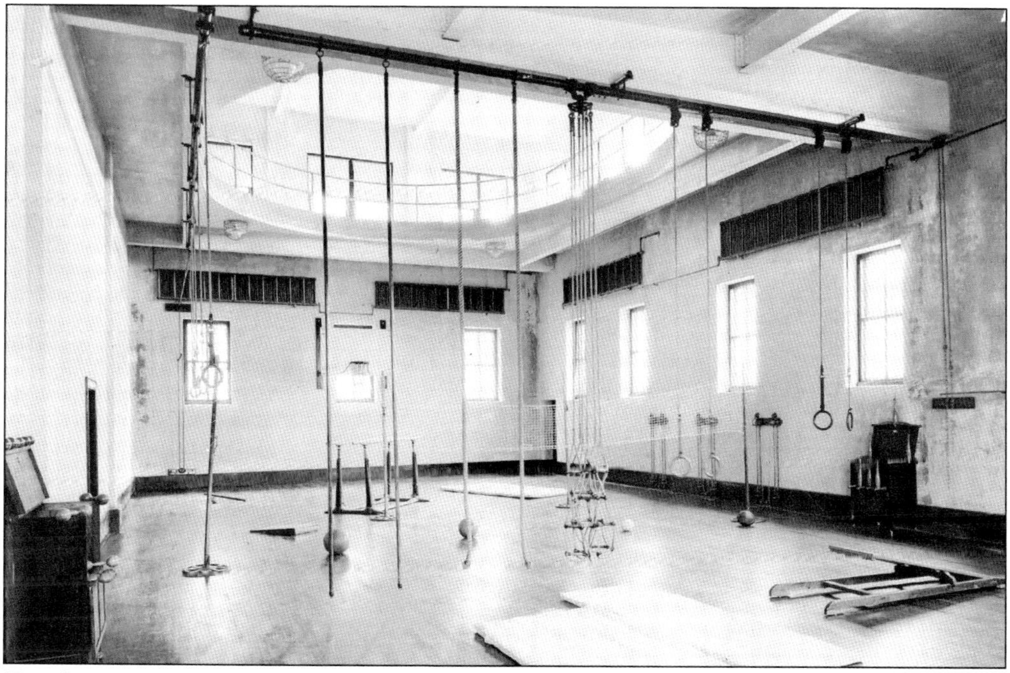

THE GYMNASIUM. At the time the Memorial Building was constructed, not even the new school had athletic facilities. This fully equipped gym in the Memorial Building was used by school and town teams for basketball and other sports. Countywide boxing matches were held here. An indoor track circled the open ceiling above the gym. Eventually the school had its own gym and appropriated much of this equipment. (Courtesy Hazel Haynes Bridges.)

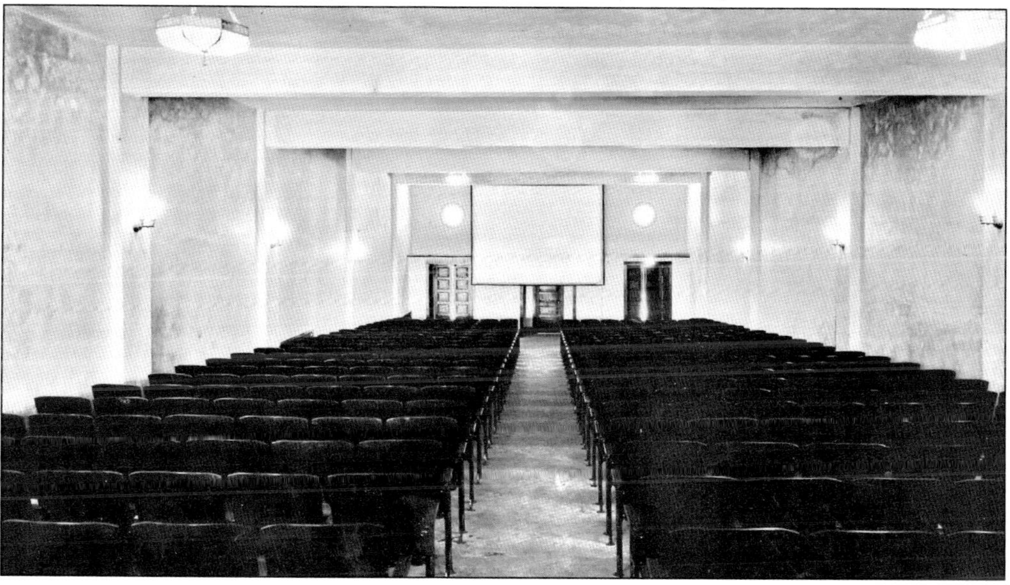

CLIFFSIDE THEATER. Prior to the Memorial Building's construction, "flickers" were shown in a long wood building a few doors north. This new "real" theater was used for the next 50 years. First-time patrons were surprised to discover they were entering the theater from the front, not the rear. They entered beside the screen, went up to their seats, and turned around to face the screen. (Courtesy Hazel Haynes Bridges.)

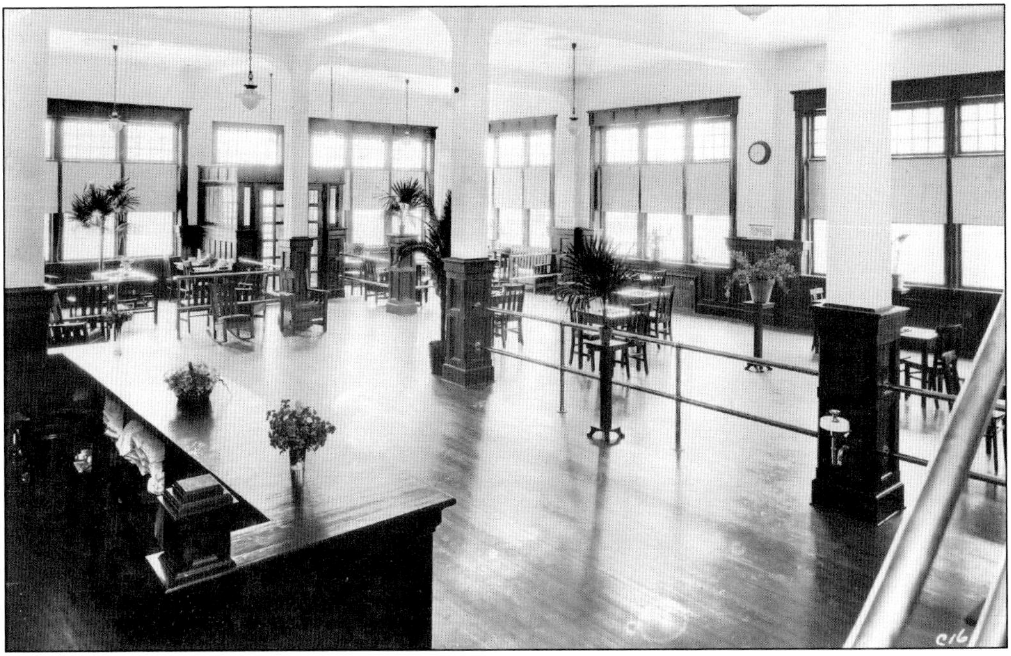

THE LOBBY. Visitors to the Memorial Building admired this spacious lobby with comfortable chairs and checker tables and a counter where drummers and other out-of-towners would register for rooms upstairs or where villagers would sign in for a shower. This photograph was one of a series made in the 1920s of the Memorial Building and other Cliffside landmarks to produce a collection of hand-tinted postcards. (Courtesy Hazel Haynes Bridges.)

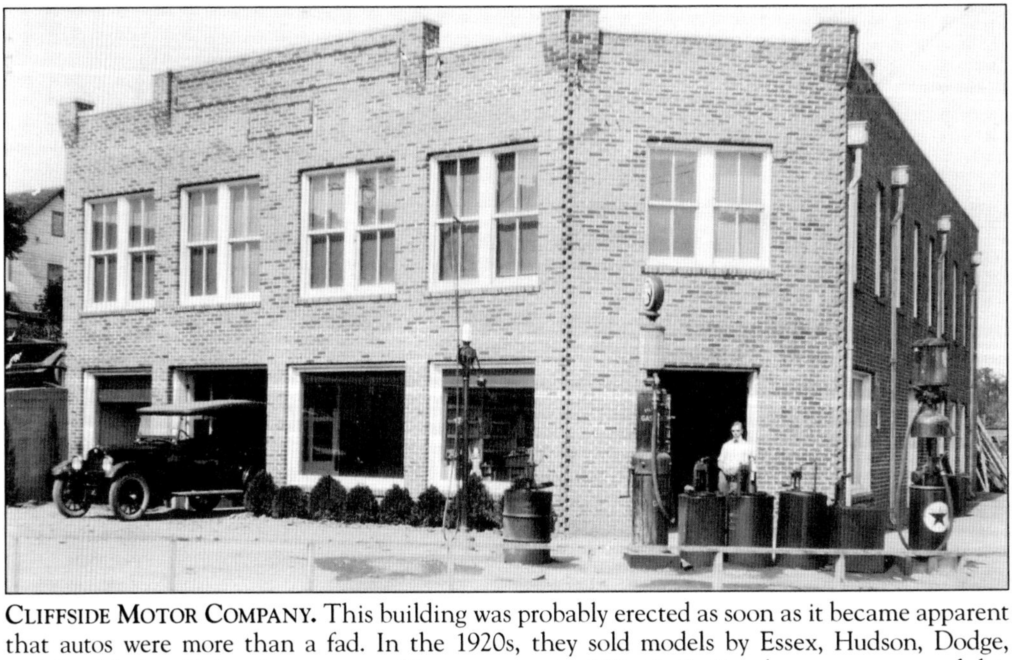

CLIFFSIDE MOTOR COMPANY. This building was probably erected as soon as it became apparent that autos were more than a fad. In the 1920s, they sold models by Essex, Hudson, Dodge, and Studebaker. Before his move to life insurance in 1931, B. B. Goode was manager of this facility. His assistant (at least in 1926) was C. B. Edwards. Later the firm evolved into a garage. (Courtesy Hazel Haynes Bridges.)

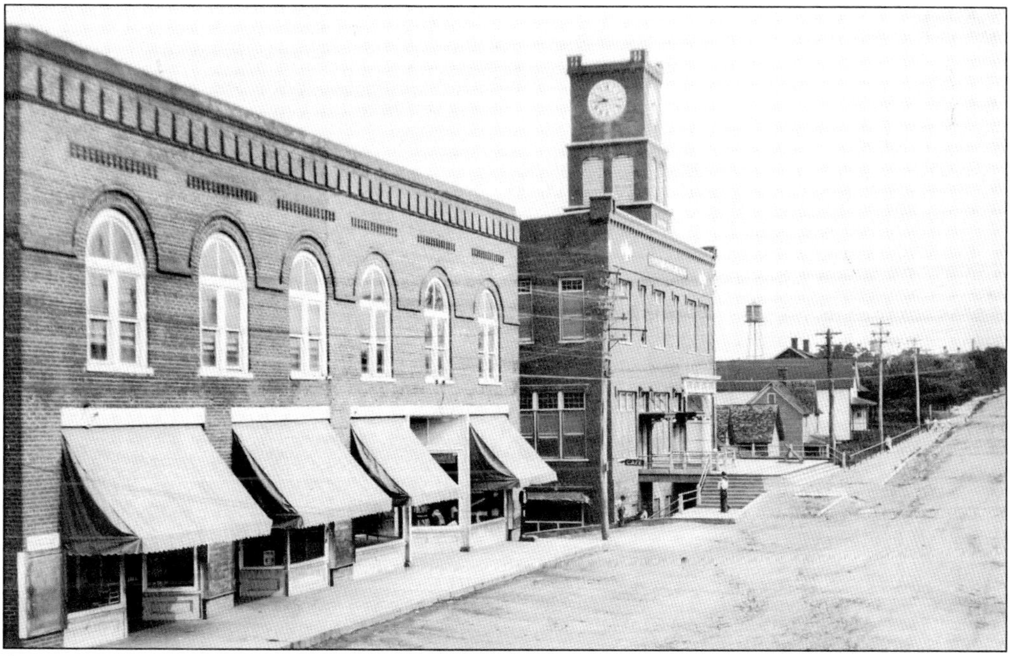

SLOW MORNING. The square is seen in the early 1920s. By now the long metal awing on the store building was gone and cloth awnings for the individual store windows had been installed. The streets were still unpaved. There are chalkboards mounted on the wall to advertise "specials." It must have been a Sunday or a holiday, for foot traffic is sparse and everything appears to be closed. (Courtesy Hazel Haynes Bridges.)

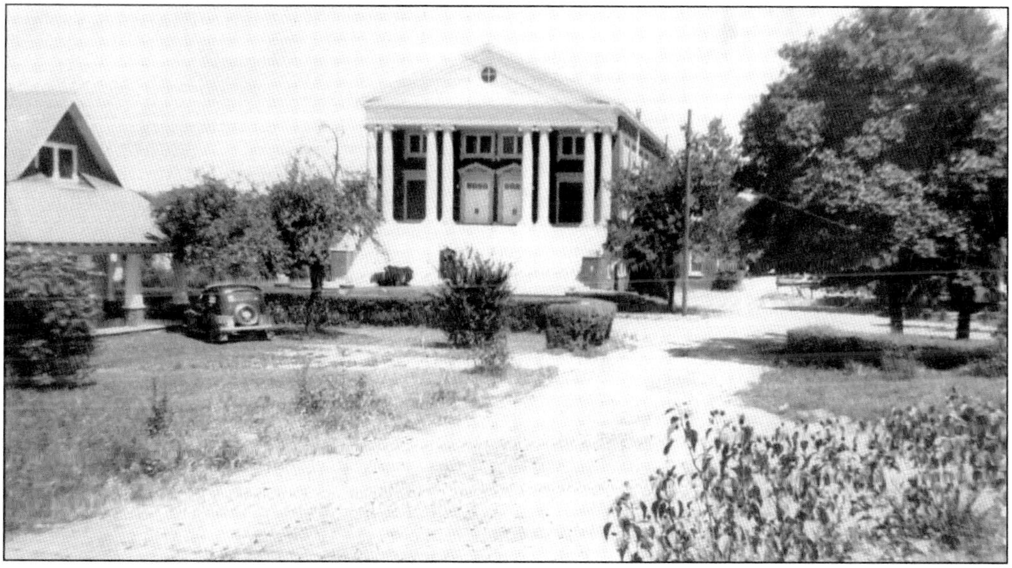

WEST THIRD AVENUE. No photograph has captured the serenity and small-town flavor of Cliffside like this one taken during World War II. The Baptist church sits just across North Main Street. Intersecting "avenues" like this one were unpaved and unmarked. They were referred to by the names of families who lived on them rather than the names of the avenues—it was common to say something like, "She grew up next door to the Vic Fortunes." (Courtesy Mack Hendrick.)

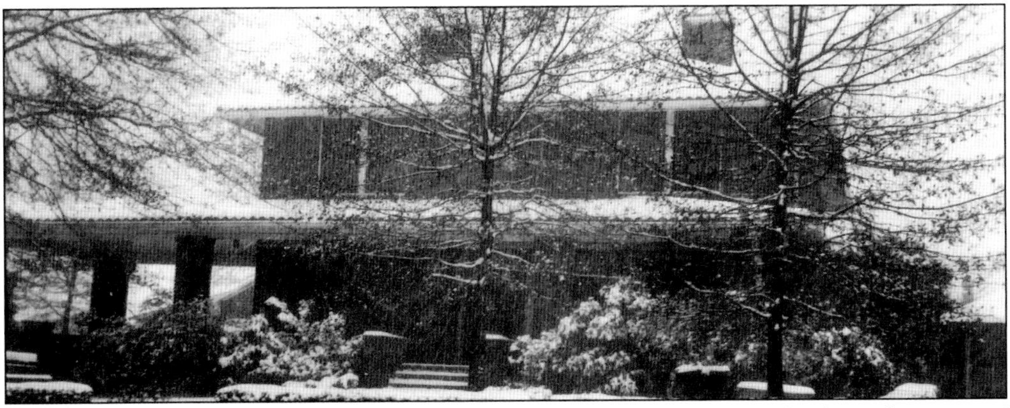

General Manager's House. This 11-room brick home with the Spanish-tile roof was one of a kind in Cliffside and fairly lavish by local standards. Built in the 1920s, it was only the second house to stand on this site in the heart of town, across a narrow street from the mill office. The company kept its officials close by in case they were needed quickly. (Courtesy Shirley Crawford Thompson.)

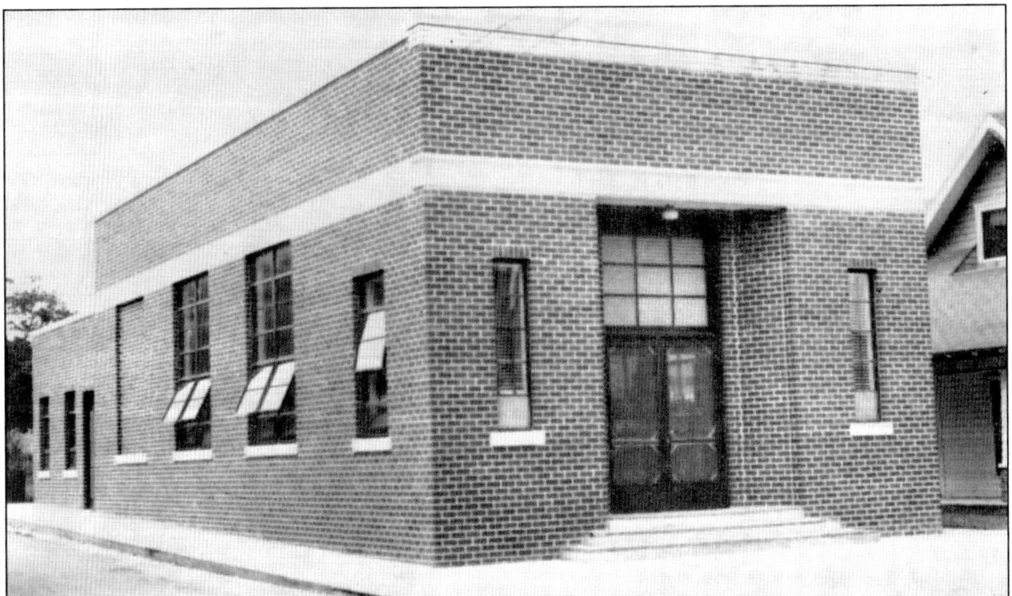

The Haynes Bank. Begun in Henrietta and then moved to Cliffside, the bank was housed at various locations. Until the late 1940s, it was downtown in the store building, next to the drug store. This stand-alone structure across from the Baptist church was built in 1947 and closed its doors in 1972. Some of its top executives over the years were John B. Watkins, J. C. Hames, and Paul Bridges. (Courtesy Hazel Haynes Bridges.)

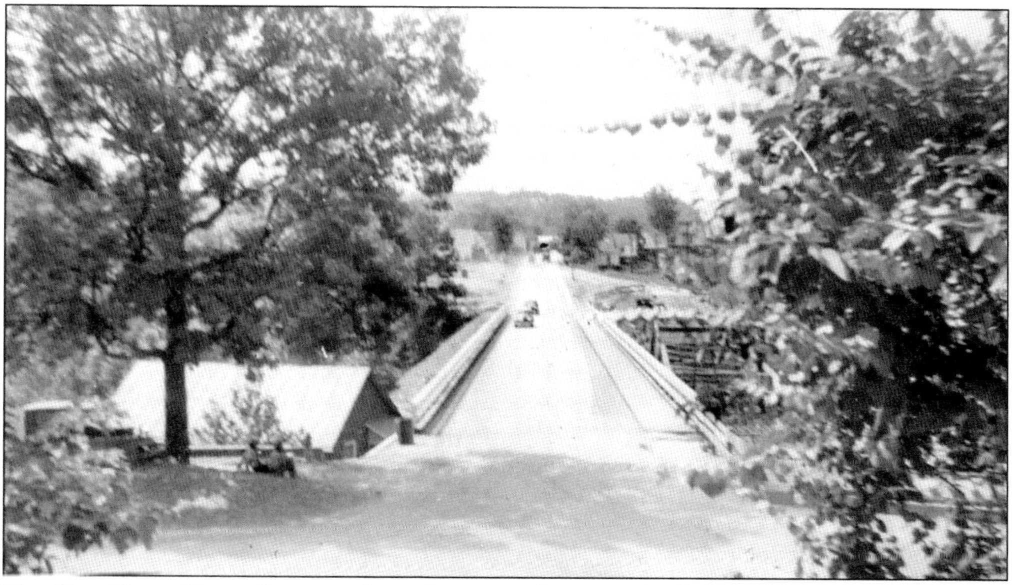

THE OAK TREE. Down the street from the square, between the forks in the road, stood a sturdy oak tree. If one said "I'll meet you at the oak tree," anyone would know which tree was meant. It provided a nice shade for loafing, waiting, or peddling wares. To the right of the bridge are the remains of the old iron bridge from earlier days. (Courtesy Loree Harrill Steele.)

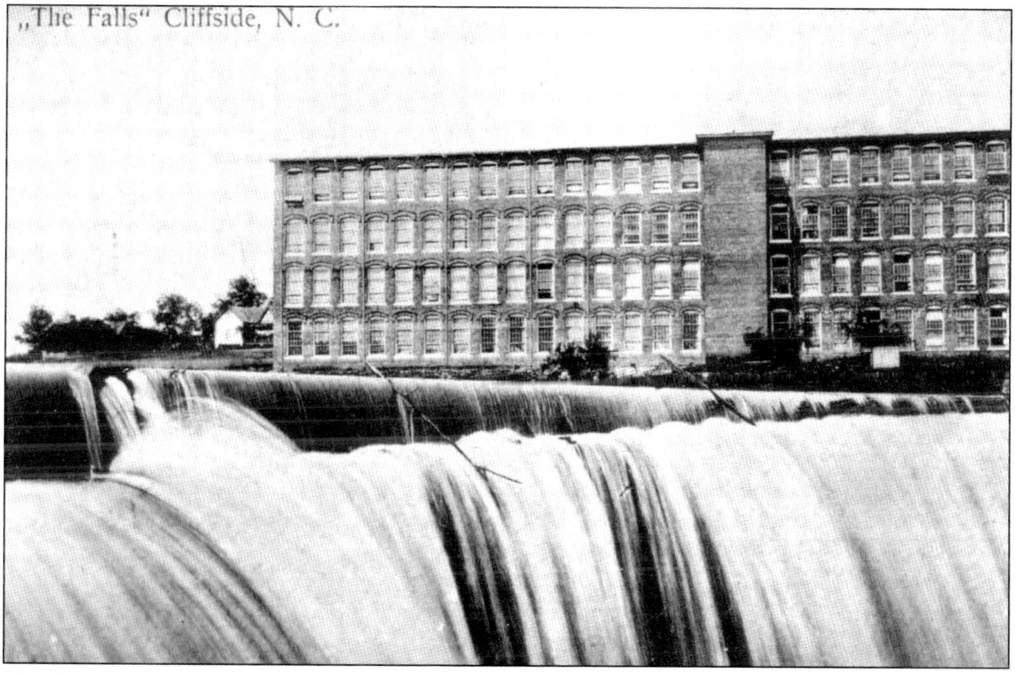

THE FALLS. A news item from 1926 reported, "Coming toward Cliffside from Spartanburg there is a splendid view of a great dam, some 25 feet high, which impounds a volume of water sufficient to make a lake of over 50 acres in extent. The water pouring over the dam harmonizing with the humming sounds from the mills beguile the eye and ear and make a visit fascinating beyond words." (Courtesy Hazel Haynes Bridges.)

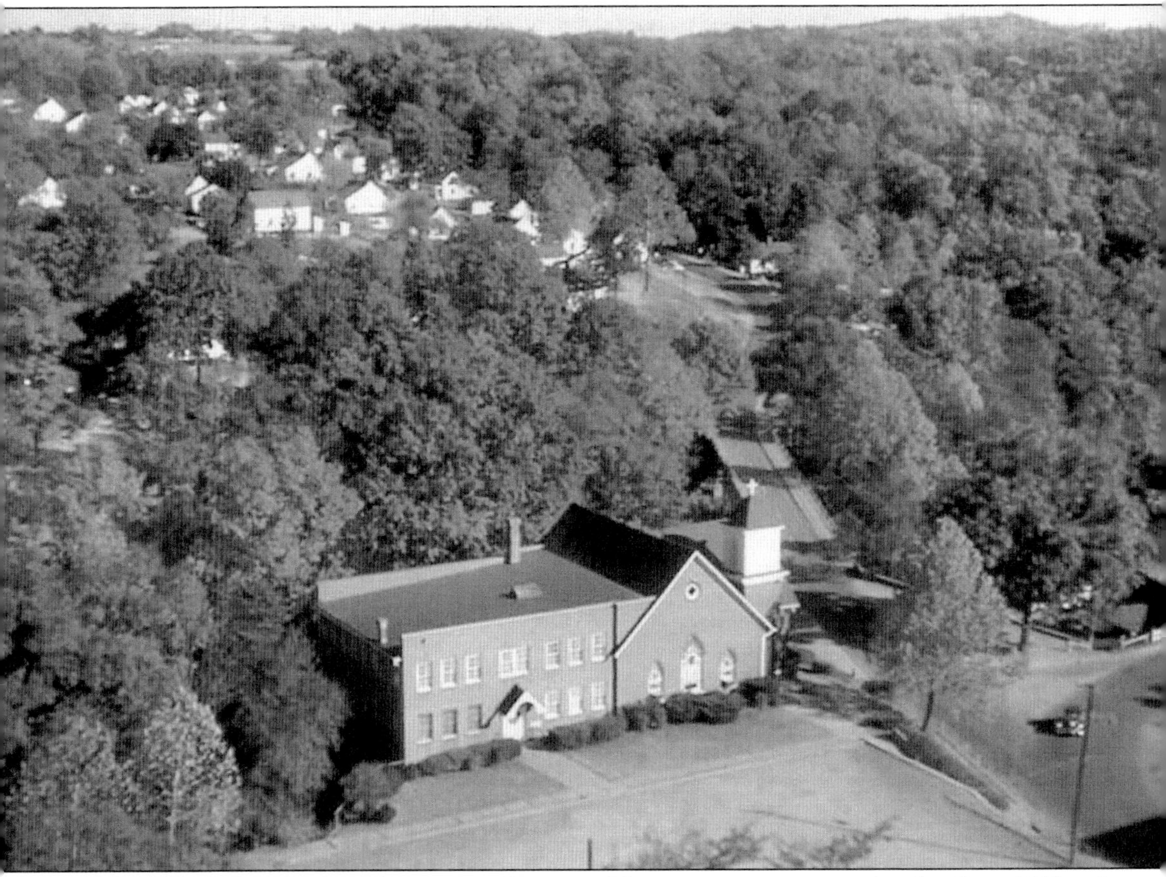

THE CLIFFSIDE UNITED METHODIST CHURCH. The sanctuary was completed in June 1912 and the "Education Building"—the wing at left—was added in 1927. The congregation still meets here, although membership, due to the changes in the town and downsizing of the mill, has dropped from over 400 in 1950 to 53 in 2005. It was a lovely fall day in 1954 when this was taken from atop the water tower. In the lower right, one fork of the road turns to the south, crosses over the river, and goes up River Street. The other leads over the "creek bridge" (shown just over the church steeple) that runs east toward Boiling Springs and Shelby. At the upper left, the white houses (all the town's houses were white) perched on the steep hillsides of Cliffside and Highland Streets glisten in the autumn sun. (Courtesy Harold Clardy.)

Five

The Cliffside Railroad

Our run may not be as long as some, but the track is just as wide.

–Cliffside trainman

It was obvious from the beginning that Cliffside Mills would need a better means of transport than horse-drawn wagons to bring in the raw materials—cotton, dyes, oil, starch, machine parts—and take out the tons of finished product.

The Seaboard Air Line (SAL) Railroad's tracks were just four miles away from the plant, and perhaps Mr. Haynes was waiting out the SAL to see if they intended to extend their service into Cliffside. They were a little slow in coming, so, naturally, he started his own railroad. At first, it focused on passenger service as well as freight, taking travelers to the newly named Cliffside Junction near Henrietta to connect with the SAL. The little line started with a couple of small, used engines purchased from the New York City elevated system; as the mill's output increased, the line graduated to bigger, more powerful engines.

The Cliffside Railroad (CRR) always had two "main" engines, so that if one needed repairs the other could take over. There was no turntable, so the engines always faced the same direction—north. If you saw an engine moving forward, it was on its way to the Junction. If in reverse, it was returning to Cliffside.

The little railroad was the pride of Cliffside throughout its 87 years. Photographers, writers, and train buffs would show up from time to time to show their appreciation for its colorful existence.

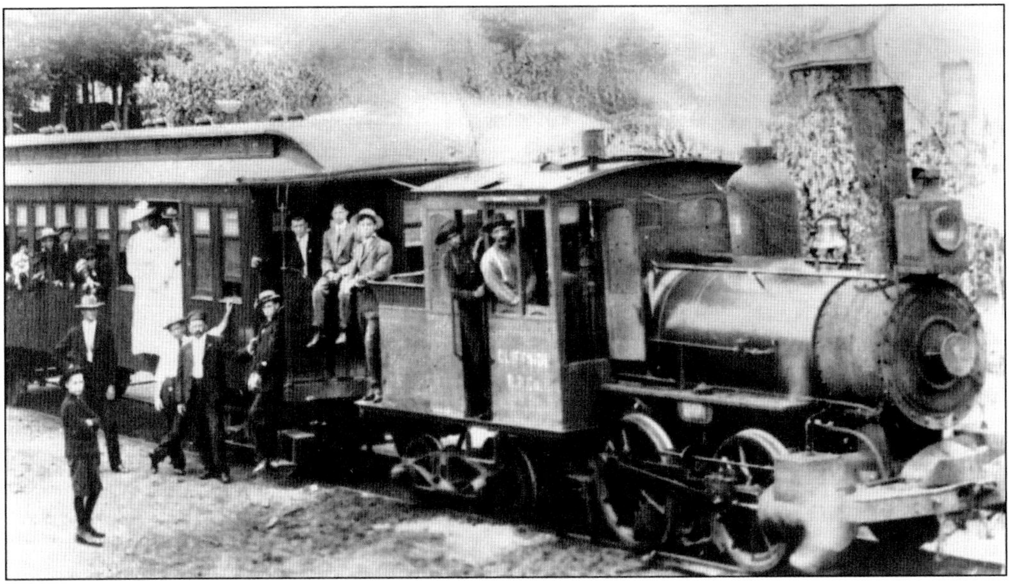

EXCURSION. On special occasions, such as Sundays, the little "dummy" line would fill up a couple of cars with nicely dressed passengers and chuff up the road to Cliffside Junction. Not much is recorded of what they would do there—perhaps have a picnic or visit friends in nearby Avondale. Later they would return, exhilarated from the ride, with photographs and memories of a grand time. (Courtesy Hazel Haynes Bridges.)

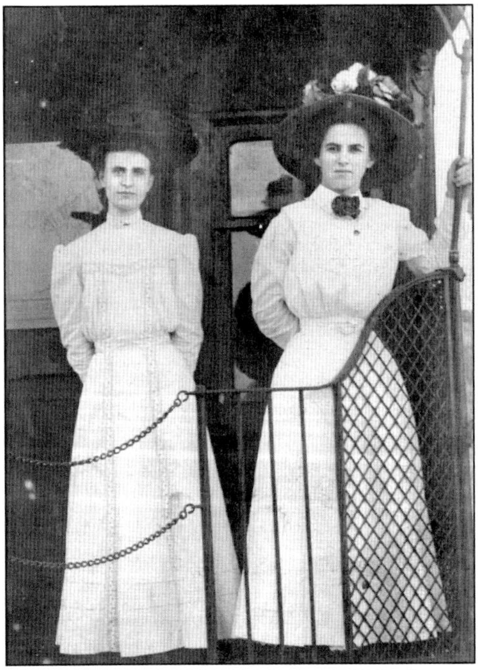

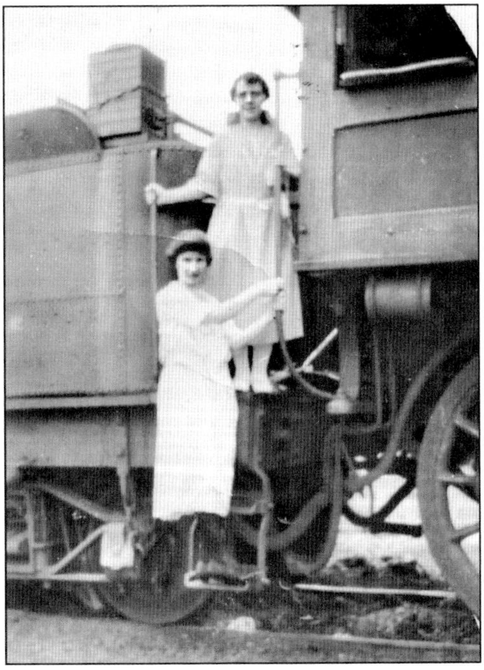

LADIES ON TRAINS. Women of Cliffside were not the least bit shy about traveling. The woman in the flowered hat at left is Ina Fortune Haynes. The picture at right must have been taken at the Junction on a Seaboard engine, because its design does not match any engine the CRR ever owned. The lady lowest on the steps is Pamelia Pruette. (Courtesy Hazel Haynes Bridges and Virginia Padgett Biggerstaff.)

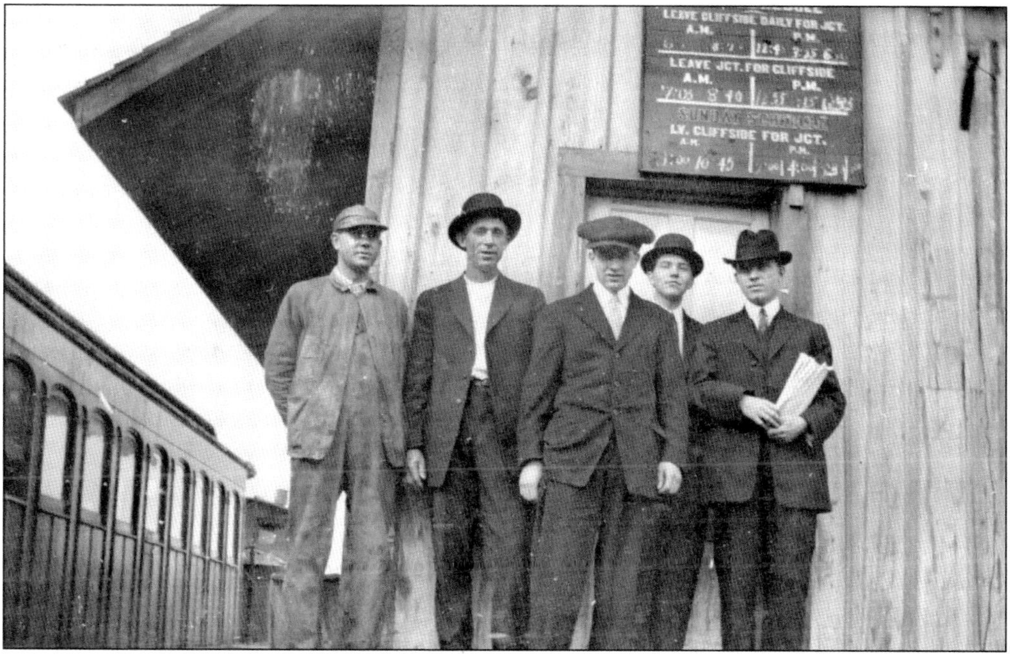

CLIFFSIDE STATION. The men are not identified in this photograph, taken in the era of passenger travel on the Cliffside around 1914. The schedule board shows the train made about four runs per day to the Junction. At some point, tracks were extended down into Henrietta, which must have increased the line's ridership. It is unknown where this building stood. (Courtesy Jim Ruppe.)

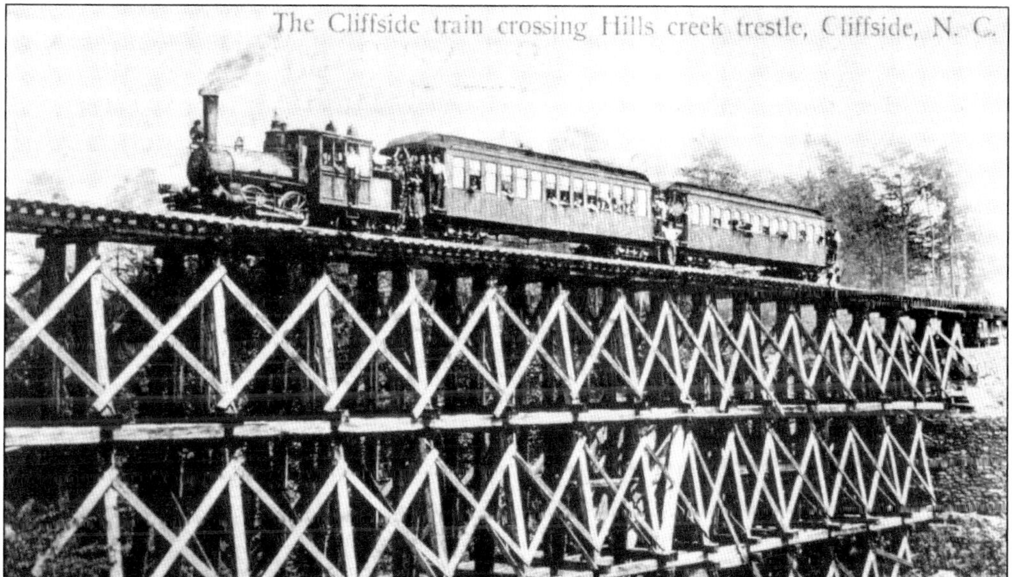

ATOP HILL'S CREEK TRESTLE. The engineer stopped the train in "mid-air" purposely for the photographer to take this picture. People are outside the train on the trestle, posing for the shot. Obviously, this was a time before liability insurance and lawsuits. All this was done on the orders of Mr. Haynes, no doubt, for the photograph was to be included in a series of Cliffside postcards. (Courtesy Hazel Haynes Bridges.)

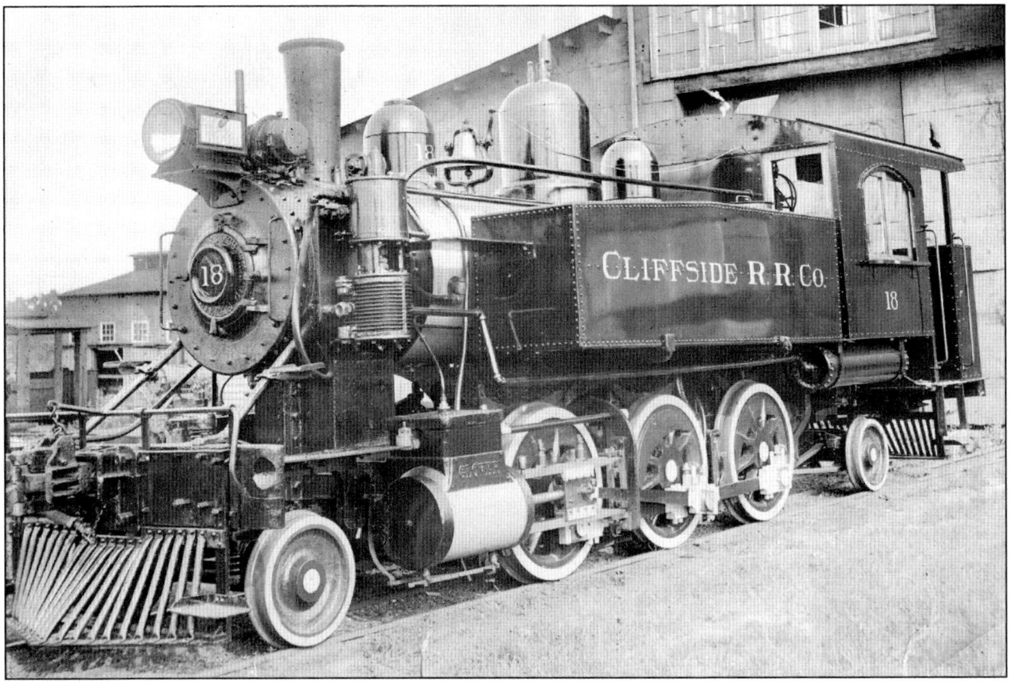

ENGINE NO. 18. In 1923, the CRR paid $10,000 for this brand new locomotive, the only new one the railroad would ever buy. It was a Glover model built in Marietta, Georgia, where this photograph was taken. Engine 18 rode the Cliffside tracks for 20 years until it was scrapped in 1943. (Courtesy Jim Scancarelli.)

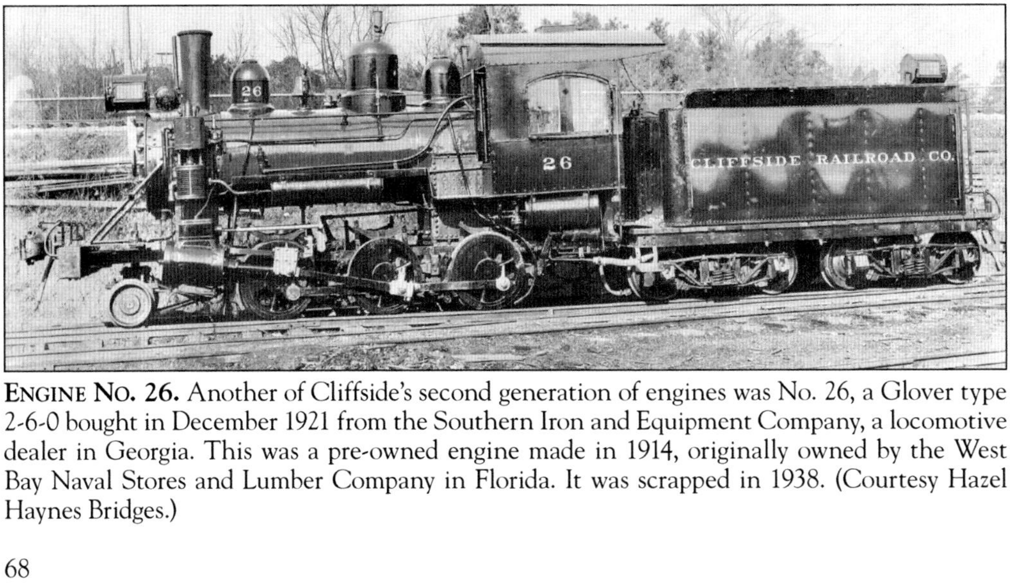

ENGINE NO. 26. Another of Cliffside's second generation of engines was No. 26, a Glover type 2-6-0 bought in December 1921 from the Southern Iron and Equipment Company, a locomotive dealer in Georgia. This was a pre-owned engine made in 1914, originally owned by the West Bay Naval Stores and Lumber Company in Florida. It was scrapped in 1938. (Courtesy Hazel Haynes Bridges.)

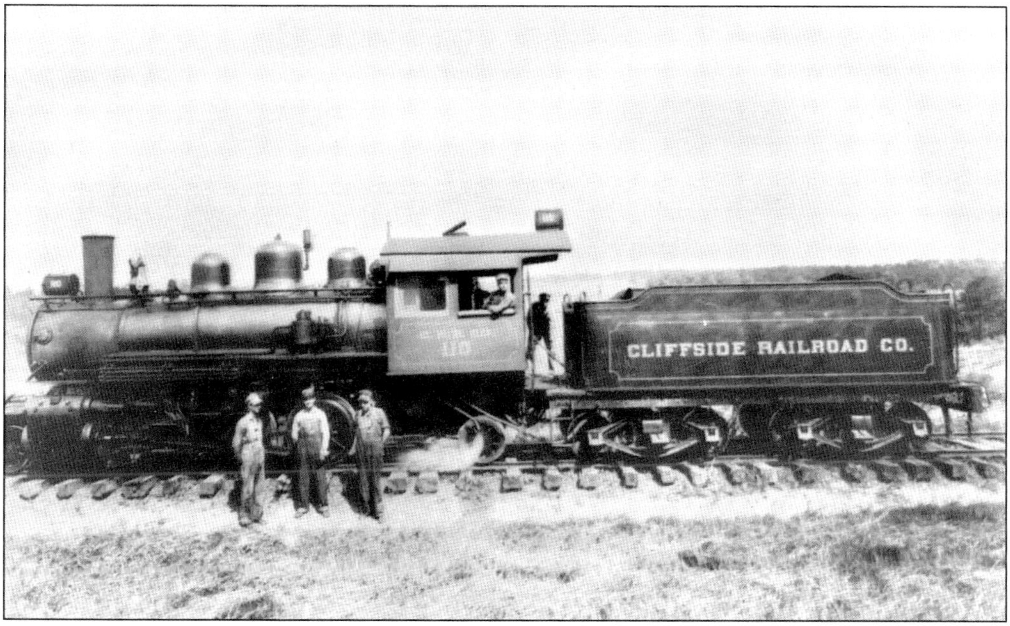

ENGINE NO. 110. One of the newer steam engines at Cliffside was the 110, a 20-year-old Vulcan. Cliffside acquired it in 1933 and used it for 30 years. From left to right are John Waters, Shirley White, and John Padgett. Cordie Freeman is in the cab, with Van Macopson on the tender. The noble 110 had the "honor" in July 1962 of hauling in its own replacement, a diesel. (Courtesy Jim Scancarelli.)

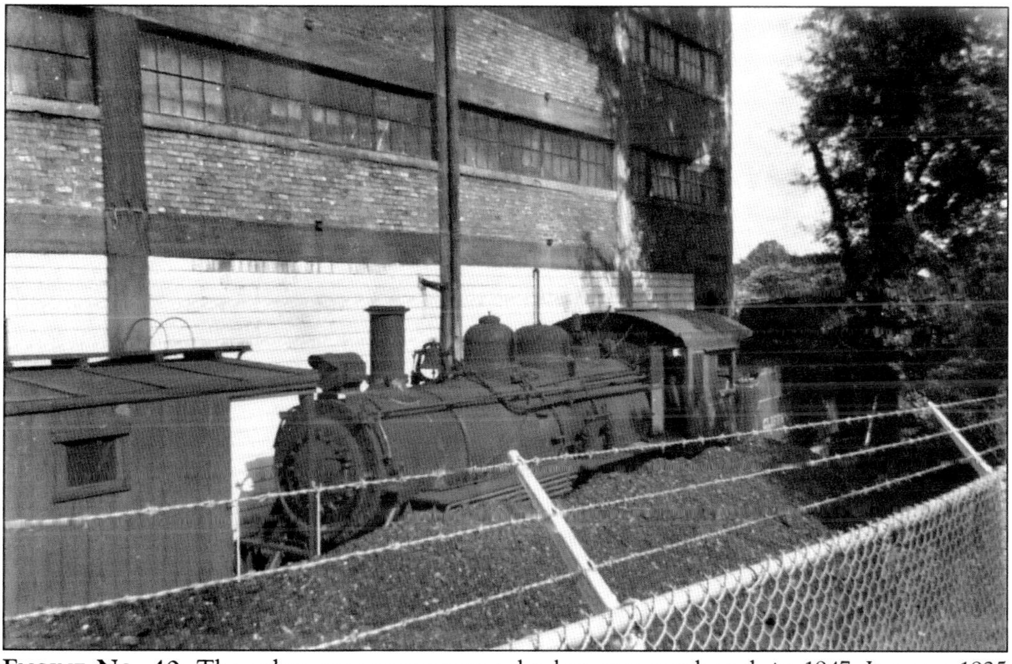

ENGINE NO. 40. The other new steamer was the last one purchased, in 1947. It was a 1925 Baldwin and it too was used until the diesels came in. It was later sold to the New Hope and Ivyland Railroad in Pennsylvania, where it still runs today. Here, in 1958, it is backed up beside the finishing room, where its fire has been banked for the night. (Courtesy Jim Scancarelli.)

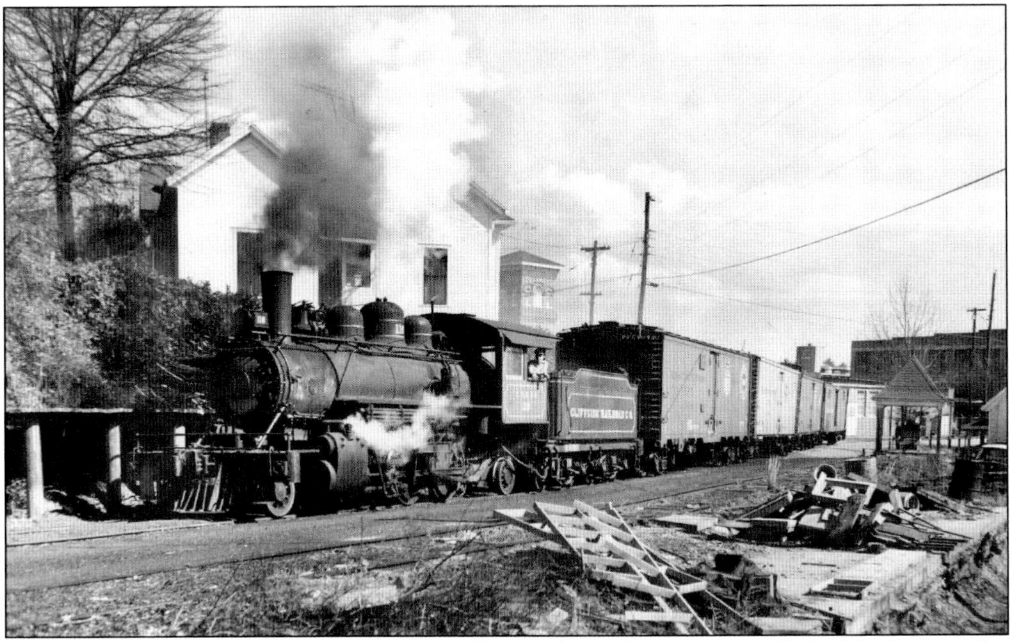

HEADIN' OUT. No. 110 has just left the mill's finishing department with Bud Padgett at the helm, crossing South Main Street and puffing smoke into someone's kitchen window. It is taking another trainload of towels to the world. Some years, these old engines would haul over 50,000 tons out of Cliffside. This photograph was taken in June 1961 by Roy Lee Harris, another fine Cliffside photographer. (Courtesy Jim Scancarelli.)

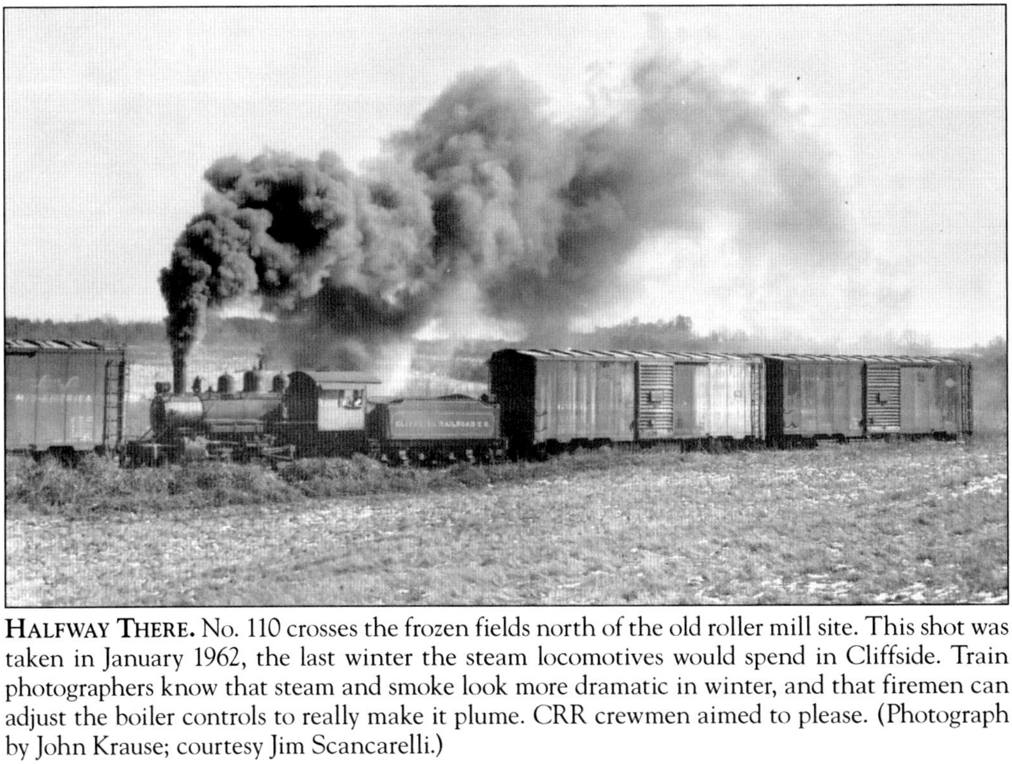

HALFWAY THERE. No. 110 crosses the frozen fields north of the old roller mill site. This shot was taken in January 1962, the last winter the steam locomotives would spend in Cliffside. Train photographers know that steam and smoke look more dramatic in winter, and that firemen can adjust the boiler controls to really make it plume. CRR crewmen aimed to please. (Photograph by John Krause; courtesy Jim Scancarelli.)

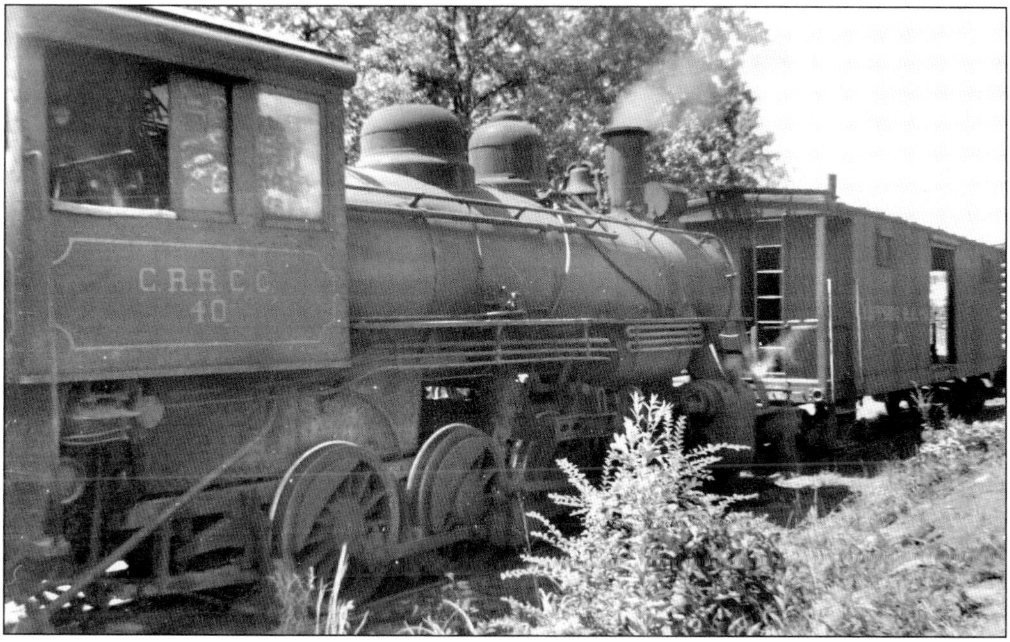

NO. 40 AND THE CUSTOM CAR. The crewmen of Cliffside Railroad were innovators. They needed a combination caboose and boxcar, so they built one, shown here in this 1958 photograph. The CRR was using steam equipment long after other roads had switched to diesel because Cliffside men, with their dedication, expertise, and improvisational skills, were able to nurse these old engines way past their predictable life spans. (Courtesy Jim Scancarelli.)

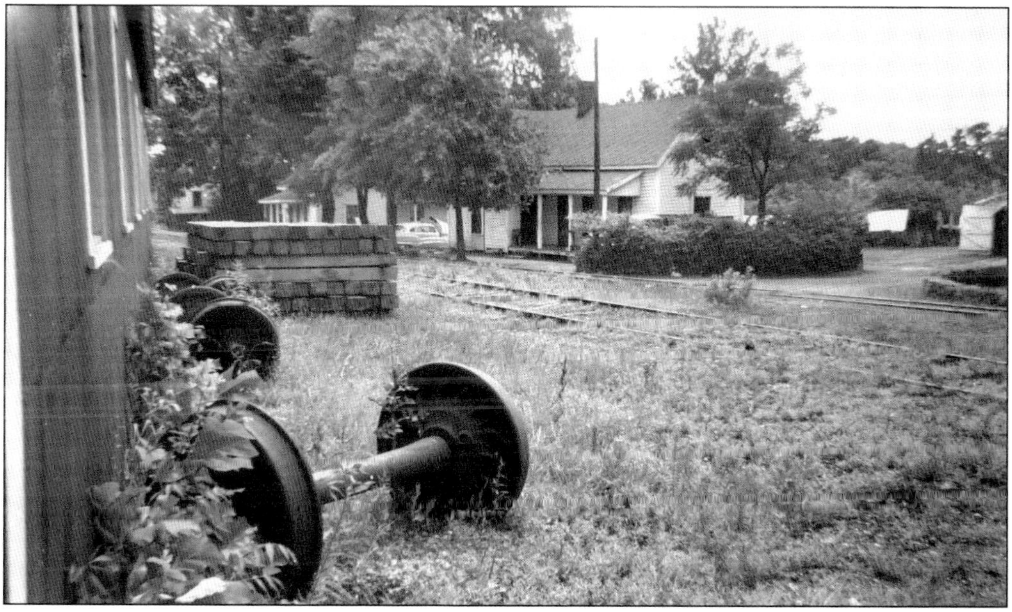

RAILROAD STREET, 1958. Alongside the engine shed spare "trucks" (wheels on axles) and crossties stand at the ready. Housewives on both sides of the tracks kept the train's daily schedule in mind so they could take their laundry in before the train rumbled by and turned their whites a little less so. But the engineers were polite; they tried their best to tiptoe by houses. (Courtesy Jim Scancarelli.)

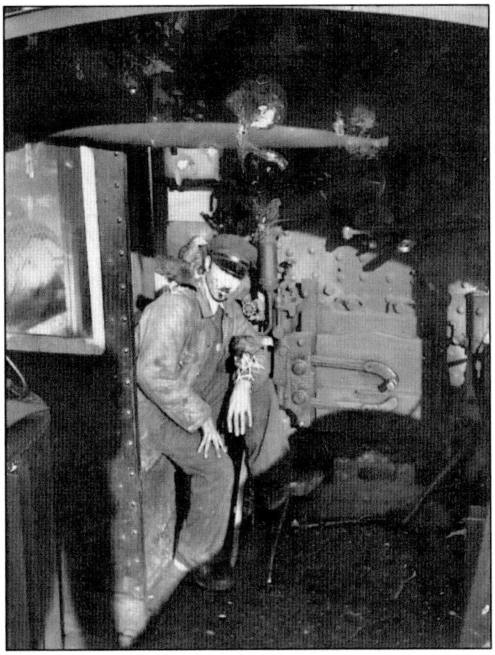

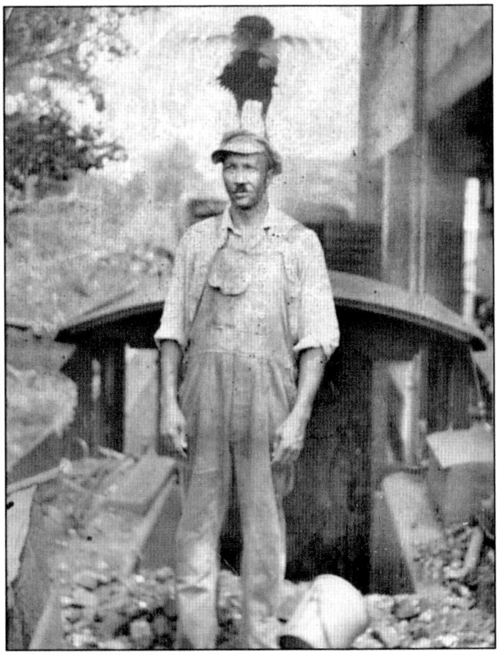

TENDER CHICKENS. A favorite story involved a mother hen and her chicks that were found trackside and placed in the tender by fireman Van Macopson, shown above. Whenever the train stopped, Van put them on the ground to scratch and forage. Soon they became trained to return to the train when the whistle blew and to jump off when the train stopped. (Courtesy Jim Scancarelli.)

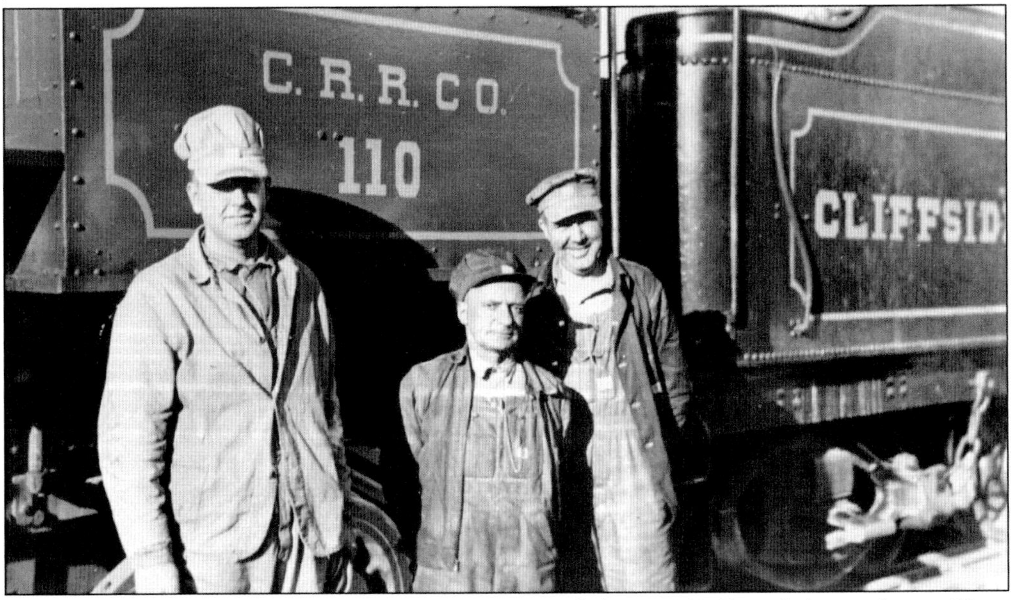

OLD-TIMERS. Three of the last steam men are pictured about 1960. From left to right are Shaw Biggerstaff, Cordie "Shine" Freeman, and Odell Biggerstaff. Shaw was CRR's shipping agent, who frequently helped out on the crew. Fireman Freeman began work on the road at the age of 15 in 1920. Engineer Odell, Shaw's uncle, started with the Seaboard as a young man and came to the CRR in 1953. (Courtesy Jim Scancarelli.)

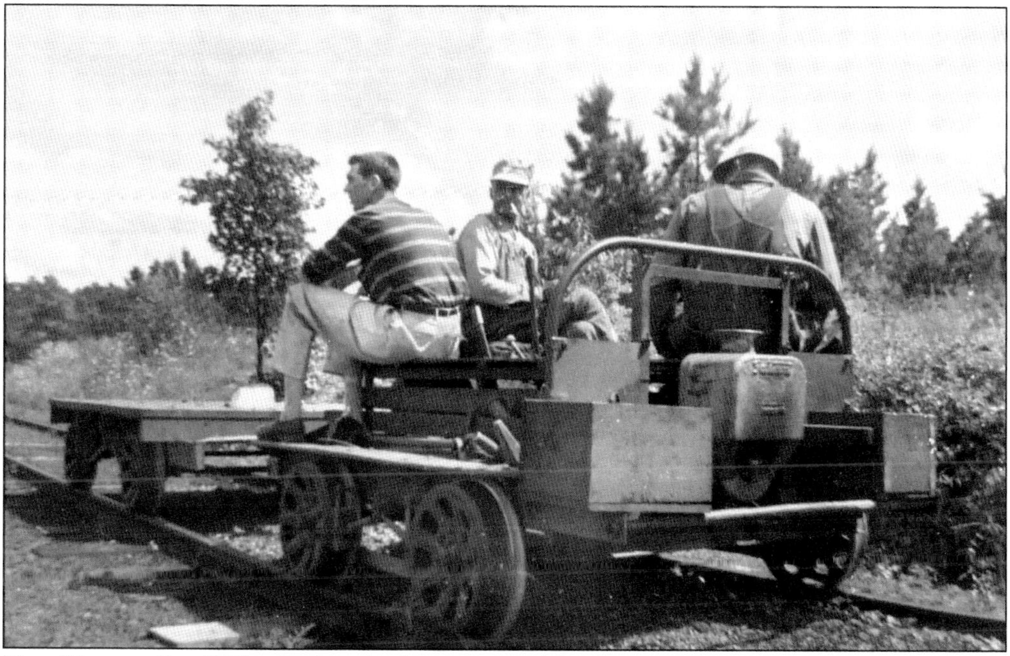

THE "PICKER-PAT." This little vehicle was named for the sound it made as it hummed along the tracks. Although it weighed close to 1,000 pounds, the crew routinely lifted it on and off the line. In the center is Cordie "Shine" Freeman, whose life and the railroad began in the same year, 1905. At left is Lee Kolbe, a visiting photographer; at right is fireman Eli Wilkins. (Courtesy Jim Scancarelli.)

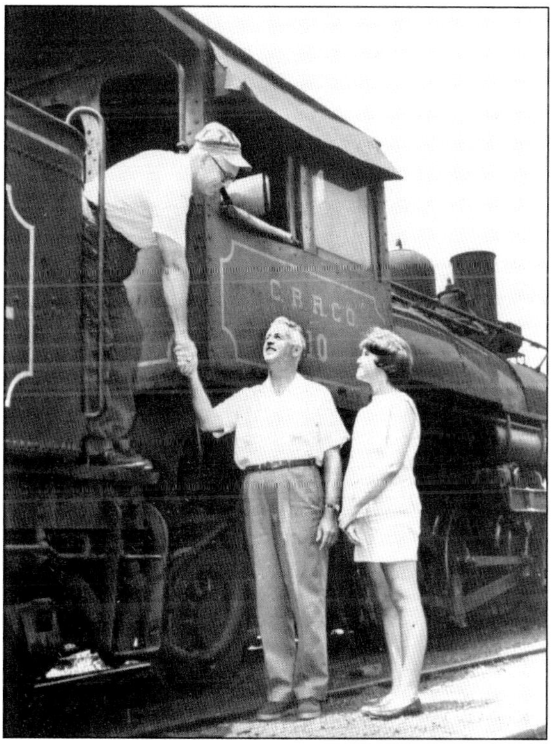

LAST RUN. On July 20, 1962, after 55 years of steam operations, the last run was made by No. 110, and both it and No. 40 were retired. Company president Paul Bridges and his 14-year-old daughter, Janice, say farewell with a handshake to conductor Shaw Biggerstaff. The CRR was the last commercial railroad in North Carolina to convert from steam to diesel. (Courtesy Hazel Haynes Bridges.)

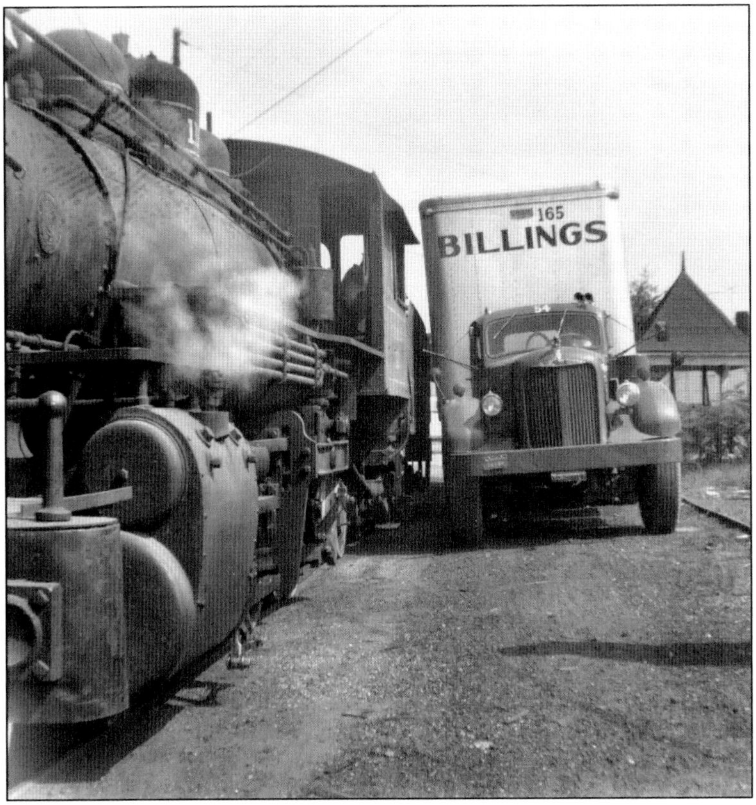

TUG OF WAR. At Cliffside, diesels were not a good long-term solution. The battle between rail and highway transport was already over: the trucks had won. As the years went by, the mill had fewer steady customers, and of those, fewer requested their goods be shipped by rail. The greater war was between domestic and foreign textile products. (Courtesy Jim Scancarelli.)

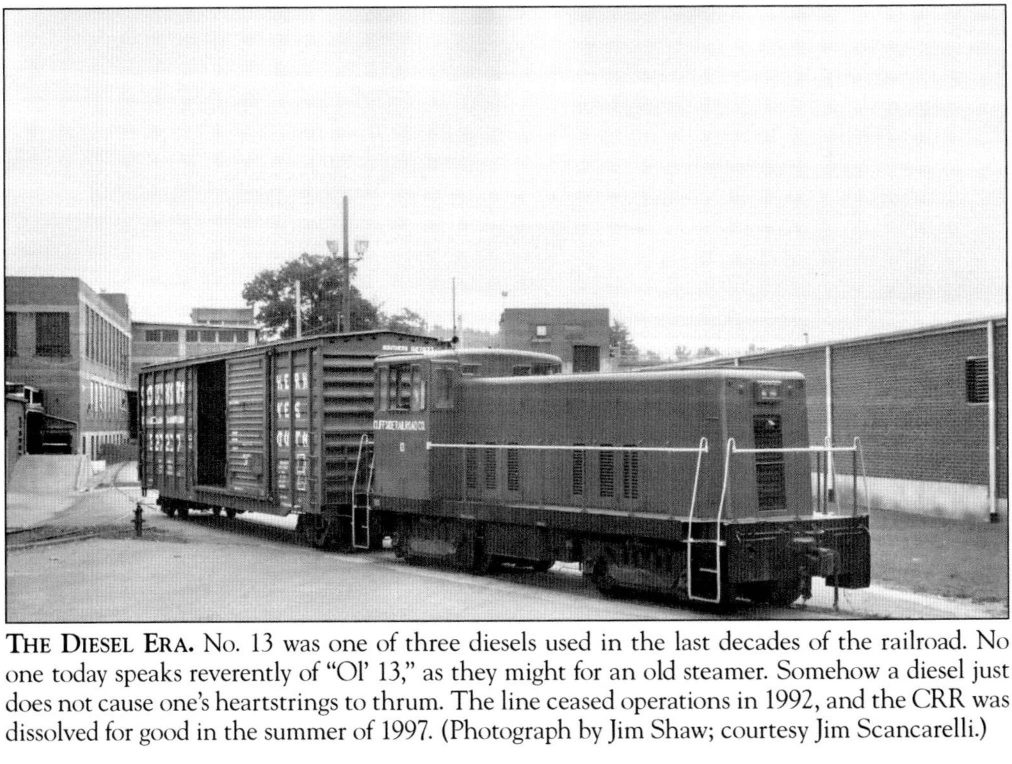

THE DIESEL ERA. No. 13 was one of three diesels used in the last decades of the railroad. No one today speaks reverently of "Ol' 13," as they might for an old steamer. Somehow a diesel just does not cause one's heartstrings to thrum. The line ceased operations in 1992, and the CRR was dissolved for good in the summer of 1997. (Photograph by Jim Shaw; courtesy Jim Scancarelli.)

Six

THE RIVER

Ben Humphries' feelings for the river run deeper than the water level. "It's hard to put in words," he says. "I know my people always lived along the river. That's where my heritage is."

–News item, 1984

It is not a grand stream like the Mississippi or the Ohio, not worthy of a diary entry ("Today we crossed the mighty Second Broad"), but in the heyday of cotton mill towns and productive farms along its banks it served its purpose, and it was a source of power and livelihood for those inclined to partake of its benefits.

The Second Broad begins as a trickle about 40 miles to the northwest near Marion, in the hills of McDowell County. Like a cornered snake, it darts its way down into Rutherford, past Union Mills, Logan, Bostic, Forest City, through Caroleen and Henrietta, and ultimately into Cliffside, where, in a final spasm, it jerks itself into a double horseshoe curve. It slithers a few more miles to the southeast before emptying into the Broad River, which, after being further engorged by the muddy waters of the First Broad, pushes southward to join with the Saluda near Columbia.

Perhaps the old river's past was but a prelude to greater things. It is said plans are afoot to "repurpose" the river and part of the old Cliffside mill to generate "green" (purely hydroelectric) energy and to turn the river in the vicinity of Cliffside into a place that will attract new generations.

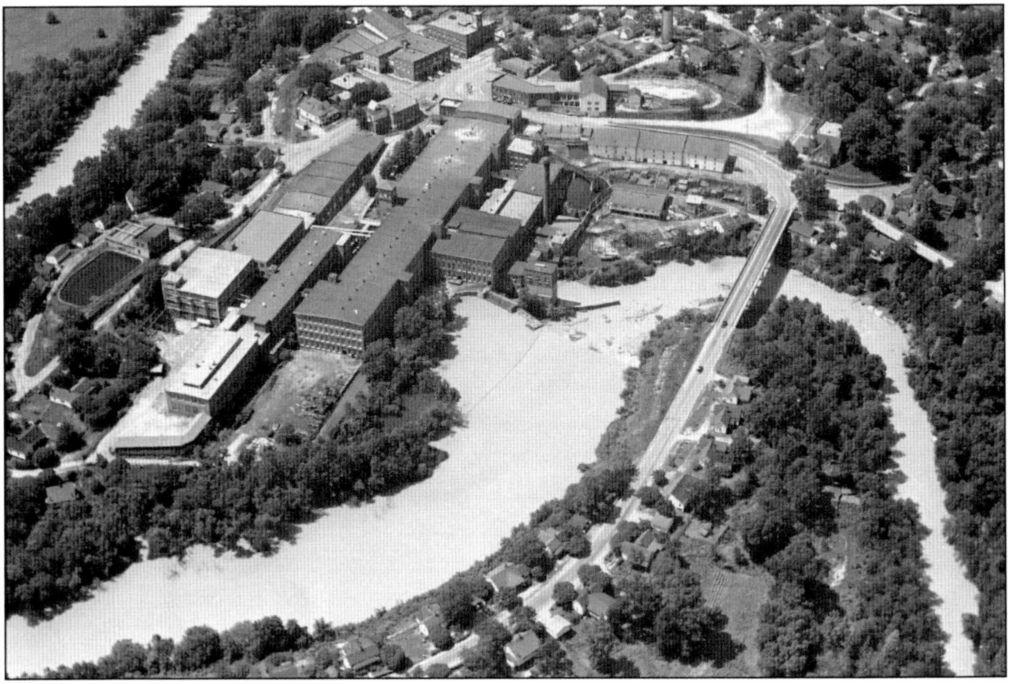

SERPENTINE. The river comes down from the north (upper left) to form a pond. The massive mill sits on the peninsula formed by the bend in the stream. At its widest point, the dam restricts its flow; the water that manages to escape makes another abrupt turn under the River Street bridge and resumes its southeast journey. (Courtesy Joan Humphries Harris.)

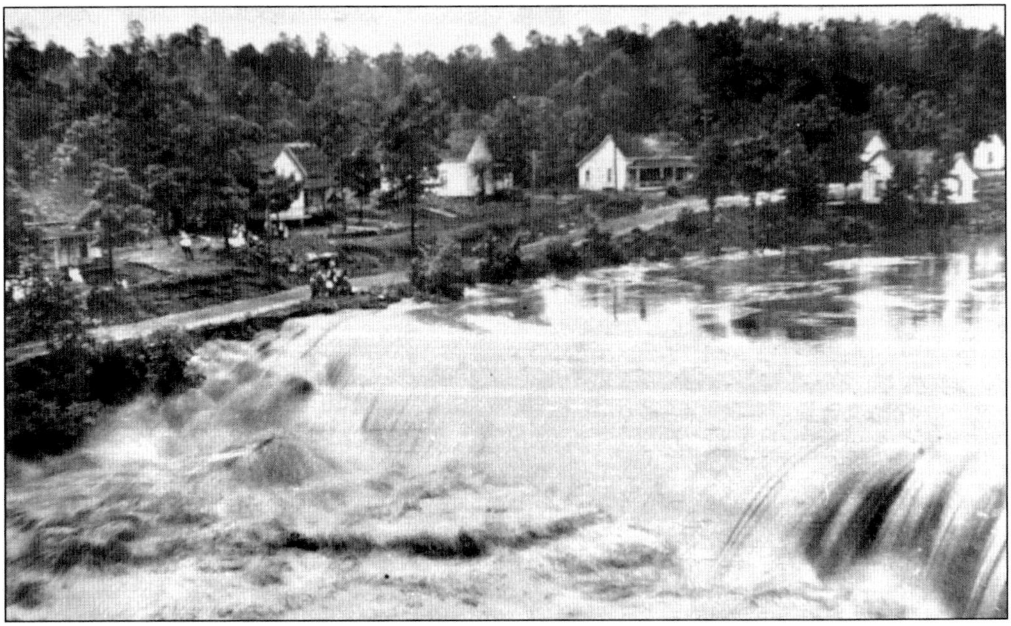

THE FLOOD. Mabel Bridges Cargill recalls, "In the year 1916, we had a terrible flood in the county. . . . The water got into the mill; it was pouring over the dam in torrents. It was about to wash away the bridge. I can remember how the men went down and tied that bridge with wires to keep it from washing away." (Courtesy Phillip White.)

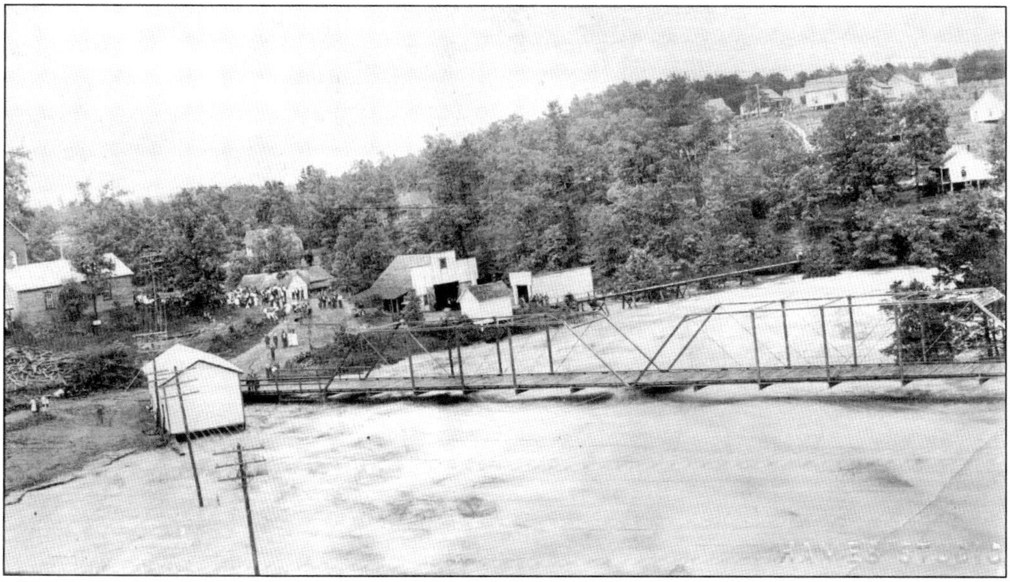

HIGH WATER. This is the bridge the men were trying to save in 1916, and they were successful. Half the town appears to be on the bank, watching anxiously. This rare view of the area shows the Methodist church and the wood shop at left. In the center is a livery stable, and farther right is a footbridge over to Highway Street. (Courtesy Ginny Greene Reid.)

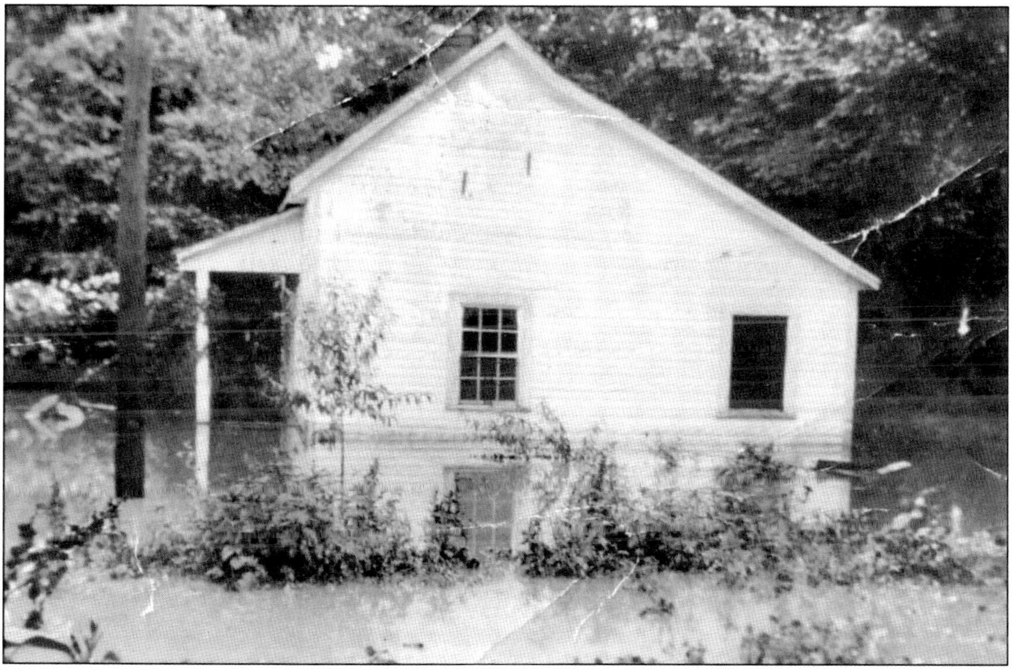

HOUSE ON GOFORTH FLAT. Tom Crow had to evacuate his family from this little house near the Sulfur Well behind the Methodist church during the Great Flood of 1916. They removed most of their furniture through the open window. The flood was devastating to other areas of the county and state, but Cliffside fared well by comparison. (Courtesy Judson O. Crow.)

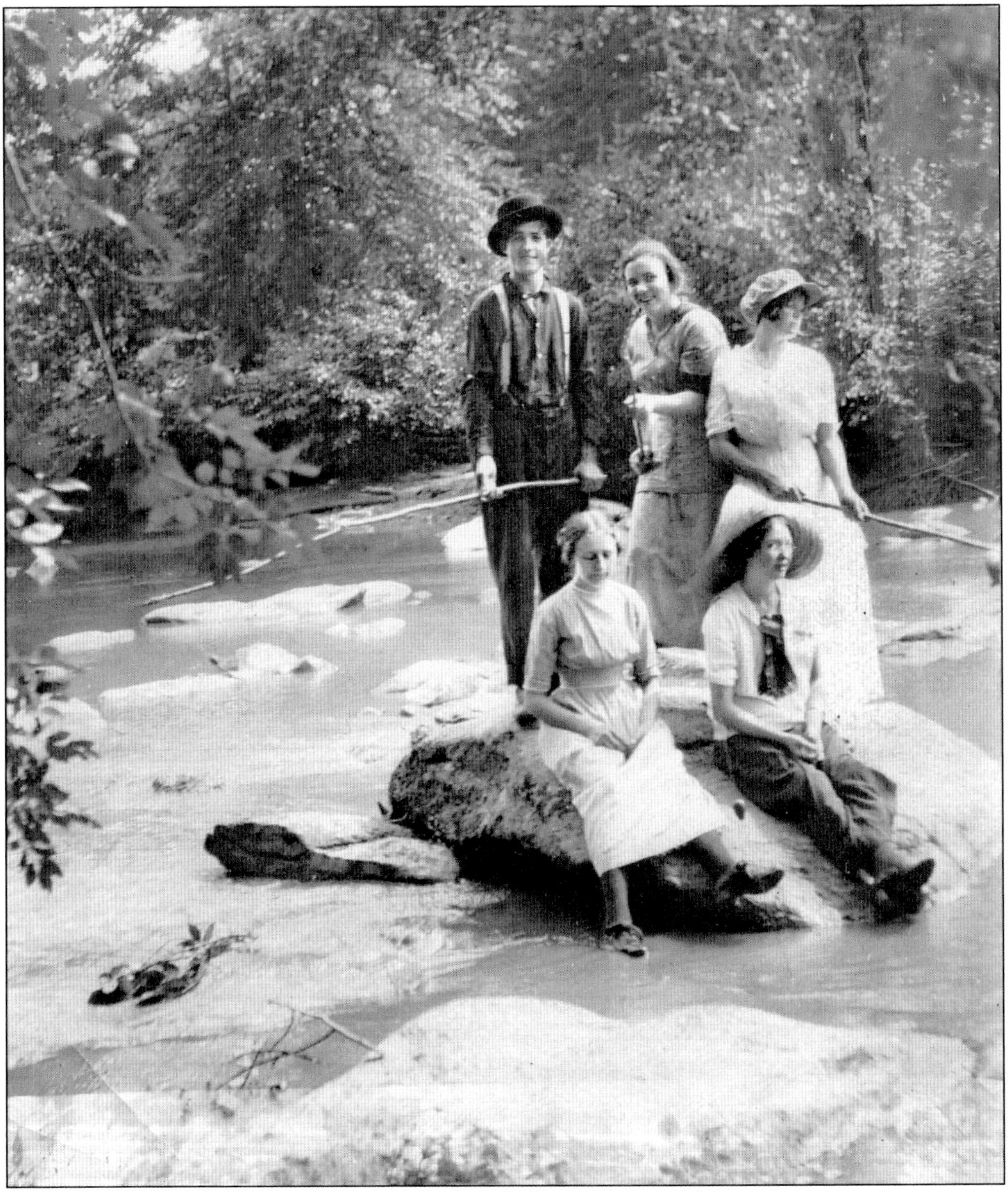

AMERICAN IDYLL. At every opportunity, Cliffside's young people gravitated to the river, to skip rocks off the water, watch minnows in the shallows, or pretend to fish. From upper left, clockwise, are Thomas Mack Crow, looking very much like a grown-up Tom Sawyer; Edna Hawkins; Lula Ricketts (later Mrs. Tom Crow); Dorcas Hawkins; and Ruth Mashburn. Dorcas and Edna were daughters of Joseph and Etta Smith Hawkins. (Courtesy Judson O. Crow.)

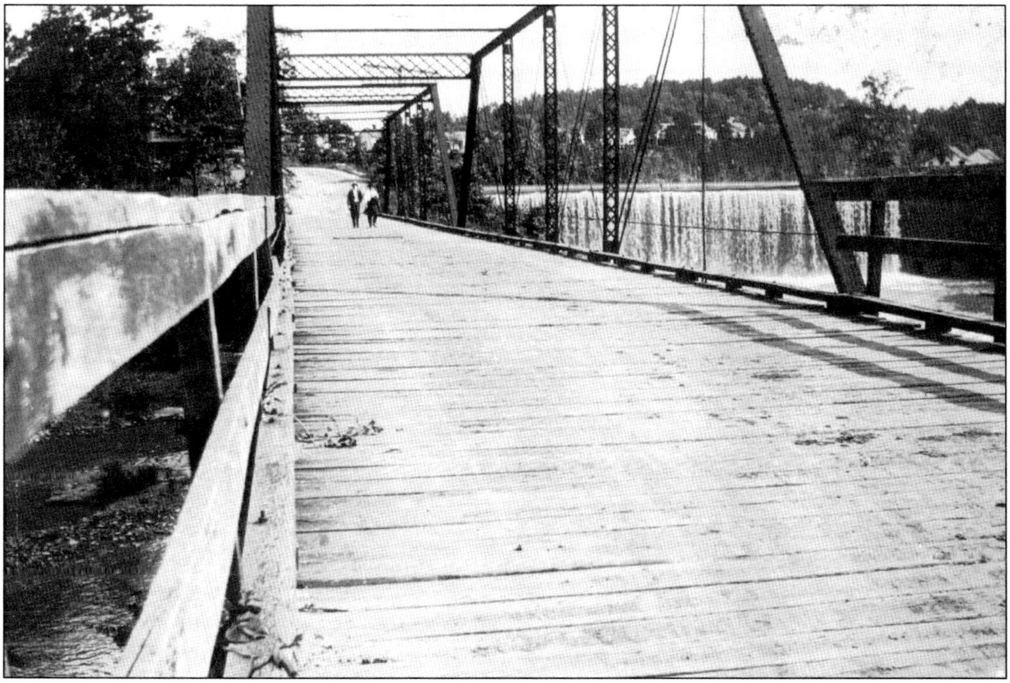

OLD IRON BRIDGE. Shown is Cliffside's first bridge, with iron supports and wooden guardrails. The men in the photograph are approaching town from River Street. Some of the houses that once lined the river at the mill's south end can be seen to the right of the waterfall. There being few cars in those years, the bridge was used more by pedestrians than vehicles. (Courtesy Carolyn Greene Waters.)

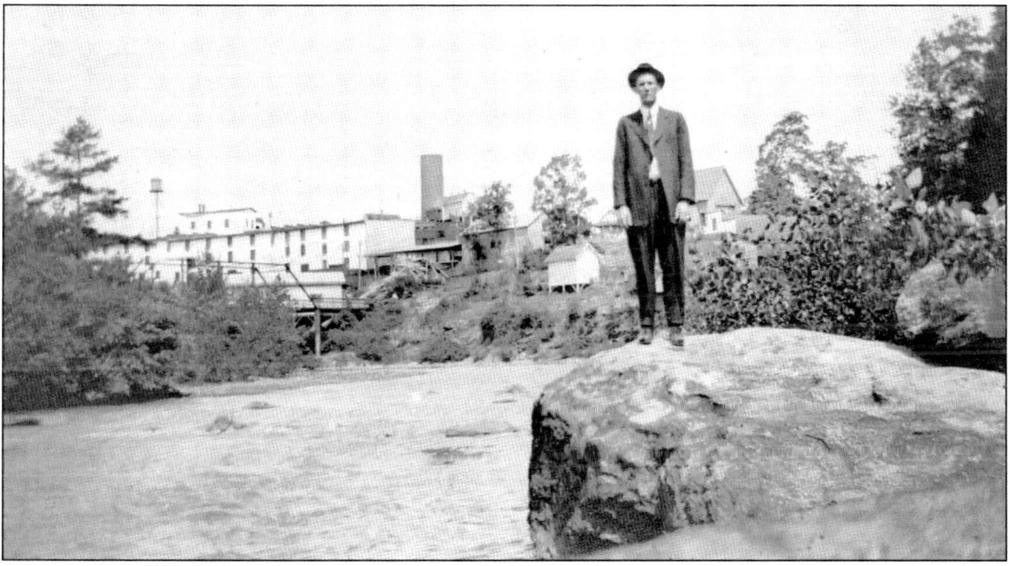

LOOKING UPRIVER. An unidentified man poses on a boulder downriver from the iron bridge, where the stream straightens out for its run to the Main Broad. In the background are white warehouses and water towers. At the end of the bridge is a sawmill. The company used lots of lumber and owned timber forests elsewhere in the state to provide it. (Courtesy Carolyn Greene Waters.)

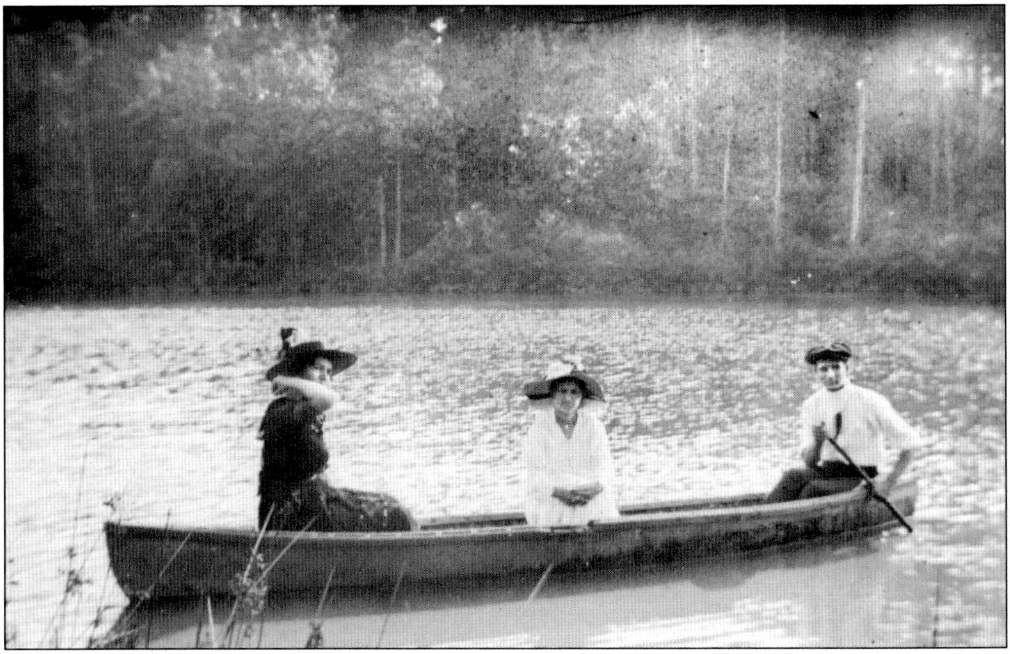

CANOEING ON THE POND. Blanche Edwards Campbell (left), Lillie McFalls (center), and Charles F. Moore take to the water. Blanche married Luther Campbell, and they lived at 30 Main Street for many years. She was one of Cliffside's librarians; he worked in Jackson's Department Store. In a 1913 *Skyland* magazine, Moore was singled out as a "mill operative" doing well at a school in Virginia. (Courtesy Carolyn Greene Waters.)

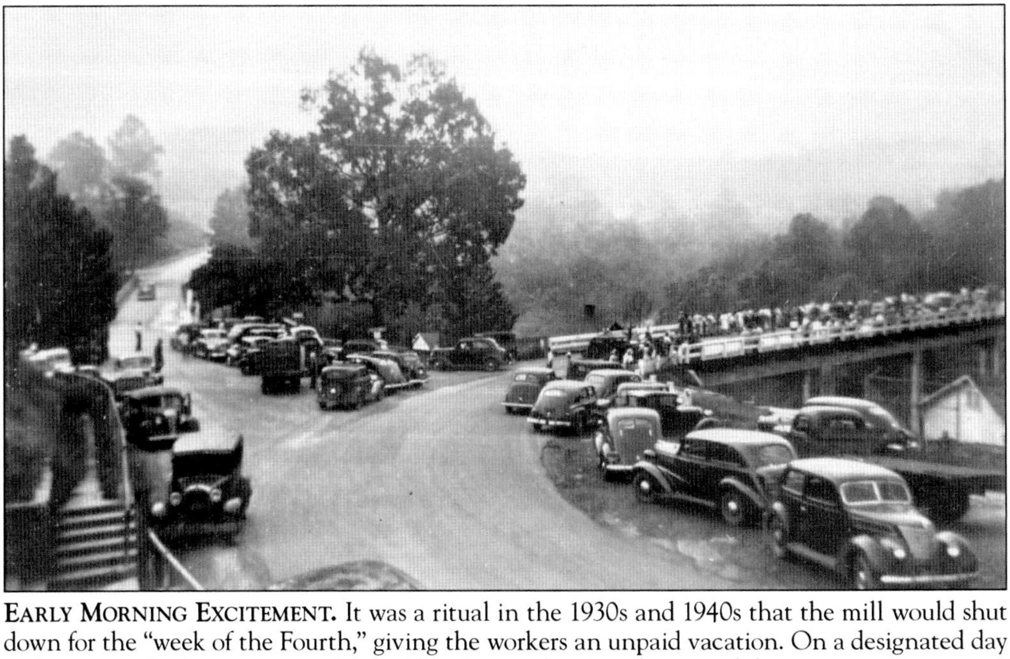

EARLY MORNING EXCITEMENT. It was a ritual in the 1930s and 1940s that the mill would shut down for the "week of the Fourth," giving the workers an unpaid vacation. On a designated day early that week, the townspeople would gather at the river for one of the most exciting events of the year. Parking wherever they could, they came to participate or to watch. (Courtesy Loree Harrill Steele.)

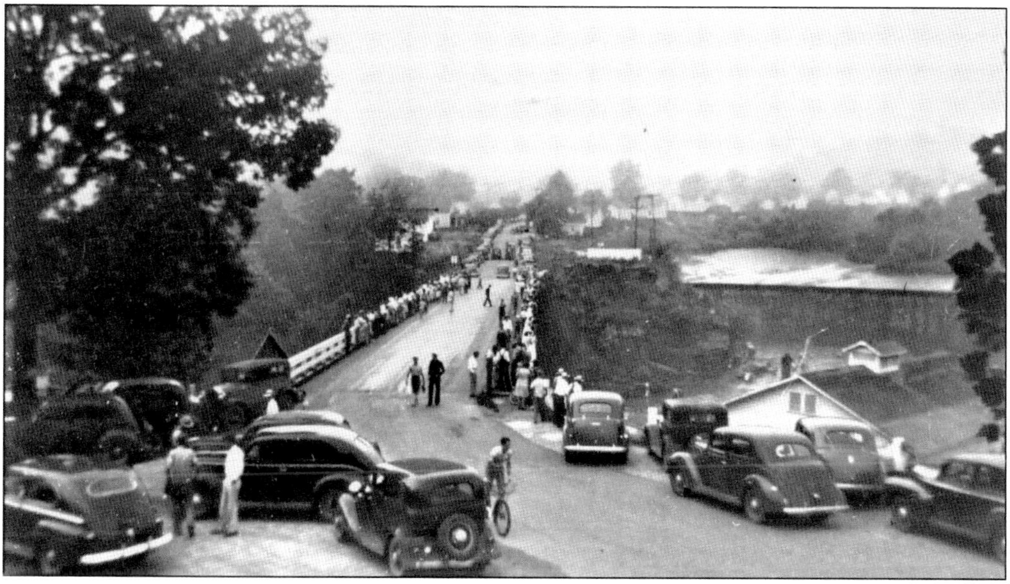

DRAWING THE POND. The dam's floodgates were opened to let the pond water escape, providing an opportunity to clean and paint the mill's water wheel. Behind the dam, the lowering water revealed a huge field of mud, some of which would gush through the gates along with hundreds of carp and catfish. Folks would fan out across the bridge to enjoy the show. (Courtesy Loree Harrill Steele.)

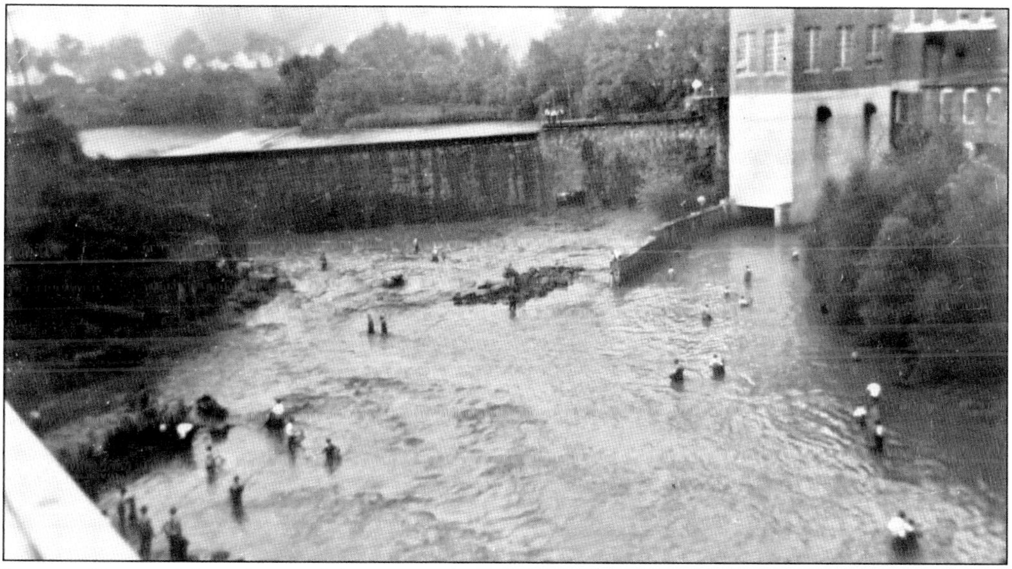

IN THE RIVER. The object of the excitement was catching, or watching someone else catch, the bewildered fish as they came tumbling down the stream. The men, in their oldest, most ragged clothes, would wade chest deep in the muddy water with wooden-handled baskets made of chicken wire and pounce on the big fish as they came swirling by. (Courtesy Loree Harrill Steele.)

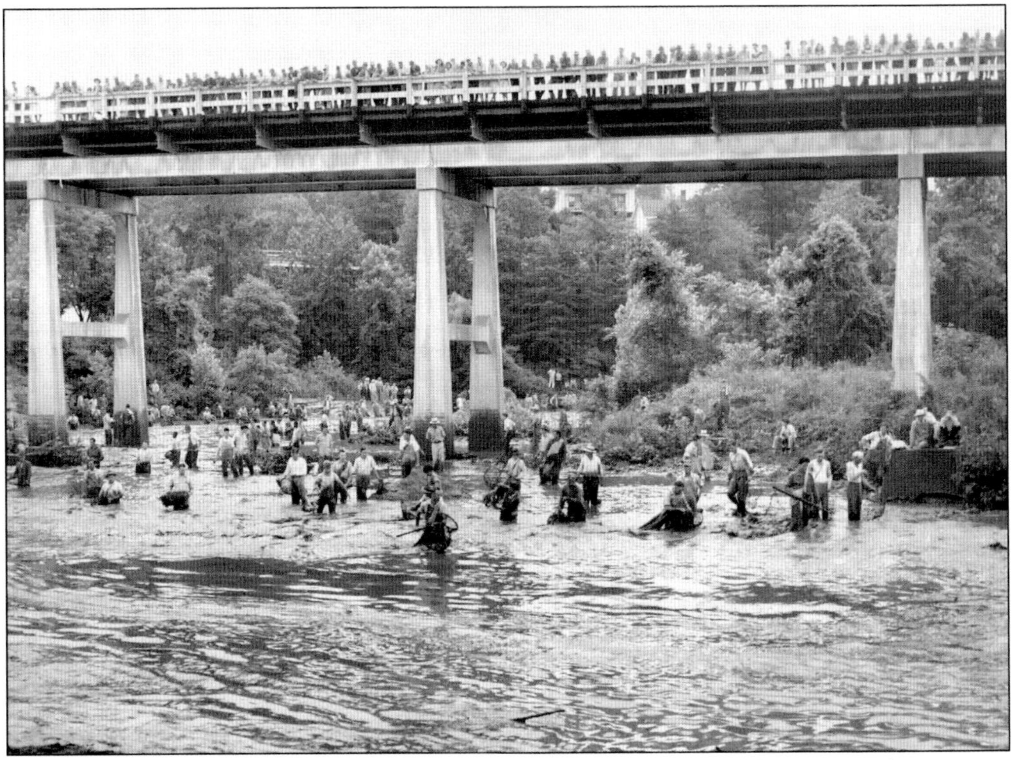

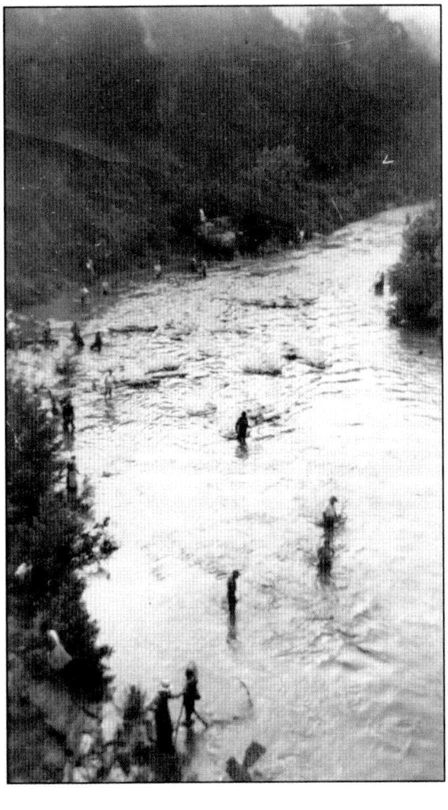

FOOD FOR THE TAKING. Not just an adventure, this was a chance for a man and his sons to provide food for their family at no expense, as their kinfolk cheered them on from the bridges. Each man wanted just enough for a meal or two as there were no freezers in those days. Those who caught an over-abundance would share with those who caught none. (Courtesy Mack Hendrick.)

AFTERMATH. After a couple of hours the water would slow down and recede. The sickest, most disoriented fish would have been caught, while the rest slipped away down river with their little fish brains wondering, "What in the world was that?" The men would slog to shore, go home, clean the fish, take a bath, and wait for suppertime. Life was good. (Courtesy Loree Harrill Steele.)

Seven

GENTLE PEOPLE

As our little family grew and grew, life in Cliffside continued to be filled with a quiet happiness built out of love, respect, and pride in each other. We were fortunate in that we always had plenty of love and plenty of good food to eat.

–Jennie Hawkins Metcalfe

It's easy to forget that our predecessors, the people "back yonder," had a large part in making us what we became. Speaking at the 1922 dedication of the R. R. Haynes Memorial Building, Rev. A. C. Swofford said, "It has been a source of great joy to me that the same spirit [Mr. Haynes] left here, that he founded in Cliffside, still abounds. You can come into the town and feel it, and be inspired by it, and rejoice in it, and glory in it."

Youngsters would listen to the old folks talk, those who had lived back then with Mr. Raleigh and other pioneers of the town who shared his manners and values. Most hoped to absorb their wisdom and advice. They would try to emulate their elders' honesty, gentle art of persuasion, guilelessness, and respect for their fellow man.

Each face in this book might bring back a fond memory of a day, a place, a remark, a story, or a tender moment that fills the heart and puts readers back in a little house on a hilly Cliffside street, where it seemed life would never change, and they would all stay young forever.

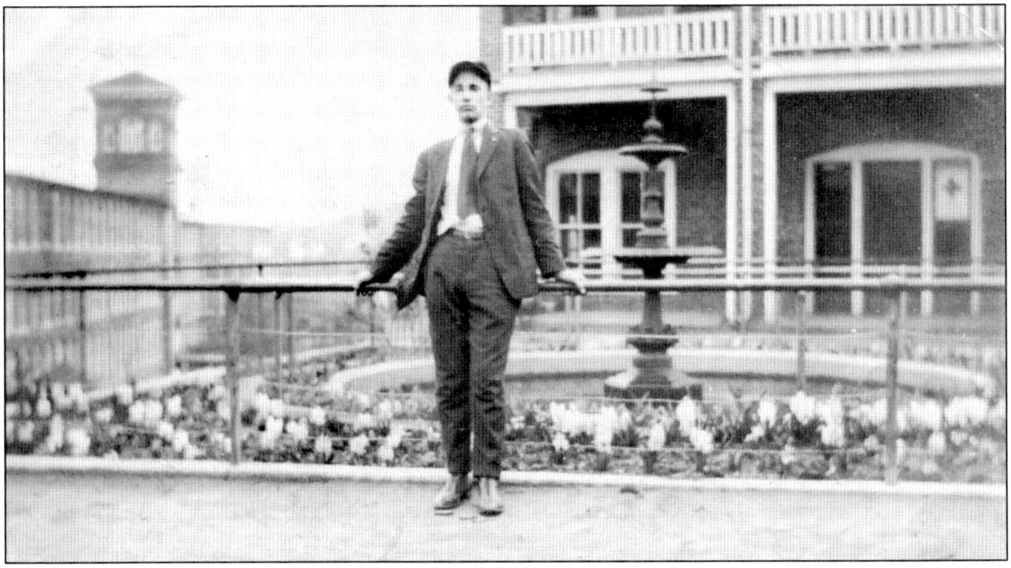

FLAY FREEMAN. Born in 1902, Flay died at only 23 in a tragic accident at the dairy north of town. He and Gordon Philbeck were swimming in a deep hole where sand had been pumped out. Flay called for help, but Gordon was unable to save him. Ironically, 52 years later, Flay's brother Cordie would also die from drowning when his car plunged into the millpond. (Courtesy Peggy Blanton Hadden.)

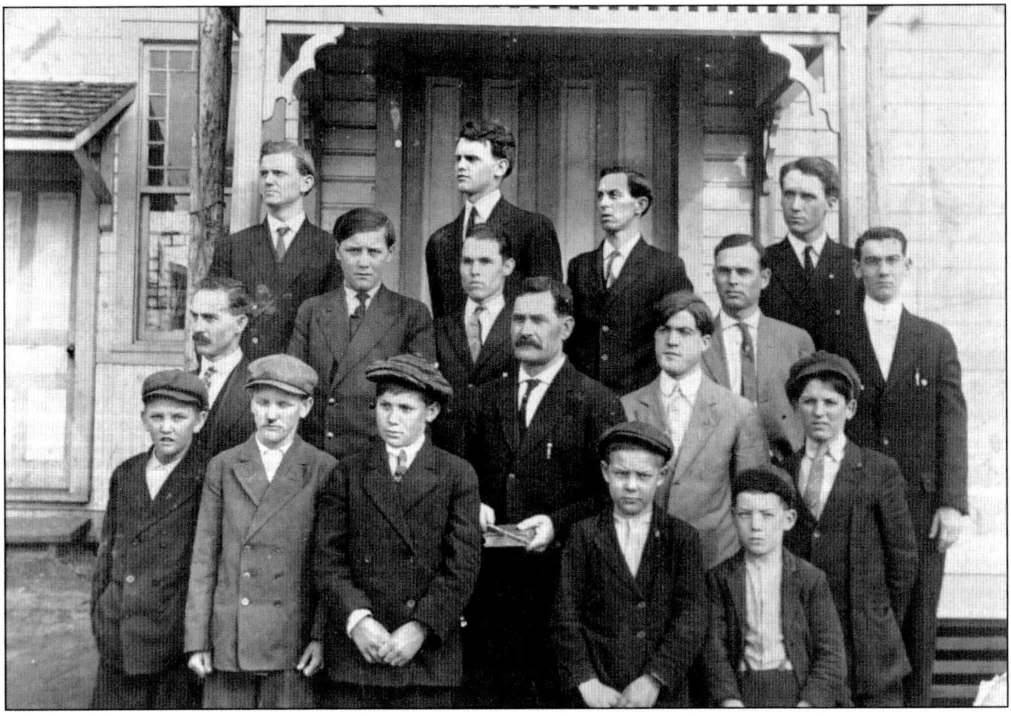

MEN AND BOYS. At the entrance to Cliffside's first schoolhouse, the principal, Dr. J. L. Hunt (also the Baptist minister), assembles a study group around 1918. Dr. Hunt, holding a book, is front and center. To his left is Thomas Mack Crow. Behind Dr. Hunt and to his right is Robert Sparks. On the second row at left is R. B. Watkins. (Courtesy Judson O. Crow.)

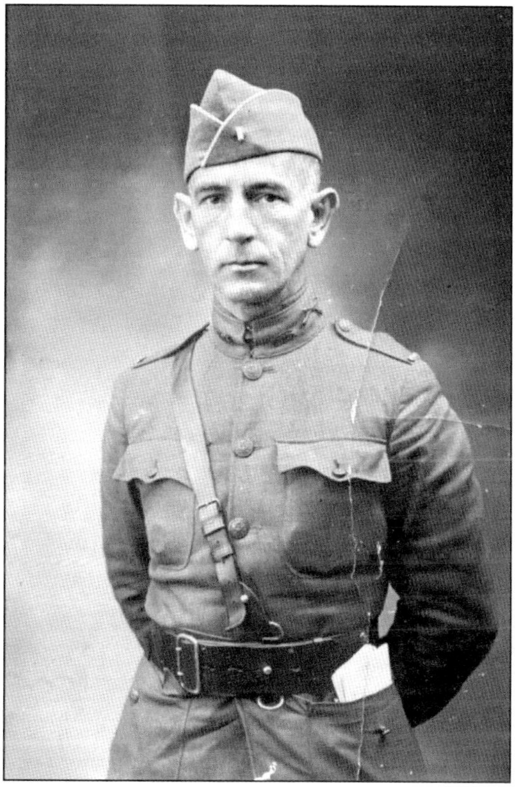

"YOURS IN THE FIGHT." Barron P. Caldwell, husband of R. R. Haynes's youngest child, Virginia, was a first lieutenant in the American Expeditionary Force in France. The picture was made October 28, 1918. Mr. Caldwell filled a number of roles in Cliffside, including superintendent of the school. He is said to have worn his old army uniform at every opportunity. (Courtesy Hazel Haynes Bridges.)

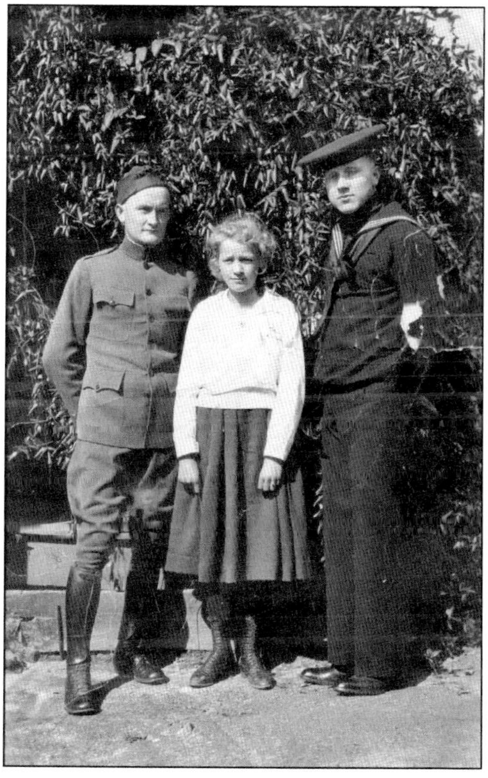

ON LEAVE. From left to right are Elifus Jarrett, Mary Quinn Womick, and B. B. Goode. Mary Quinn lived next to Gilbert's Studio (one door north of the store building) when Elifus and B. B., home on leave during the Influenza Pandemic of 1918 (probably because both their mothers were widows), had arrived to have their pictures made. They persuaded Mary Quinn to pose with them. (Courtesy Mary Quinn Womick Prewitt.)

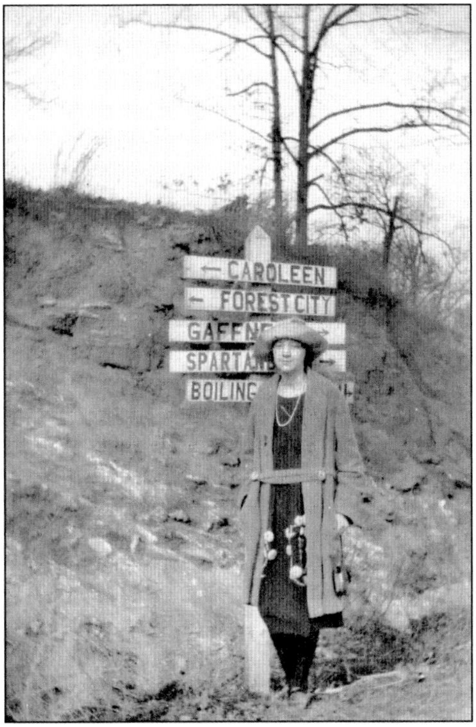

Sign Post. Mary Quinn Womick posed at the road sign that proved what everyone knew: Cliffside was the center of the universe. This was before the slats pointing to London and Tokyo had been added. The sign stood where the road forks at the Methodist church. Mary Quinn was daughter of Quinn and Eva Cole Womick, and she was about 15 when this was taken around 1920. (Courtesy Mary Quinn Womick Prewitt.)

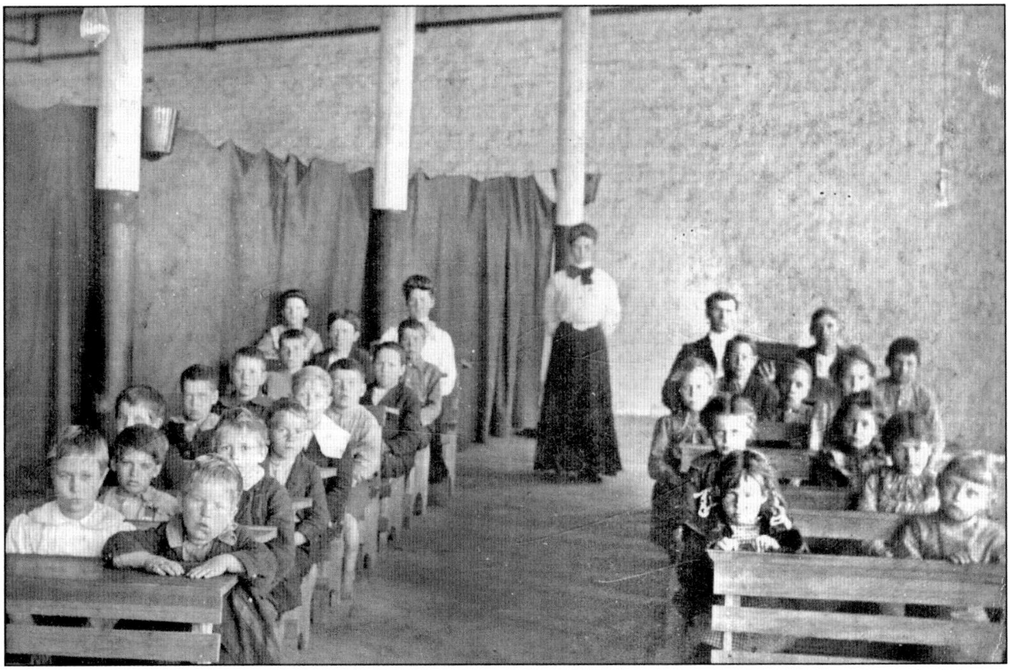

Learning In Progress. A schoolroom in Cliffside is shown in 1907, in a curtained off area of the mill. Later, classes were held in the store building and other locations. Notes for the photograph tell us Clarence Watkins is one of the students, and Winnie Davis Shelby is the teacher. Some of the old fire buckets hanging on the posts were still there a half century later. (Courtesy Dena Watkins Chandler.)

"CLIFFSIDE JACK." Lawrence Blanton was a beloved young man of Cliffside who in the late 1920s enjoyed a brief career as a boxer. The son of Clinton and Orah Bland Blanton, Jack was an exemplary student, winning the school's highest average award in 1929. He married Juanita Crawford, and they had a daughter, Peggy. In 1934, following an appendicitis attack, he died from gangrene at age 27. (Courtesy Bob Hawkins.)

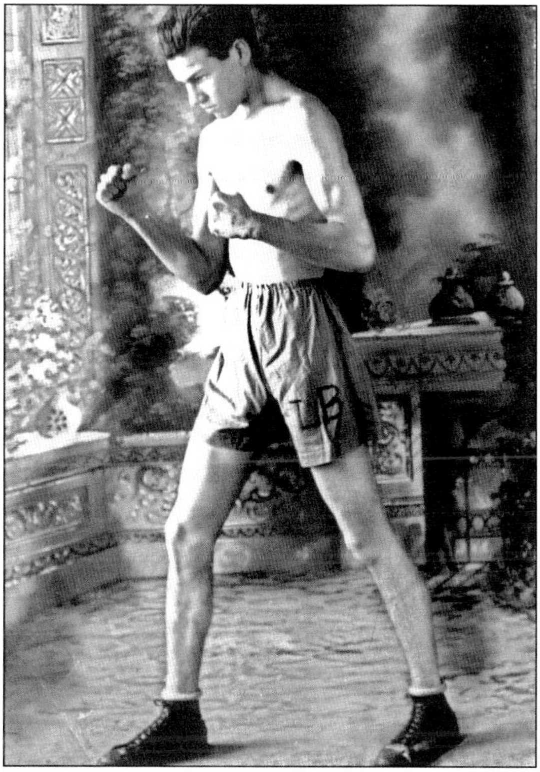

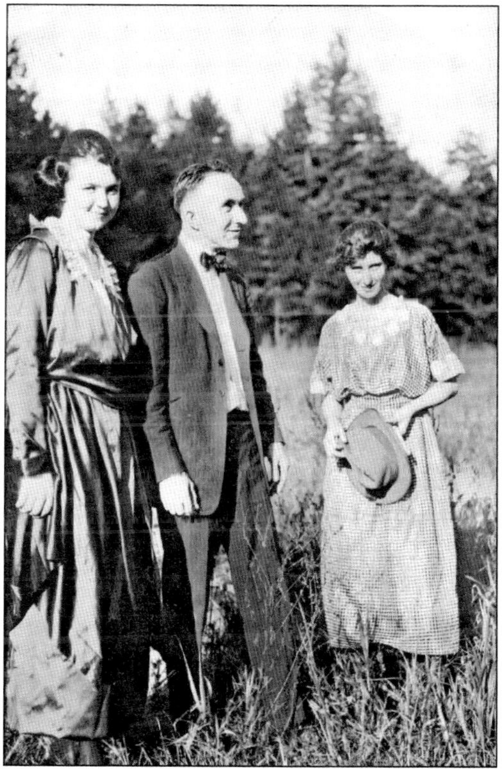

MR. COLE. Dee Christopher Cole, Cliffside's "Music Man," had a 45-year career of organizing and leading bands. He joined the Cliffside band in 1907 at age 17, and nine years later, he became its director. He taught and conducted in schools throughout Rutherford County until retirement in 1959. From left to right are Pamelia Pruette, D. C. Cole, and his future wife, Faye Best. (Courtesy Virginia Padgett Biggerstaff.)

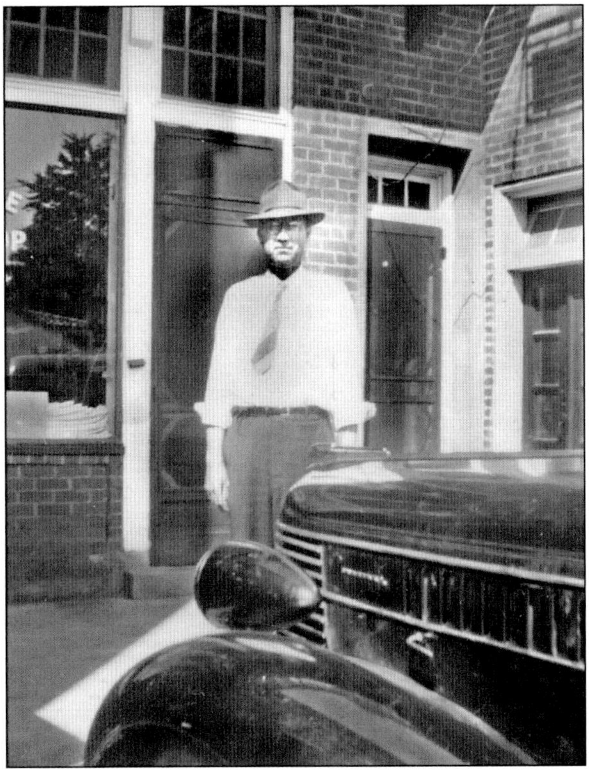

B. B. Goode. He was always called "Bum," although his name was Broadus Bumber. He was Cliffside's Metropolitan Life Insurance man for half a century, a friend to everyone he met, and one of the most respected men in town. If Cliffside had an Atticus Finch, the beloved character in *To Kill A Mockingbird*, then B. B. Goode was it. He is seen here about 1943. (Courtesy Mack Hendrick.)

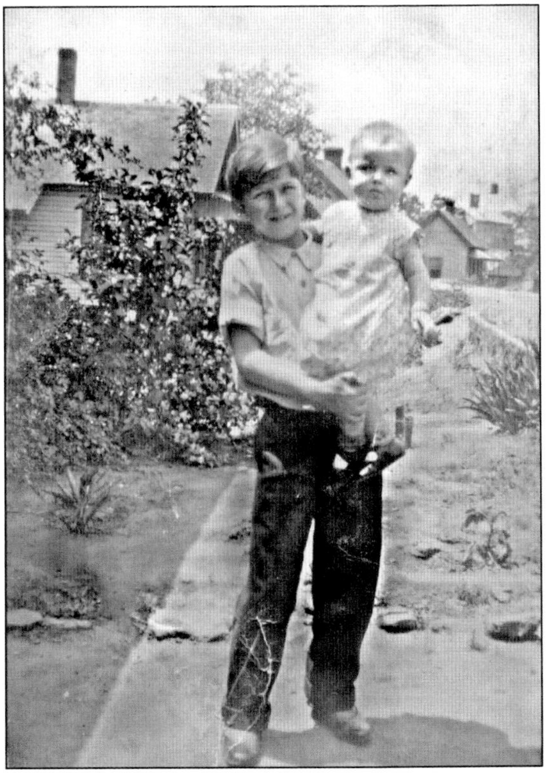

Uncle Dewitt. Dewitt Rollins holds his niece Geraldine Wall in front of his father's house on unpaved Shelby Highway. The water tanks of Cliffside can be seen in the distance. The year is 1931, and Dewitt, a son of L. D. Rollins, is 14 years old. Geraldine is the daughter of Leon and Era Rollins Wall. (Courtesy Geraldine Wall Evans.)

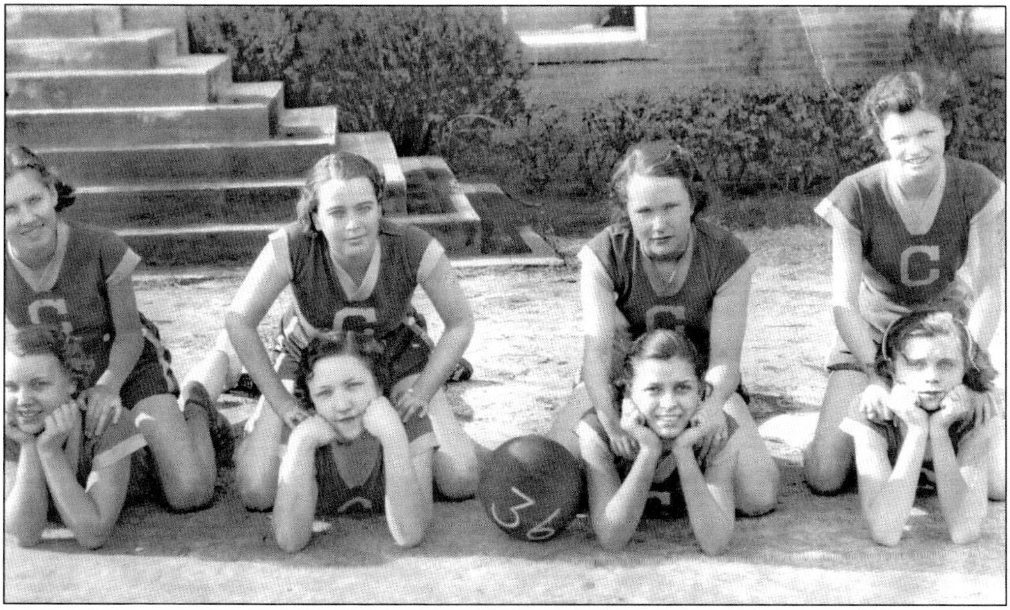

GIRLS' BASKETBALL TEAM 1936. Posing in front of Cliffside High School, are the district champions. From left to right, they are as follows: (first row) Mildred Neal, Ruth Scruggs (Porter), Maude Scruggs (Dalton), and Betty Simmons; (second row) Mary Frances Moss, Pauline Scruggs (Moore), Ola Mae Price (Cash), and Ruth Fowler (Glenn). (Courtesy K. D. Scruggs; identifications by Al Dalton.)

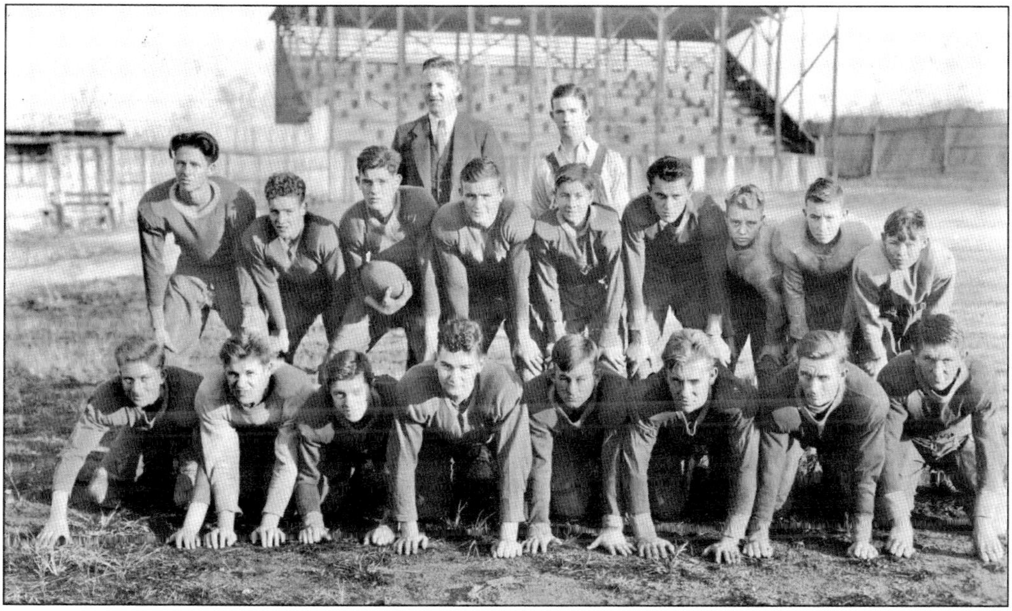

BOYS' FOOTBALL TEAM 1933. The team is seen at the Cliffside athletic field on Highway 120, site of the present Honeysuckle Park. Note the grandstand. From left to right, they are (first row) Francis Fowler, Clarence McKinney, Mal McMurray, Harry Hawkins, Oliver Prewitt, Jim Frye, unidentified, and ? Matheny; (second row) unidentified, Herman Green, Leon Dedmond, G. C. Fisher, William D. Morgan, James Robertson, and three unidentified players. (Courtesy Mack Hendrick.)

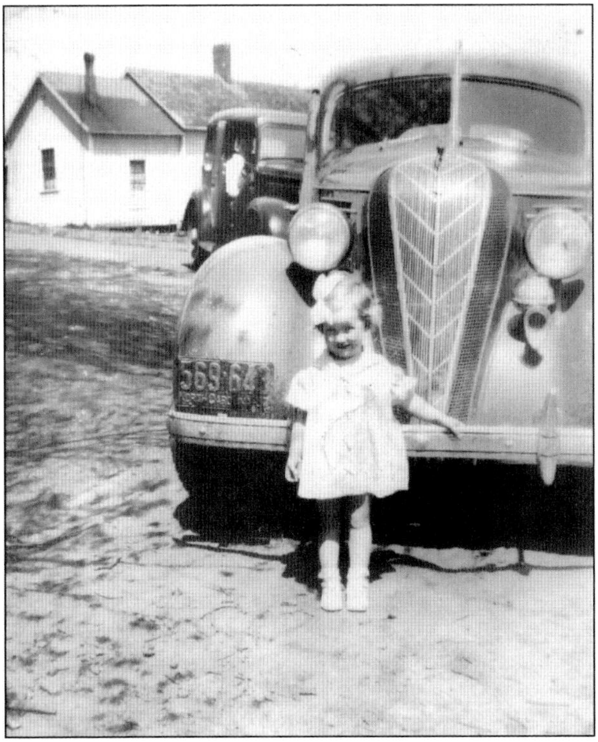

THE BELLE OF SOUTH MAIN. It was 1937 when little Joyce, daughter of Ferrell and Esther Atkinson of 34 South Main Street, posed in front of her uncle Roy Hill's 1936 Hudson Terraplane four-door sedan. In the background was the home of Mr. and Mrs. G. B. Hill. Mr. Hill was a watchman at the mill. (Courtesy Joyce Atkinson Hunter.)

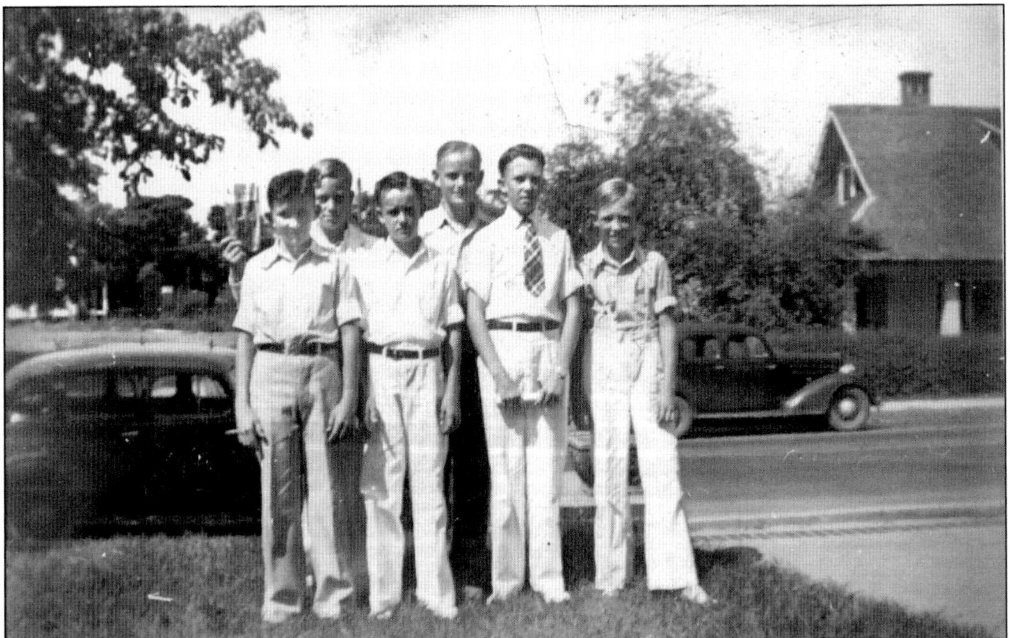

YOUNG MEN AT CHURCH. Standing on Main Street *c.* 1938 facing Cliffside's Baptist church are, from left to right, Grover Haynes Jr., Boyce Bridges Jr., Marvin McDaniel, Raleigh Biggerstaff, Maurice "Bobby" Cordell, and Buren Ledford. Within four years, five of them went off to war. Boyce did not return. A total of 366 Cliffside men and women served in World War II. (Courtesy Grover Haynes Jr.)

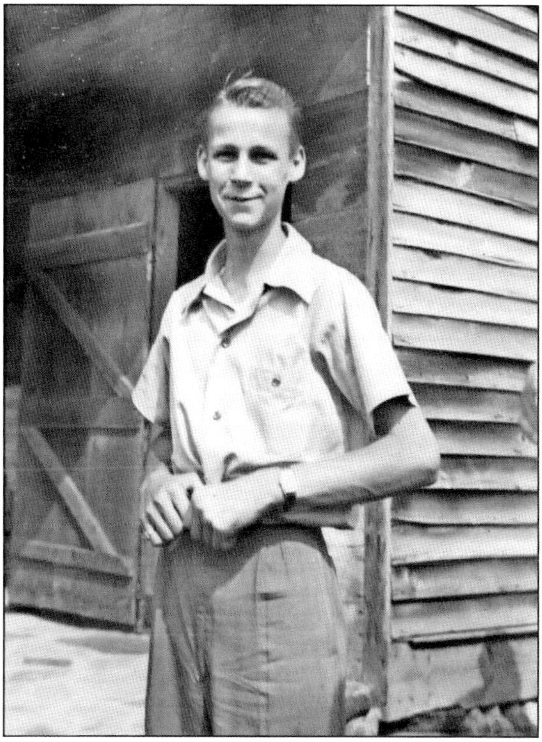

MACK HENDRICK. Mack is the son of Maurice and Lela McFarland Hendrick. He was president and valedictorian of Cliffside High School's class of 1942 and served in the army in Europe. He was wounded in Germany in 1944 near the Saar River. Mack enjoyed a long career in textiles, and he and his wife, Avis, retired in Elkin, North Carolina. (Courtesy Mack Hendrick.)

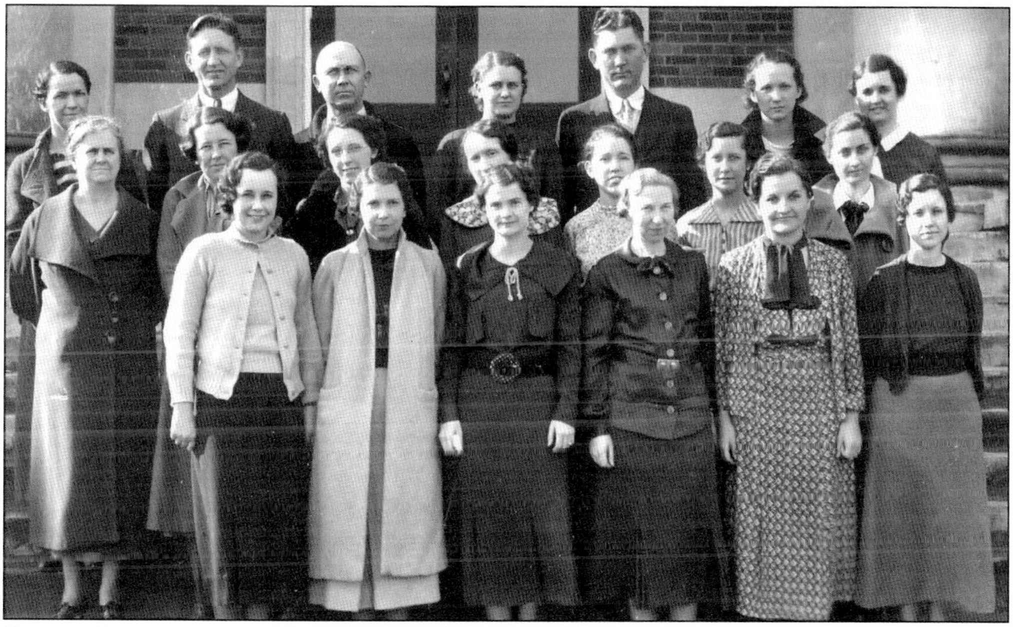

SCHOOL FACULTY, 1938. From left to right are as follows: (first row) Ruth Robertson, Corrine Bookout, ? Rikert, Letha Bame, Virginia Owens Davidson, and Amanda Haynes; (second row) Annabelle Logan, three unidentified teachers, Myrtle Mashburn (music teacher), Gladys (Mrs. John) Tinkler, and unidentified; (third row) Alice David, John Barkley, Boyce Lee Finger, Margaret (Mrs. H. C.) Beatty, H. C. Beatty (principal), Sue Whiteside, and Sarah (Mrs. Jim) Tinkler. (Courtesy Mack Hendrick.)

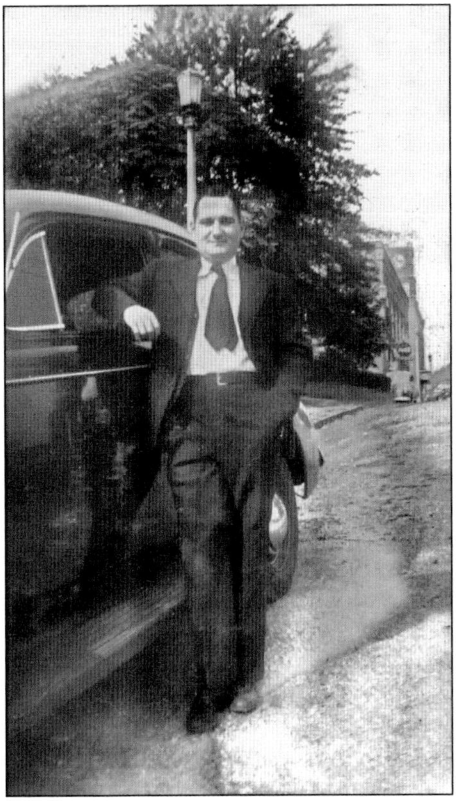

WILLIAM HAYNES MCNABB. A popular man of the community, Bill McNabb married the former Juanita Crawford Blanton, and they had two sons, Tommy and Buddy. He retired as office manager of the mill. In this 1940s photograph, he is in front of his home across South Main from the mill office. After Juanita's death, Bill married Irene Mitchell. He died in 2003 at age 91. (Courtesy Peggy Blanton Hadden.)

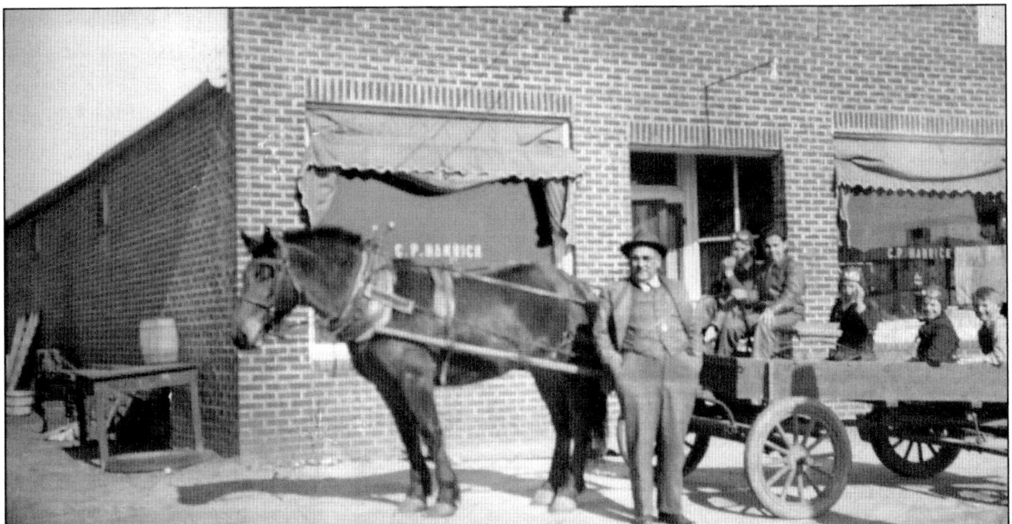

CARVES P. HAMRICK. Just before World War II, C. P. Hamrick delivered groceries from his Fairview store using this horse-drawn wagon. He is shown here with all the little Hamricks all set to go for a ride. His name was Carves, but most pronounced it "Cos" or called him "C. P." He was one of Cliffside's leading businessmen, with several retail and service operations in the area. (Courtesy Guy Hamrick.)

HENRY V. DAVIS. For many years, Henry was the face of the law in Cliffside. In the early 1930s, Charley Haynes, wanting a police presence in town, offered Henry a house and $35 a month (in addition to his county deputy sheriff's pay) to move his family from Avondale to Cliffside. Davis accepted and stayed the rest of his life. He died in 1951. (Courtesy Juanita Davis Smith.)

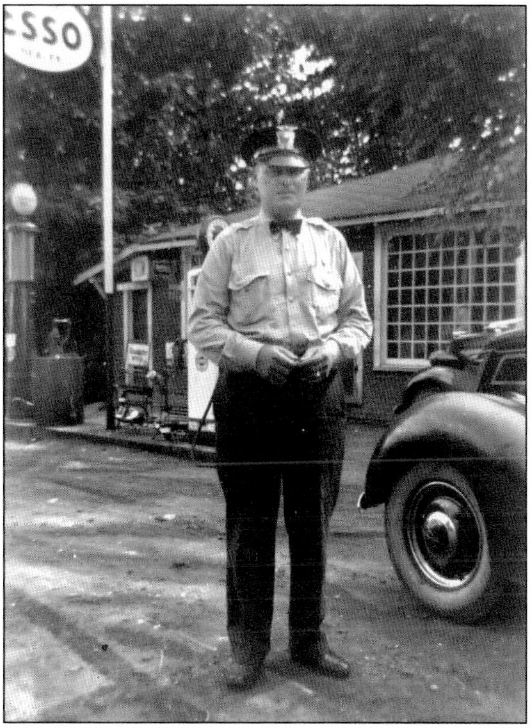

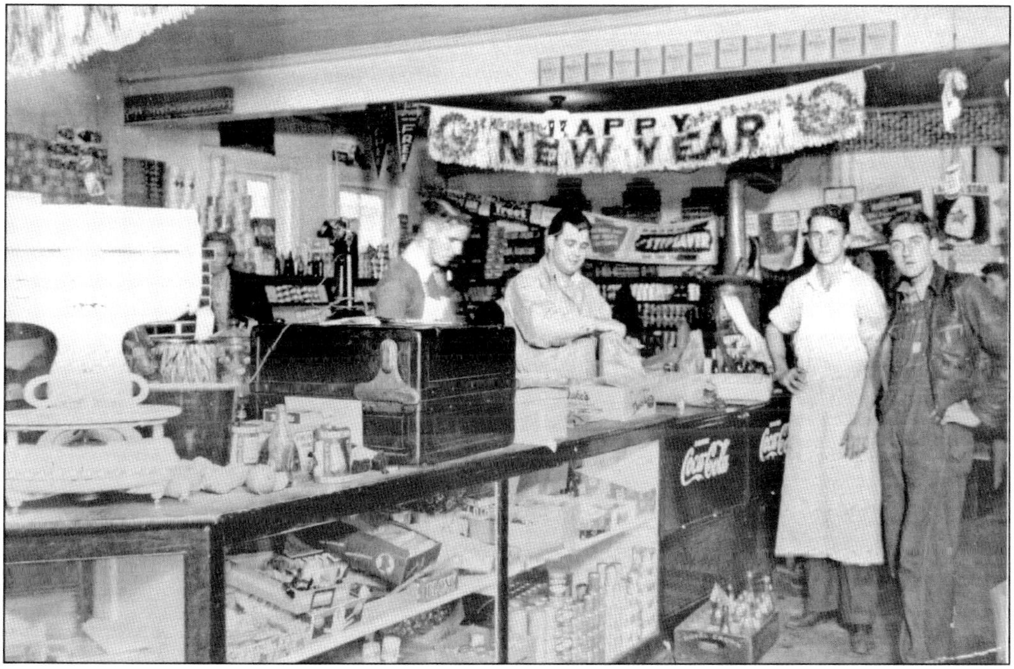

NEW YEAR'S 1943. In the late 1930s and early 1940s, the building across from the Memorial Building housed Hawkins Supermarket, run by Robert "Tubby" Hawkins. Remember when grocers wore aprons, made free deliveries, and sold penny candy? Tubby sold the store to Carves Hamrick in the fall of 1943. From left to right are Wade Bridges, Tubby Hawkins, unidentified, and Bobo Greene. (Courtesy Bob Hawkins.)

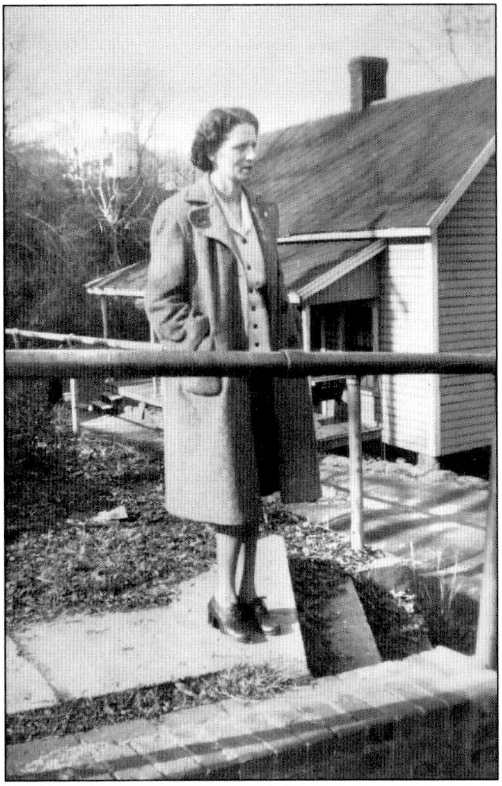

AMY BEASON HOUSER (1914–1990). The matriarch of one of Cliffside's favorite families, Amy and her husband, Ealon, raised Betty, Billy Joe, Buddy, and Terry, each of whom was a credit to the family and helped make Cliffside that much more enjoyable. Amy is buried at Mt. Pleasant Baptist Cemetery beside Ealon, who died in 1997, and not far from her parents, Paul and Lonie Greene Beason. (Courtesy Evelyn Hollifield Houser.)

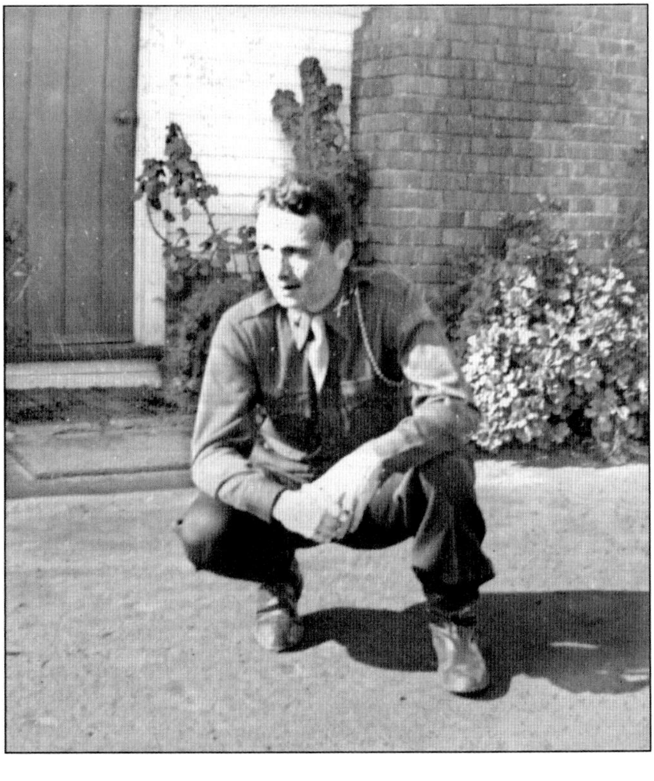

GERARD DAVIDSON. The son of Barney and Essie Davidson was called "'Fessor" Davidson, probably because he left high school at the tender age of 14, graduated from Wofford College, and returned to Cliffside High as a teacher—of many of his previous fellow students. After an illustrious teaching career, he became an executive with Duke Power Co. He was a beloved figure in Cliffside. (Courtesy Hazel Haynes Bridges.)

Radio Girl. Joan Humphries, daughter of Archie and Mary Helen Beason Humphries, loved to listen to *The Grand Ole Opry* and *This is Nora Drake*. The Humphries lived on Cliffside Street when this was taken. With five brothers (Dan, Junior, Steve, Buddy Ray, and Larry), she was something of a tomboy. Her only sister was Sara Lou. Joan grew up to marry Franklin Harris. (Courtesy Joan Humphries Harris.)

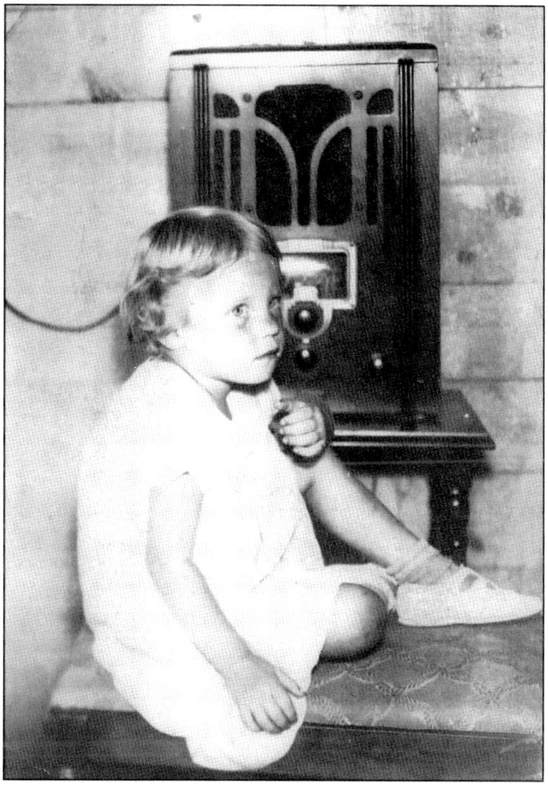

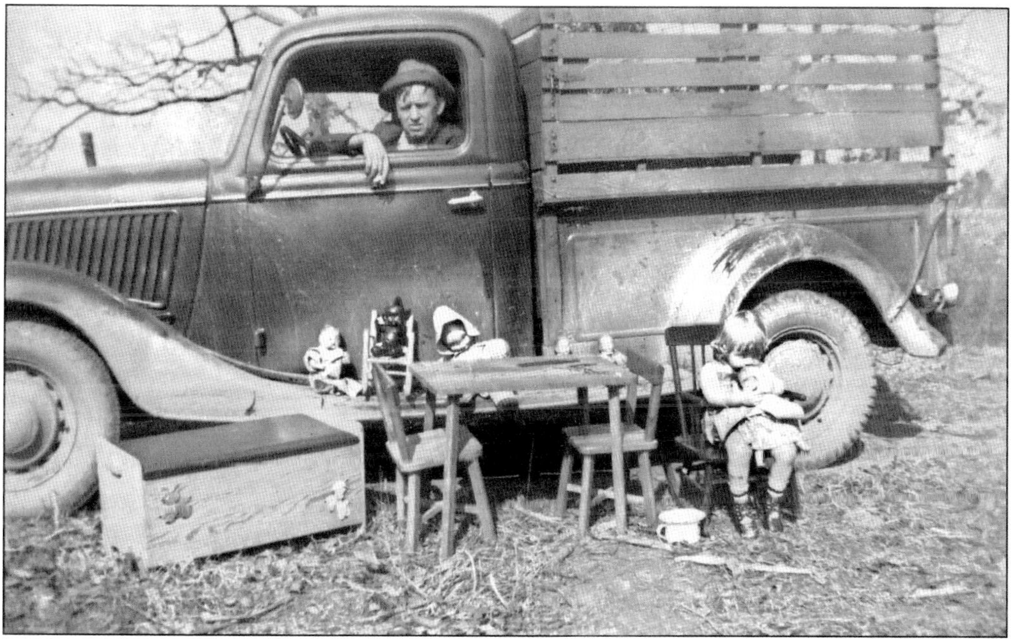

Playing House. Little Kay Lowery has set up housekeeping on the running board of her Uncle Paul Beason's truck c. 1944, and she is not about to budge. He is probably begging her mama, Dorothy Beason Lowery, to come move this stuff so he can go haul a load of shoats or go to Trade Day at Forest City. Kay's father was Perry "Cub" Lowery. (Courtesy Dot Beason Lowery.)

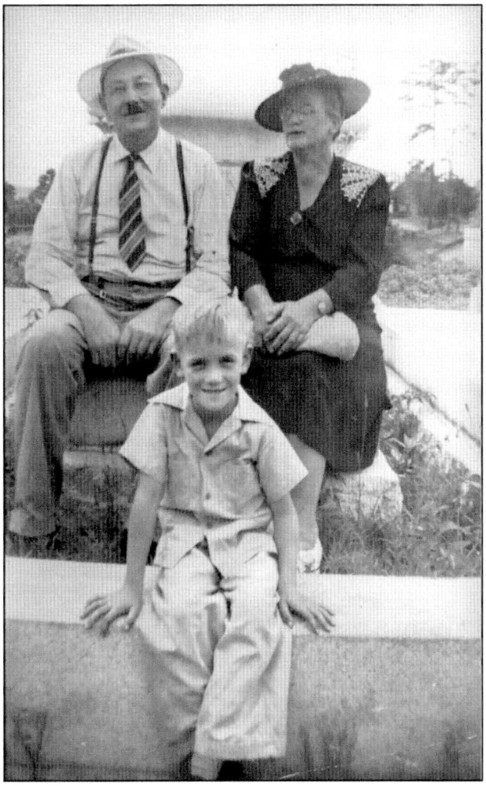

THE BIGGERSTAFFS. A favorite Sunday afternoon pastime was to take a leisurely stroll through the cemetery and maybe even take pictures around the R. R. Haynes burial site. Such was the case here with B. F. "Pick" Biggerstaff, his wife, the former Katie Goode, and their youngest child, Bumber Broadus, nicknamed "Buzzy." Buzzy was nicknamed to avoid any confusion with his uncle, Broadus Bumber Goode. (Courtesy Peggy Blanton Hadden.)

ERA ROLLINS WALL (1910–1982). Era and her daughters, Louise and Geraldine, lived with Era's parents, Delpha and Corria Rollins, on Cliffside Street. During the Depression, Geraldine remembers her mother picking cotton and gathering dried peas to earn money for her daughters' school clothes and doing laundry for a neighbor for their lunch money. During the war years, she worked in the weave room at the mill. (Courtesy Geraldine Wall Evans.)

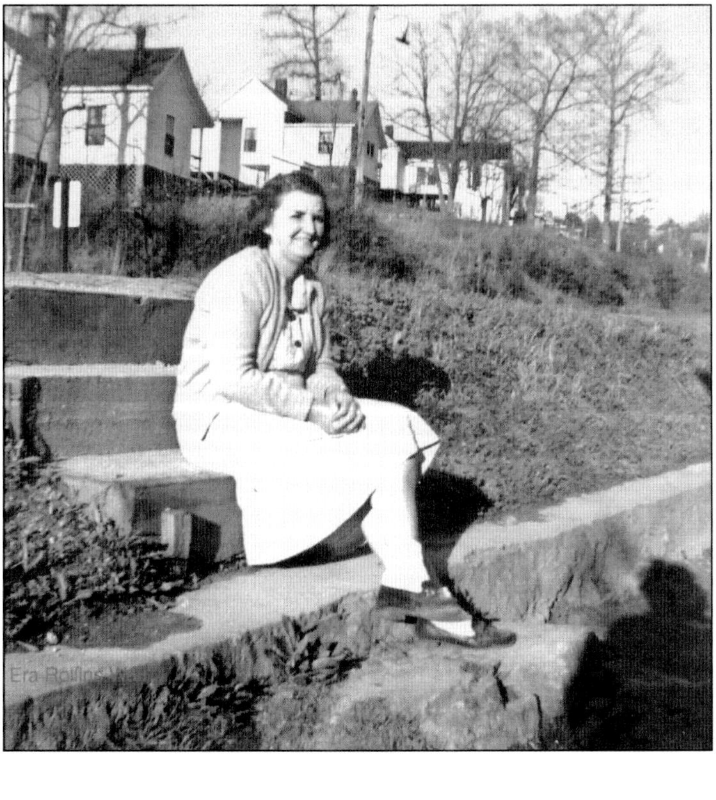

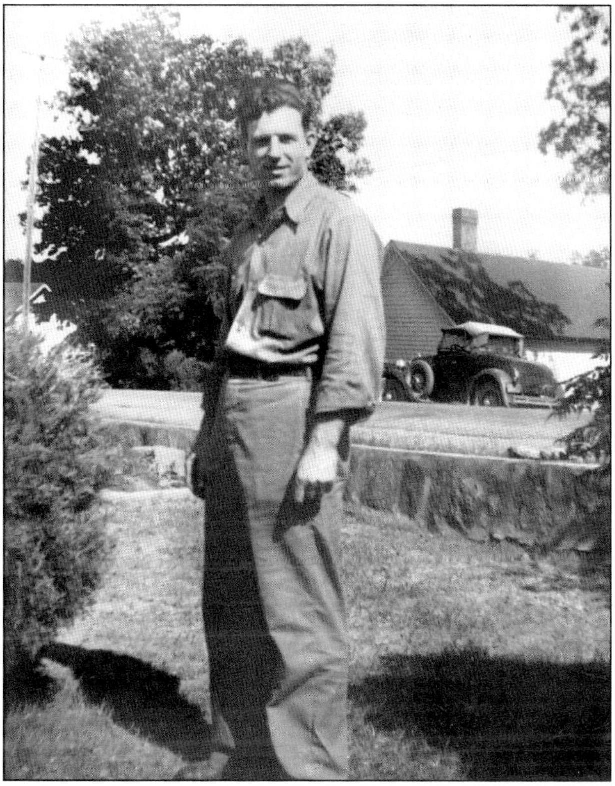

William Thomas Ingram Jr. (1913–1999). In February 1945, Technical Sergeant Ingram, serving in the famed 29th Infantry Division, won the Silver Star for gallantry in action at Julich, near the Roer River in Germany. Bill married Jewell Davis, and their children were Billy, Patsy, and Gene. The Ingrams lived on River Street when this pre-war photograph was made. (Courtesy Patsy Ingram Dothard.)

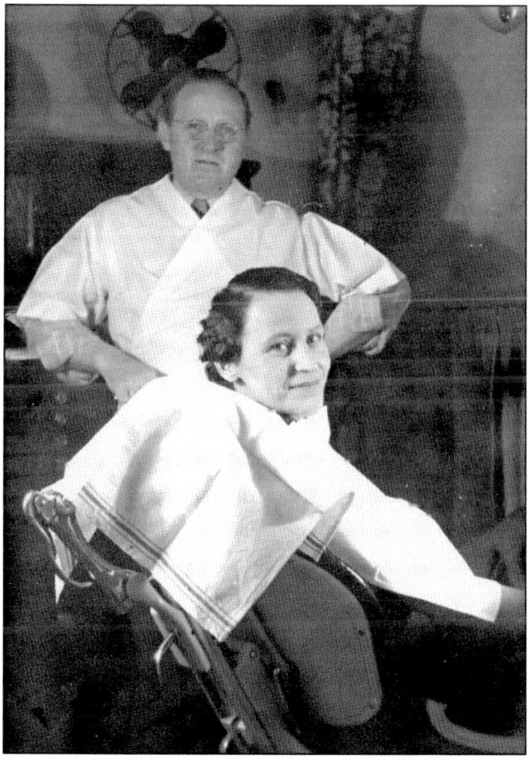

Dental Care. Cliffside always had a dentist, whether it wanted one or not. His office was up the creaky wooden stairs between the drug store and the bank. It was equipped with the latest equipment: a padded chair that pedaled up and down and an oscillating fan to prevent patients from expiring from the summer heat. Here is Dr. H. L. Robertson and his patient of the moment, Ethel Jackson. (Courtesy Mack Hendrick.)

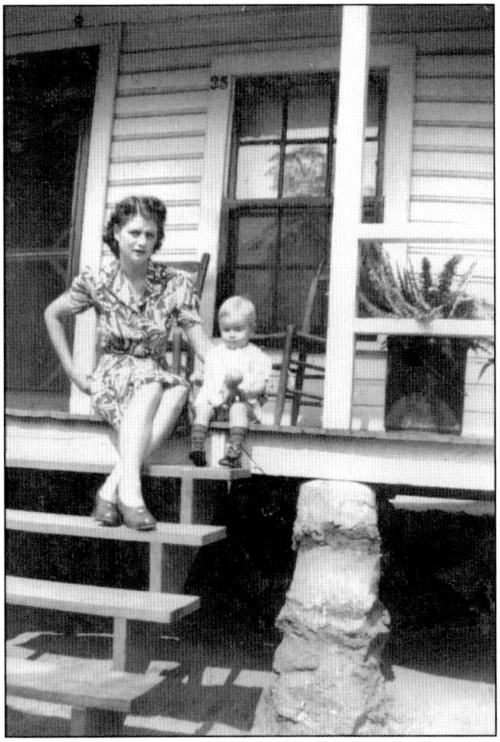

Dorothy Beason Lowery. "Dot" was the daughter of Paul and Lonie Greene Beason and wife of Perry "Cub" Lowery. She is pictured with her daughter Kay on their porch at 35 Cliffside Street. Cement blocks were unheard of in those days, at least in Cliffside; carpenters and masons propped up the mill houses with stacks of rocks and mortar that resembled termite nests. (Courtesy Dot Beason Lowery.)

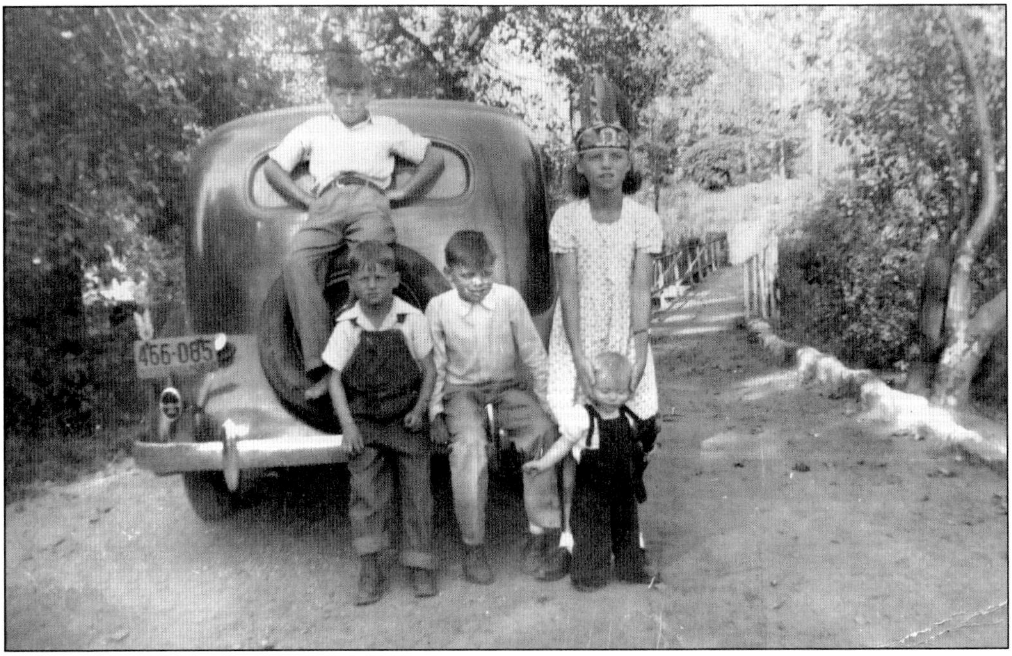

Playing at the Footbridge. Seen here is Ealon Houser's old Pontiac in the early 1940s, when the Housers lived off to the left near the Sulfur Well. The kids are mostly Housers with a Lowery and a Beason added for flavor. Betty's genuine Indian headdress probably came from Hamrick's store. Clockwise from right are Betty Houser, Kay Lowery in the headlock, Billy Houser, Buddy Houser, and Doris Beason. (Courtesy Dot Beason Lowery.)

DEWITT ROLLINS AND JACK SUGGS. Like many houses in Cliffside, Dewitt's father Delpha Rollins's was built high off the ground in back because of the hilly terrain. It was a perfect storage area for coal and stove wood. Delpha would jack up a Model T and hook a belt over its rear hub to pull his homemade wood saw. Jack's father, Walt, was the town cobbler. (Courtesy Geraldine Wall Evans.)

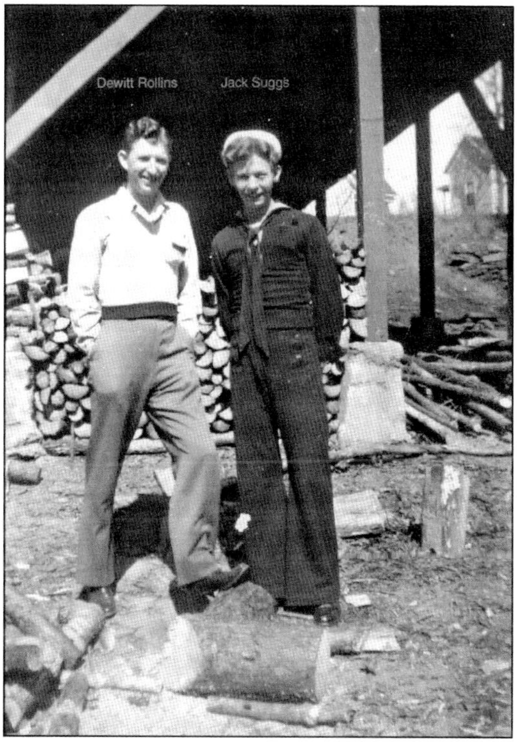

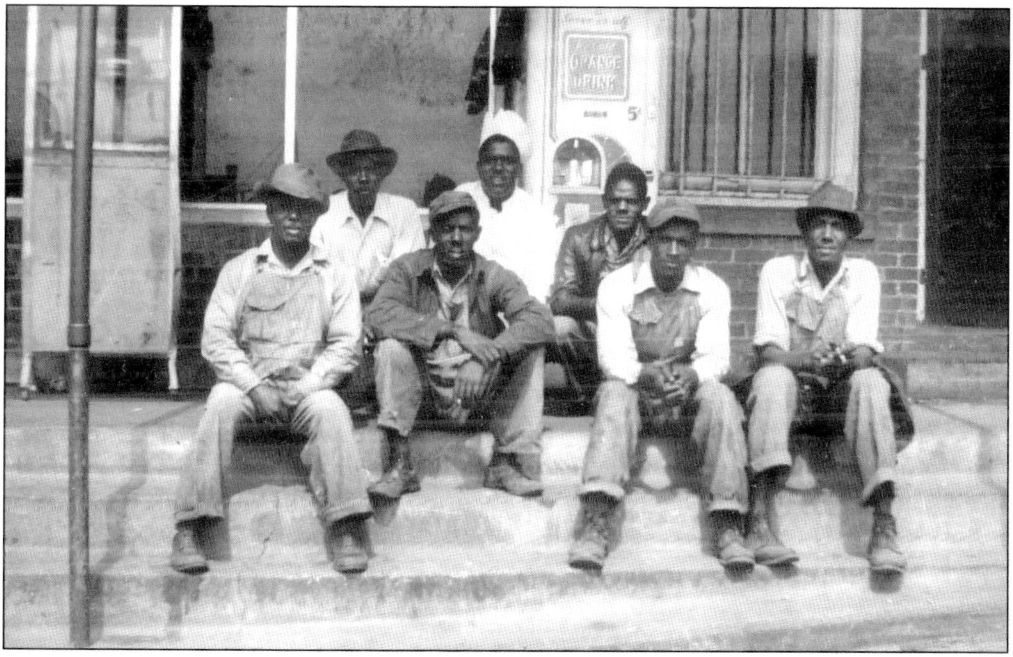

LUNCH TIME. It was about 1944 and these workmen were on a break beside C. P. Hamrick's downtown store. From left to right are (first row) Henry Wiley, Amos Surratt, Ned Hill, and Buster Gaston; (second row) Ezell Phillips, June Webster, and Babe Mercer. June was the cook for the family of the company's general manager, Maurice Hendrick. They were kind, hard working, good-hearted men who gave much to the community. (Courtesy Mack Hendrick.)

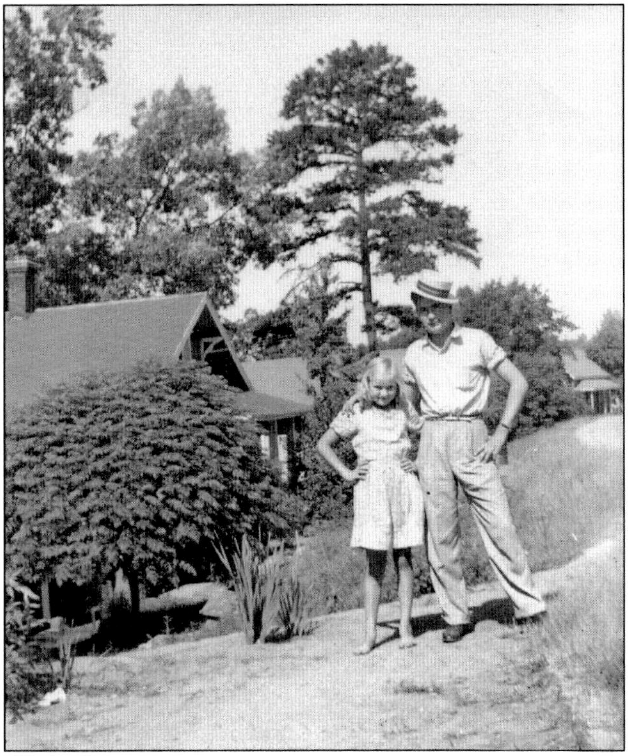

GINNY AND JOE. Ginny Ann Greene stands with her brother Joe in front of their father's house on Shelby Highway. They were the children of Raudy and Prella Beason Greene. Raudy was a butcher in several groceries in Cliffside and also worked in the mill. Joe, a trader, married Eloise Bailey. Ginny wed Ashley Reid. For many years, the Reids operated a clothing store at Sandy Mush. (Courtesy Ginny Ann Reid.)

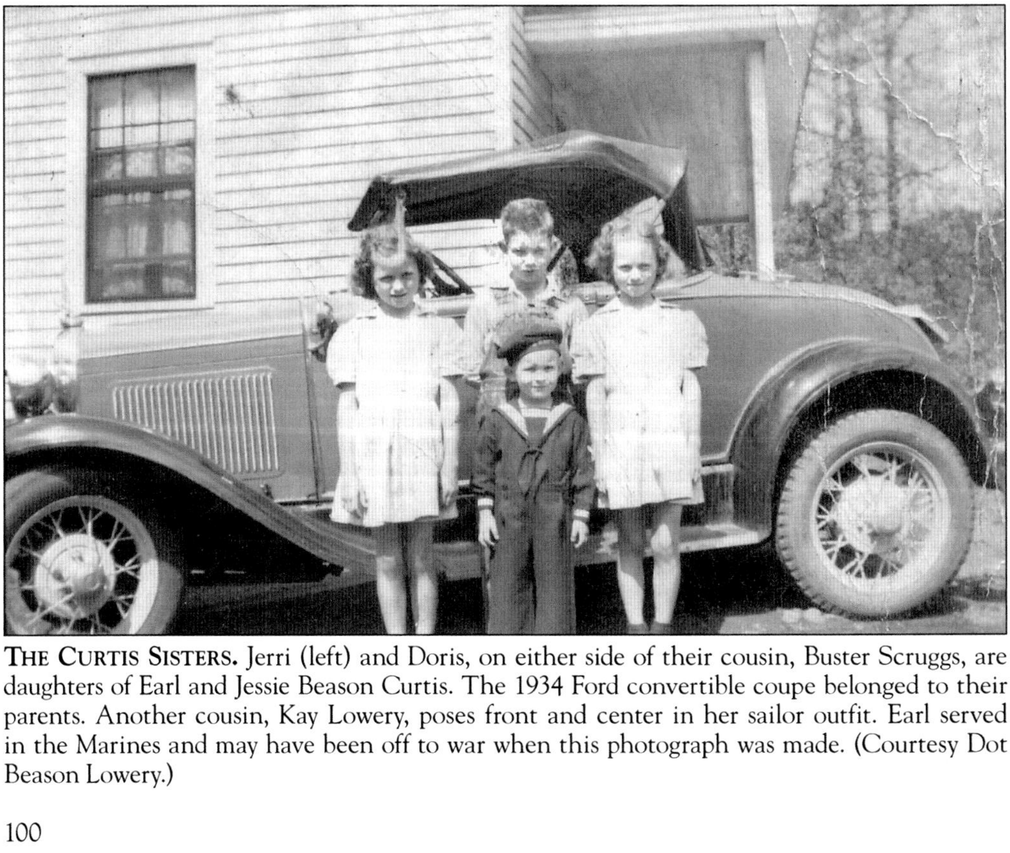

THE CURTIS SISTERS. Jerri (left) and Doris, on either side of their cousin, Buster Scruggs, are daughters of Earl and Jessie Beason Curtis. The 1934 Ford convertible coupe belonged to their parents. Another cousin, Kay Lowery, poses front and center in her sailor outfit. Earl served in the Marines and may have been off to war when this photograph was made. (Courtesy Dot Beason Lowery.)

SAM AND GRANDPA. Out by the woodpile in 1949, George W. Bird (1870–1959) stands by his grandson Sam Davis. George was a farmer in the State Line community. His daughter, Nora Betty Bird (Sam's mother), was the wife of Henry V. Davis. Nora would buy a cord of wood and have Lester Ledford saw it with his Model A–driven wood saw. (Courtesy Sam Davis.)

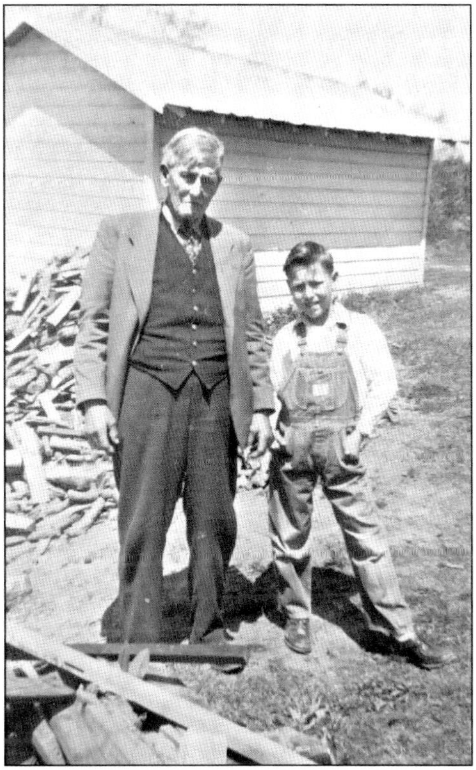

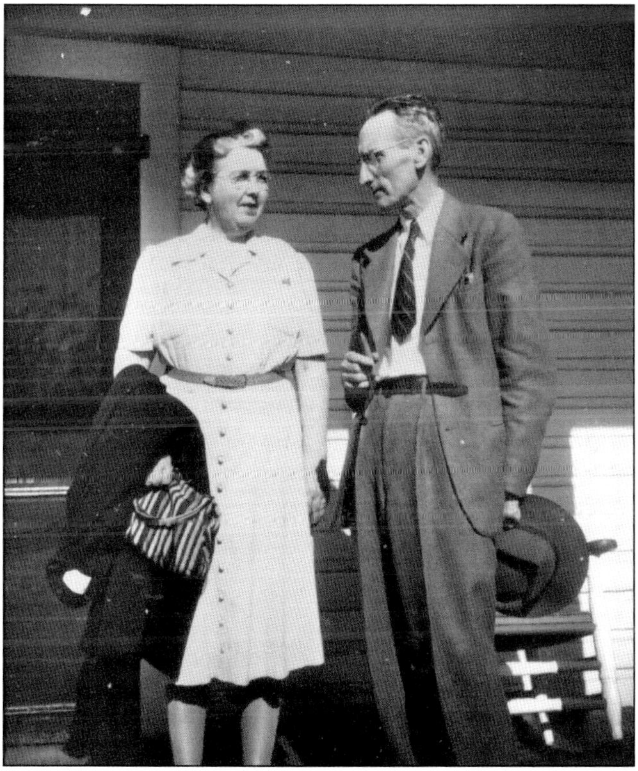

ALTONIA AND VIC FORTUNE. Victor was a son of Drury D. and Brunhilda Hollifield Fortune. As a young man, Vic worked at the marble yard. Later, his role at the mill was as overseer in the supply room. In his spare time in the 1930s and 1940s, he painted marquee banners for Cliffside Theater, gaining free admission for his family. He and Altonia Lancaster Fortune had a daughter, Rachel. (Courtesy Peggy Blanton Hadden.)

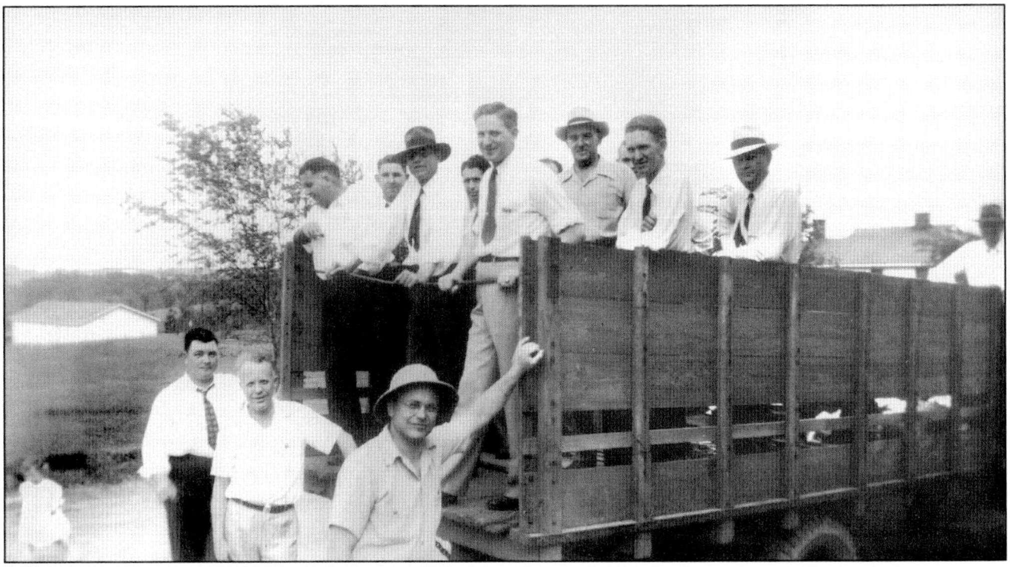

SCRAP DRIVE. On this day during World War II, volunteers drove up and down the streets in someone's truck collecting scrap metal for the war effort. From left to right are (first row) Elise Brown (far left corner), Tubby Hawkins, Edgar L. Davis, and Harry Tarleton; (second row) Jesse Honeycutt, Otto Matheny, B. B. Goode, Pete Hill, Francis Fowler, Ike Biggerstaff, James Tinkler, H. C. Beatty, and J. C. Hames. (Courtesy Shirley Crawford Thompson.)

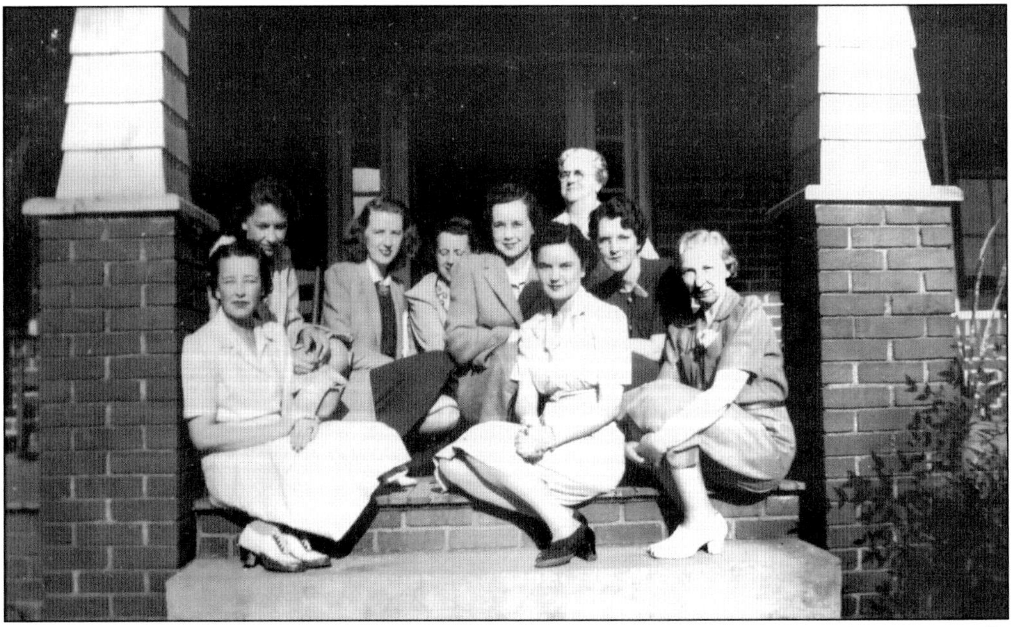

TEACHERS' INN. Until the 1950s, special housing was provided for teachers in what was usually called the teachers' home or the teachers' inn. The last of these was at 25 North Main. Seen here c. 1942 are, from left to right, (first row) Emily Hilliard, Ellen Dickerson, and Letha Bame; (second row) unidentified, Daisy Bolin, Macy Ezell, Ruth Robertson, Annabelle Logan, and Ethel Fagan. (Courtesy Peggy Blanton Hadden.)

PONY PICTURES. Every summer in the 1940s, some photographer would lead his pony through Cliffside and pose the little ones on his animal—for a fee, of course. Nearly every family from that period has a picture like this one of Bill and Jewell Ingram's brood posed in front of the car shed. Gene, the youngest, is riding with Billy, while Patsy remains on the ground. (Courtesy Patsy Ingram Dothard.)

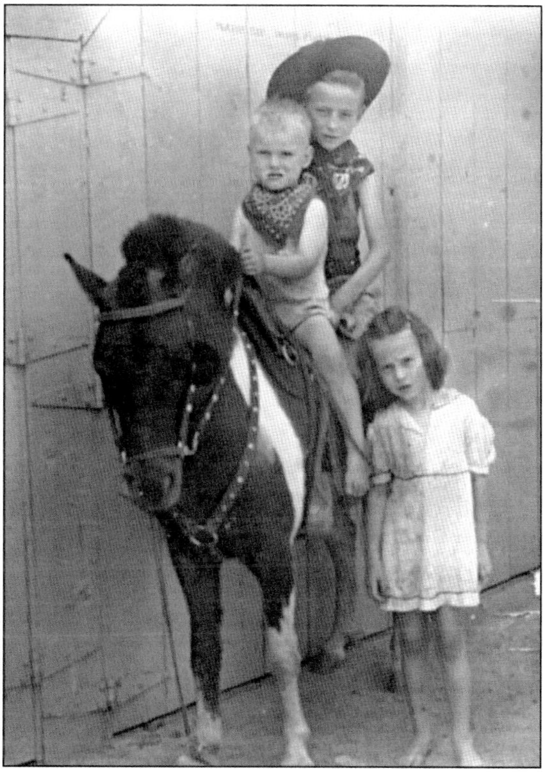

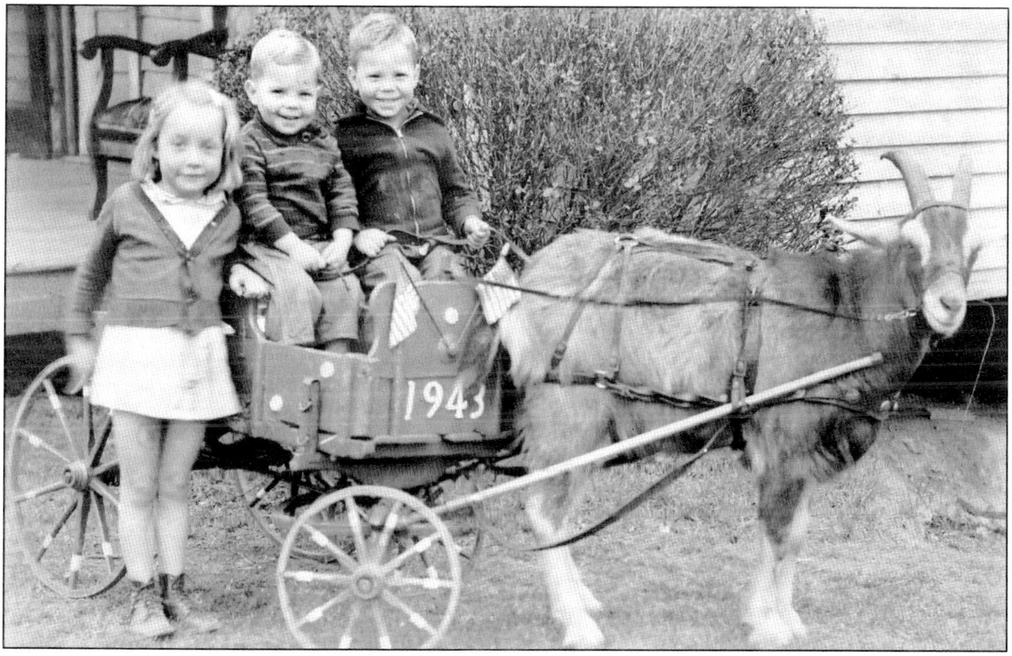

GOAT WAGON. One photographer used a goat-drawn wagon that, for posterity, displayed the current year. This was probably a Hollywood goat, for it knew how to pose for the camera. Sara Lou Humphries is at left, with her brothers Steve and Archie Jr. holding the reins. Their parents are Archie and Mary Helen Beason Humphries. (Courtesy Joan Humphries Harris.)

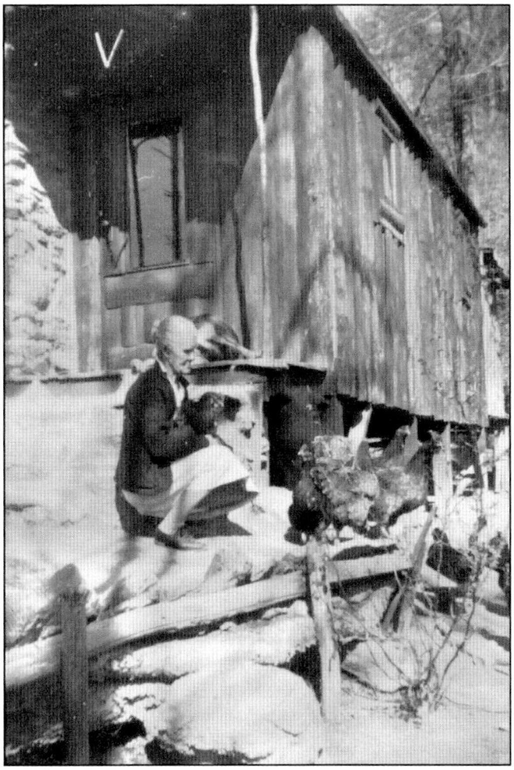

Mary Ella Bright Padgett. Mary Ella is sitting with her chickens at her husband Jim's cabin, the legendary site Jim built downriver in the 1930s for isolation. He was not a hermit by choice; he had tuberculosis and was told by his doctor to avoid the "dirty air" of Cliffside. James Young Padgett (1881–1962) and Mary Ella (1873–1962) were the parents of Flossie and Ovia Koeyu Padgett. (Courtesy Peggy Blanton Hadden.)

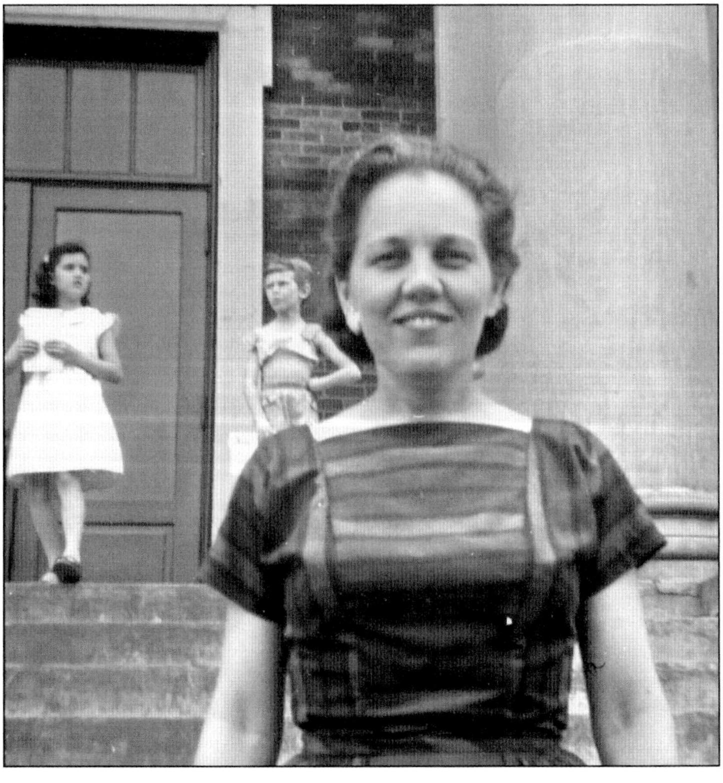

Miss Christy (1914–2004). Although an Avondale native, the beloved music teacher, Virginia Christy, was herself a Cliffside High graduate (1932). She attended the University of North Carolina at Greensboro (graduating in 1936), then returned to Cliffside School for a 29-year career directing choruses and glee clubs. She was also a music director at Cliffside Methodist Church. In 1965, she left Cliffside and spent 11 more years teaching music in Charlotte schools. (Courtesy Hazel Haynes Bridges.)

ROBERT CLYDE "TUBBY" HAWKINS (1914–1980). Everyone knew "Tubby" Hawkins. He was a bundle of energy, an entrepreneur, a doer, and a shaker. He operated groceries, hardware stores, and shoe stores; he would create whole new businesses to dispose of the salvaged cargo of train wrecks. When his Hoggly Woggly shoe outlet outgrew his garage, he moved it to a vacant school in Henrietta. It attracted shoppers from miles around. (Courtesy Mack Hendrick.)

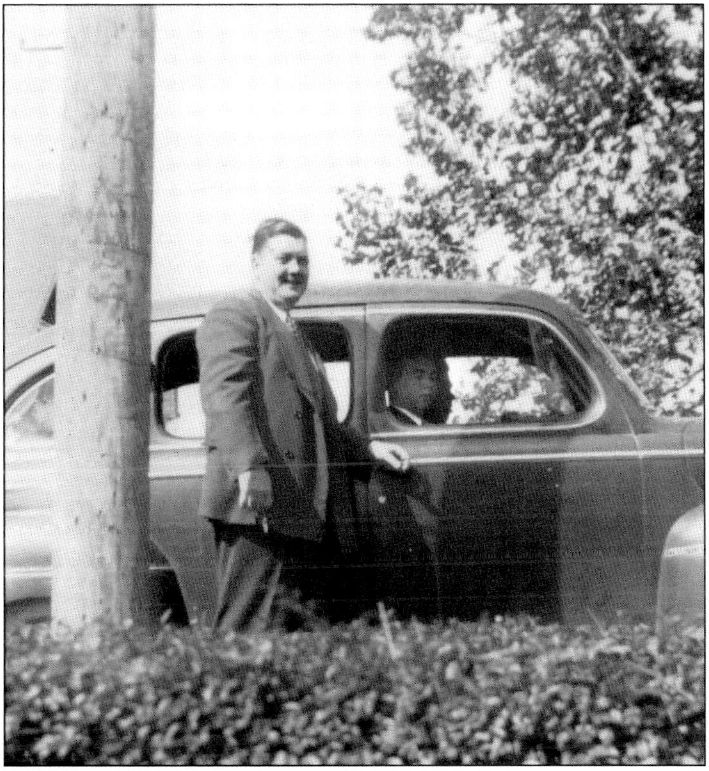

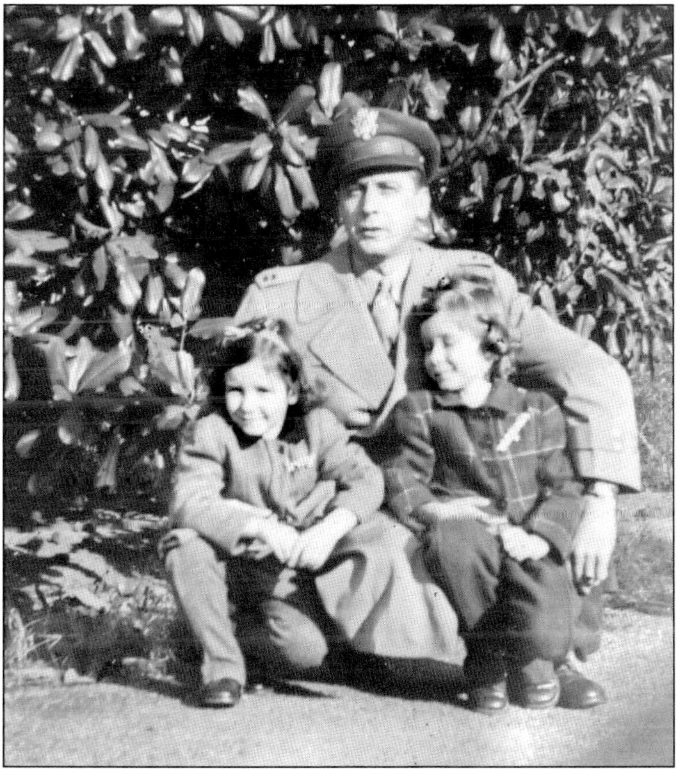

HUGS ALL AROUND. It was a glorious and sweet time when servicemen returned to their families. Capt. James Padgett, on leave from the army, hugs his daughter, Virginia (right), and her cousin, Betty Nantz. James, a son of Roscoe and Frances "Fannie" Scruggs Padgett, was a designer at the mill. Both Virginia and Betty had long careers as teachers. (Courtesy Virginia Padgett Biggerstaff.)

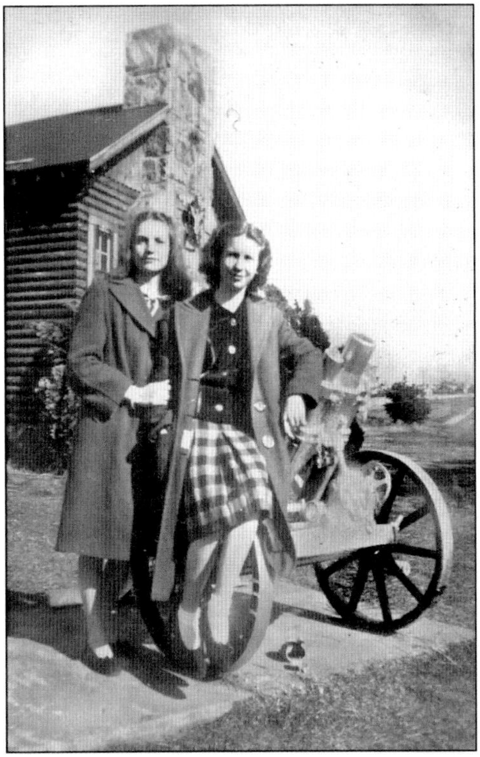

Two Peggys. At the Scout cabin on North Main, Peggy Harris and Peggy Blanton pose around 1943 with one of the two World War I mortars that sat for years on the grounds. The cabin was built in 1936 for the Boy Scouts on the site formerly occupied by Cliffside's first schoolhouse. In later years, it was used by the Rescue Squad. It still stands today. (Courtesy Mary Edna Hamrick McCraw.)

Miss Essie Matheny's Bible Class. The students are assembled in 1947 on Cliffside High's back steps behind little Margaret Beatty, the principal's daughter. From left to right are as follows: (first row) Sara Lou Winn, Betty Jean McGinnis, Clemmie Sparks, and Elizabeth Jolley; (second row) Maude Stephens, Nellie Jo Scruggs, Osteen Gosey, Geraldine Wall, and Essie Matheny (teacher); (third row) Flossie Cash and Mavorine Sparks; (fourth row) Jack Biggerstaff, Vivian McDaniel, and Earl Scruggs. (Courtesy Ginny Greene Reid.)

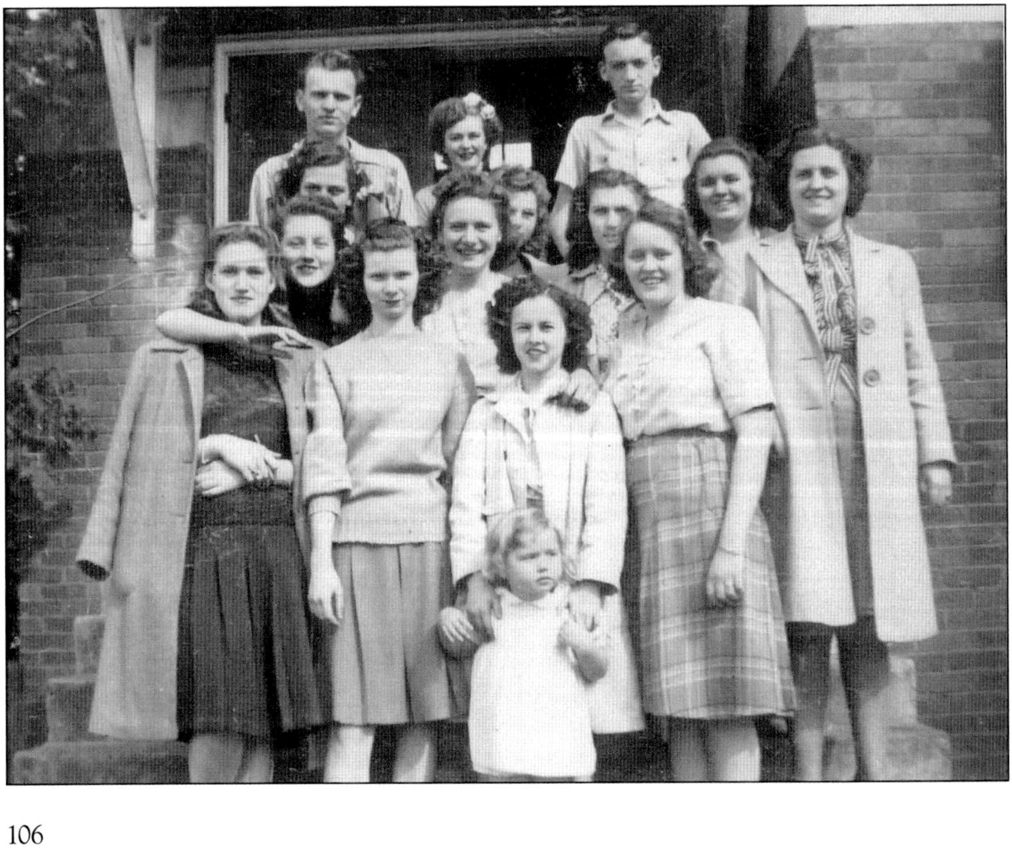

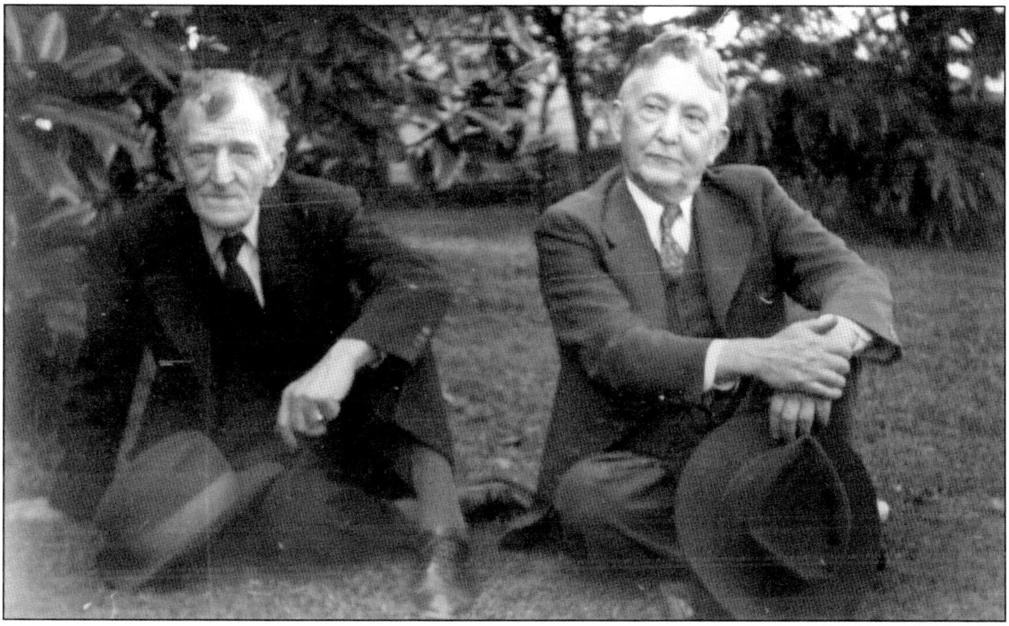

THE OLD GUARD. Brothers Walter (left) and Charley Haynes are seen around 1955, in their later years. They were the last living sons of R. R. Haynes. By now, Charley had retired from the company; Cone Mills had taken over. He would live another three years. Walter, always a farmer and entrepreneur and four years younger than Charley, would die first, in 1957. (Courtesy Hazel Haynes Bridges.)

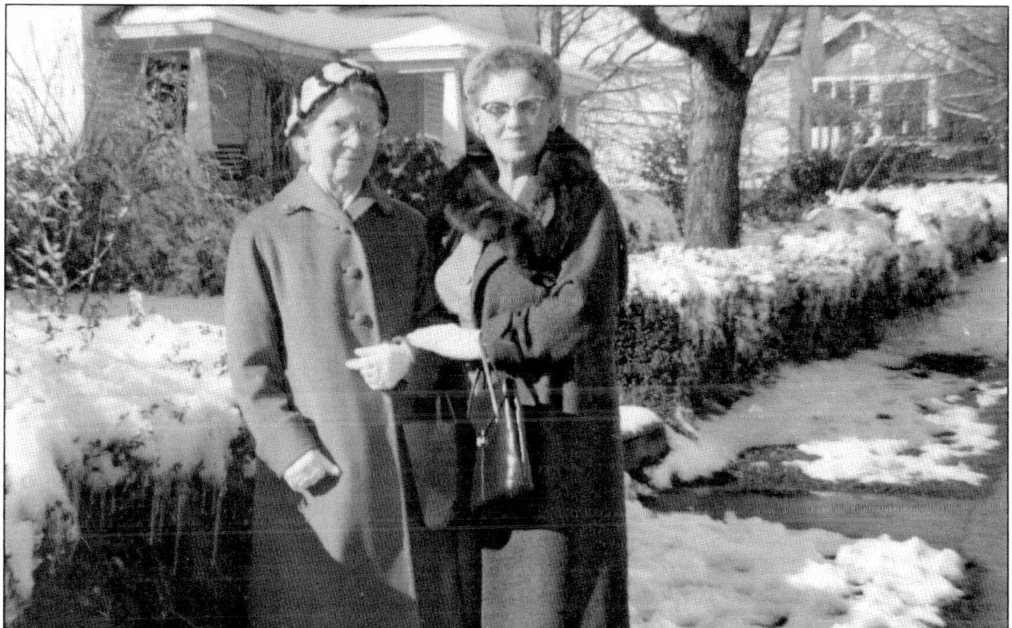

FORTUNE SISTERS. On a snowy Main Street in the late 1950s, Ina Fortune Haynes (right) and her sister Grace Fortune Troutman, from Southern Pines, stand in front of Ina's daughter Hazel and son-in-law Paul Bridge's house. In those years, Paul was superintendent of the mill. (Courtesy Hazel Haynes Bridges.)

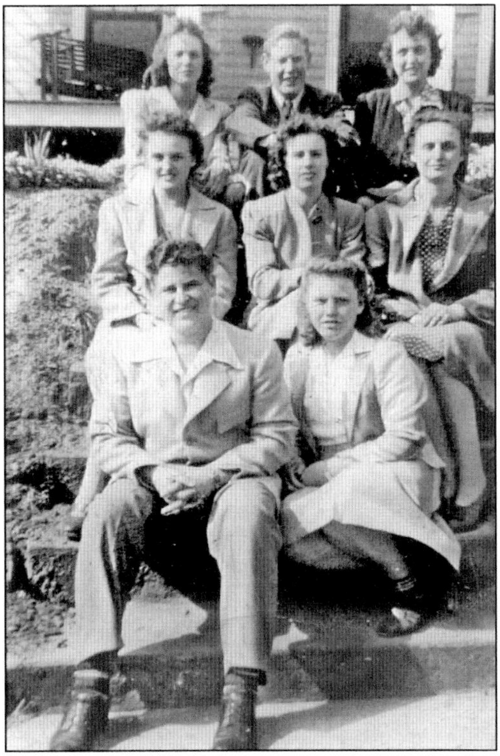

FRIENDS ON SHELBY HIGHWAY. From left to right are (first row) Sam Hill and Mary Edna Hamrick; (second row) May Ruth Scruggs, Melrose Robinson, and Louise Scruggs; (third row) Willie "Sister" Greene, Broadus Robinson, and Ruby Scruggs. They are in front of Mary Edna's house about 1940. Her parents, Raleigh and Ethel Robinson Hamrick, often invited the group to have dinner after church. (Courtesy Mary Edna Hamrick McCraw.)

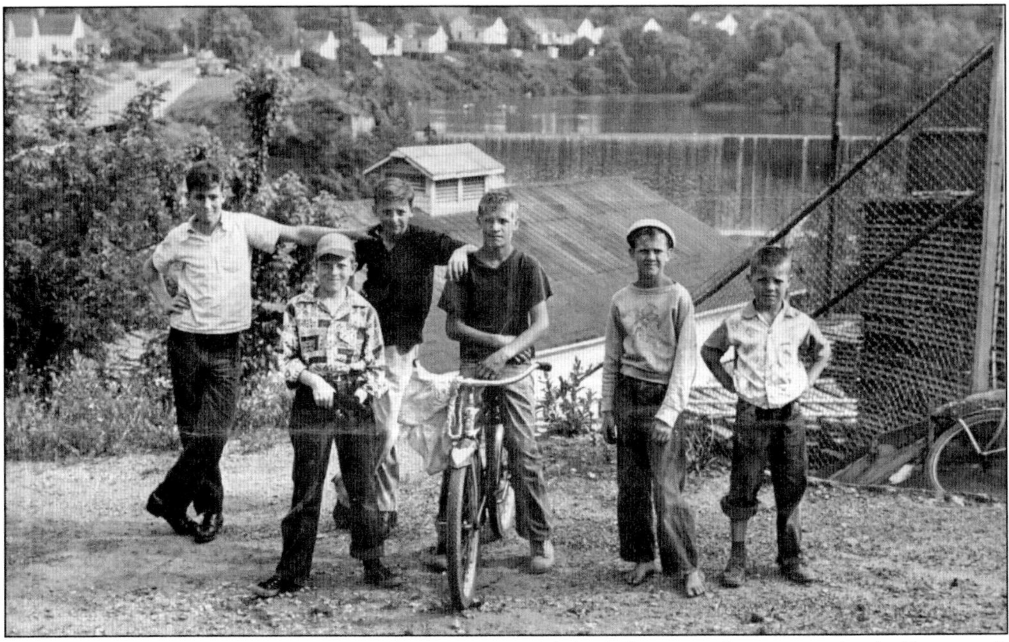

BLUE JEANS AND BIKES. Boys in the 1950s could find fun anywhere—at the ball ground, riding their Schwinns, or taking a hike. Shown from left to right, Knox Mintz, Dean Ledbetter, Herbert Scruggs, Don Harrison, Jerry Harrison, and Steve Humphries constitute a quorum at a spot overlooking the dam and the houses of River Street. Remember when boys rolled up their right pant leg to keep it out of the sprocket? (Courtesy Joan Humphries Harris.)

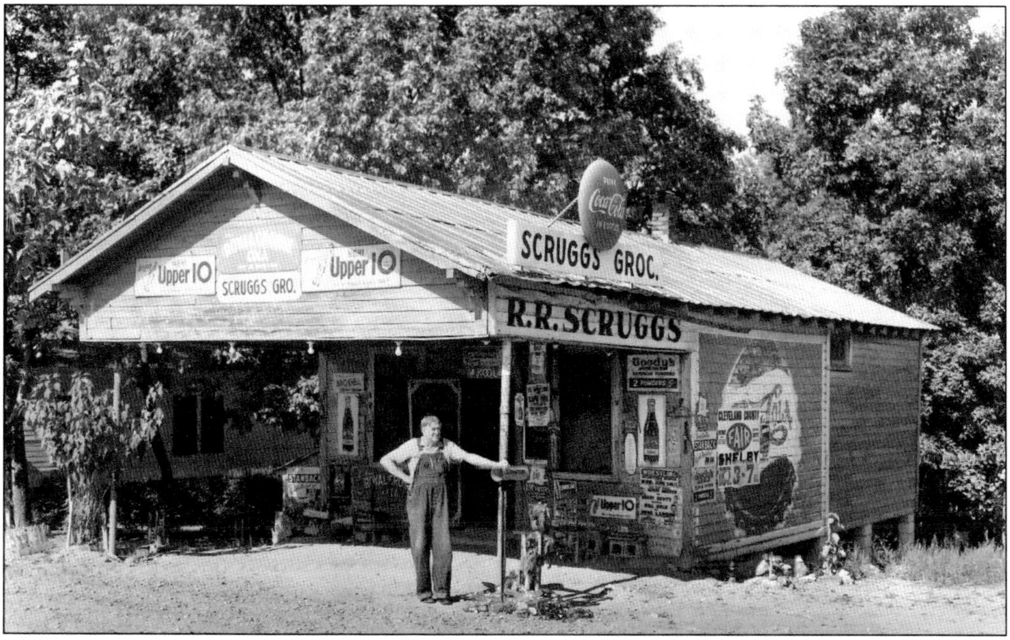

R. R. SCRUGGS'S STORE. Roy Rucker Scruggs ran this ramshackle old store at the top of River Street from before World War II for at least 35 years. He and his wife, Ina Mae, lived next door. It was a favorite meeting place for the men of the community, who would stop to buy a plug of Brown's Mule and maybe drink a Sun-Drop. (Courtesy Mary Scruggs.)

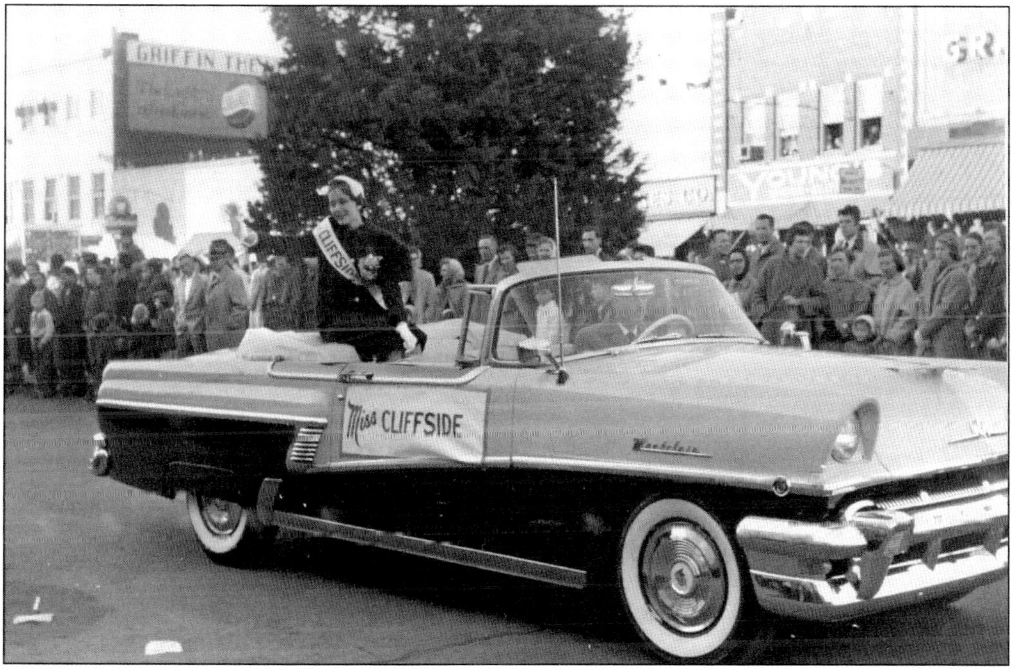

BEAUTY QUEEN. Aboard her royal coach—a spiffy Mercury Montclair convertible—Miss Cliffside of 1956, Virginia "Gigi" Padgett, waves to the throng along the Christmas parade route in Forest City. Her parents, James and Ferne Pruette Padgett, were surely in the crowd, bursting with pride and dying to tell those close by, "That's our daughter!" (Courtesy Hazel Haynes Bridges.)

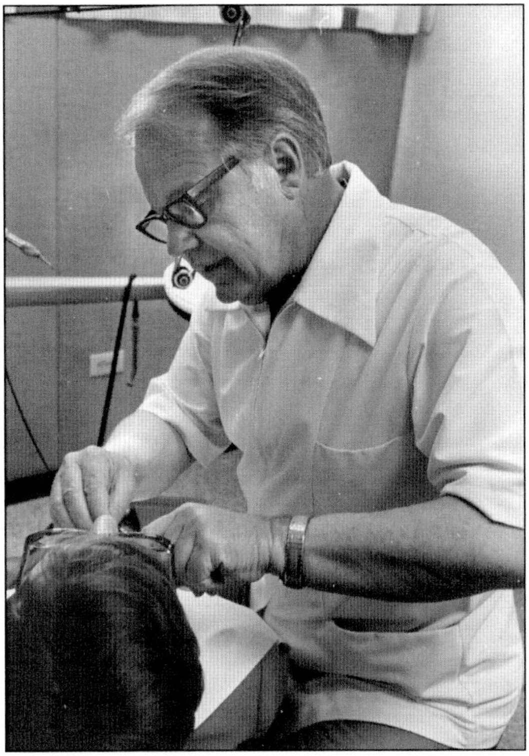

Dr. John Jackson "Jack" Hunt. In 1946, this young Lattimore dentist came to Cliffside to relieve Dr. H. L. Robertson for two months. He stayed 50 years. In 1972, Dr. Hunt began a 22-year tenure in the North Carolina House of Representatives, all the while maintaining his practice in Cliffside. He is back in Lattimore now but still remembers those wonderful Cliffside years. (Courtesy Dr. Jack Hunt.)

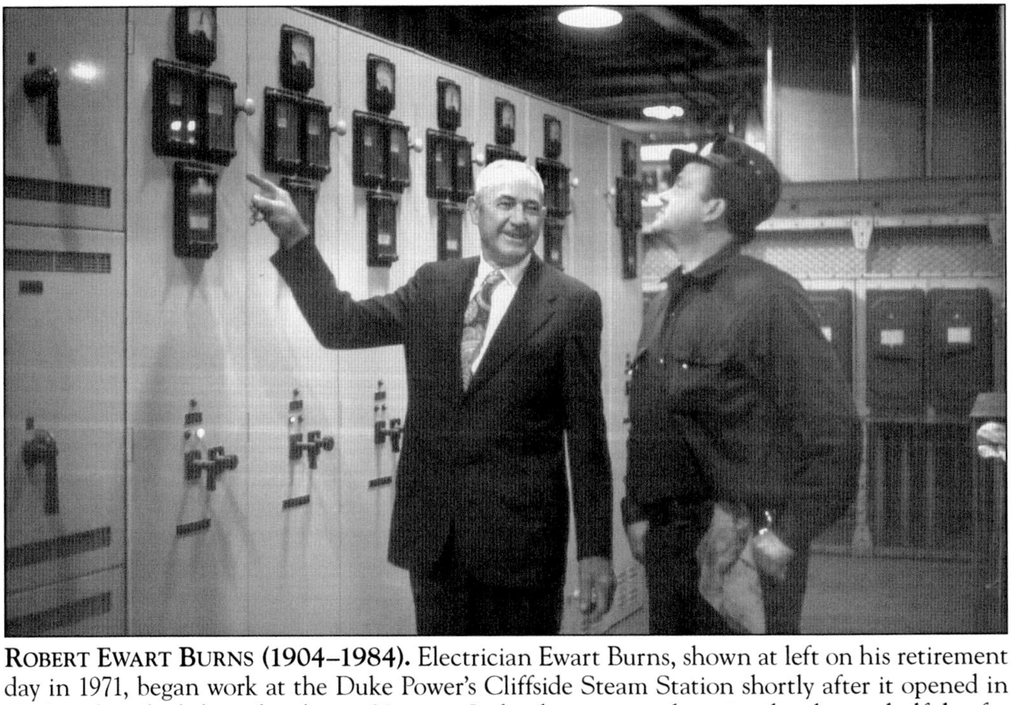

Robert Ewart Burns (1904–1984). Electrician Ewart Burns, shown at left on his retirement day in 1971, began work at the Duke Power's Cliffside Steam Station shortly after it opened in 1940 and worked there for almost 30 years. In his long career, he missed only one half-day for illness, when a crowbar flew up in his face and opened a gash on his forehead that required multiple stitches. (Courtesy Anita Price Davis.)

Eight

UPHEAVAL

But in this world nothing can be said to be certain, except death and taxes.

—Benjamin Franklin

In the 1950s, who could have guessed what was to come? There was no hint that Cliffside's way of life would not last forever. With America's population soaring, couldn't Cliffside remain competitive with terry-cloth industry giants like Cannon and Springs Mills? Weren't the homes good enough? After all, practically all of them now had indoor toilets. Wouldn't the majestic Memorial Building stand as long as the pyramids? If anyone anticipated that in a few years Cliffside would start a sad decline, he kept such provocative thoughts to himself.

The end began in the early 1960s, with civil rights changes, the dictates of OSHA, and the decision by Cone Mills that it would be impossibly expensive to upgrade the homes to meet new, modern standards. The era of mill owners providing nearly free housing was over, and the slow and sorrowful task began of urging employees to make other living arrangements for their families. The old houses—and then the downtown buildings—were razed, a few at a time.

To this day, the folks who love Cliffside are in denial. Few photographs were taken of the deconstruction (if you ignore it, it isn't happening). It lasted a couple of decades, but few can recall any significant details or dates of the town having been torn down. "I don't know," they say, "one day you just looked around, and it was gone."

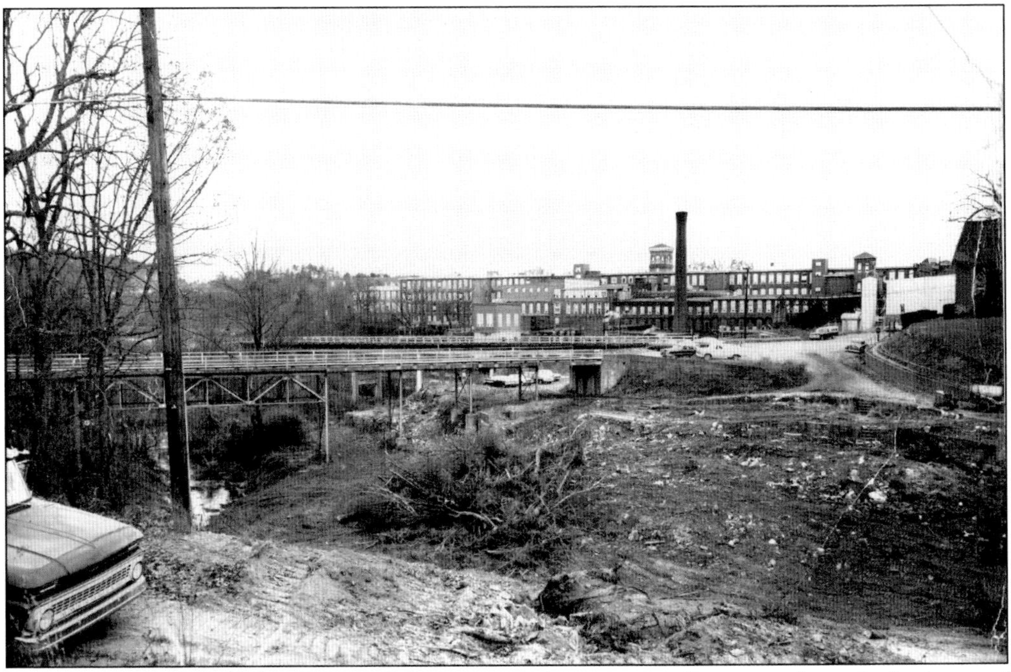

The Bypass. After all those years of the main road twisting and turning through the heart of town, state authorities decided it must go somewhere else. Thus the bypass was born. Here, the way is being cleared to tear down the creek bridge, build a new bridge over the river, and fill in the chasm near the mouth of Riddle's Creek. (Courtesy Larry McDaniel.)

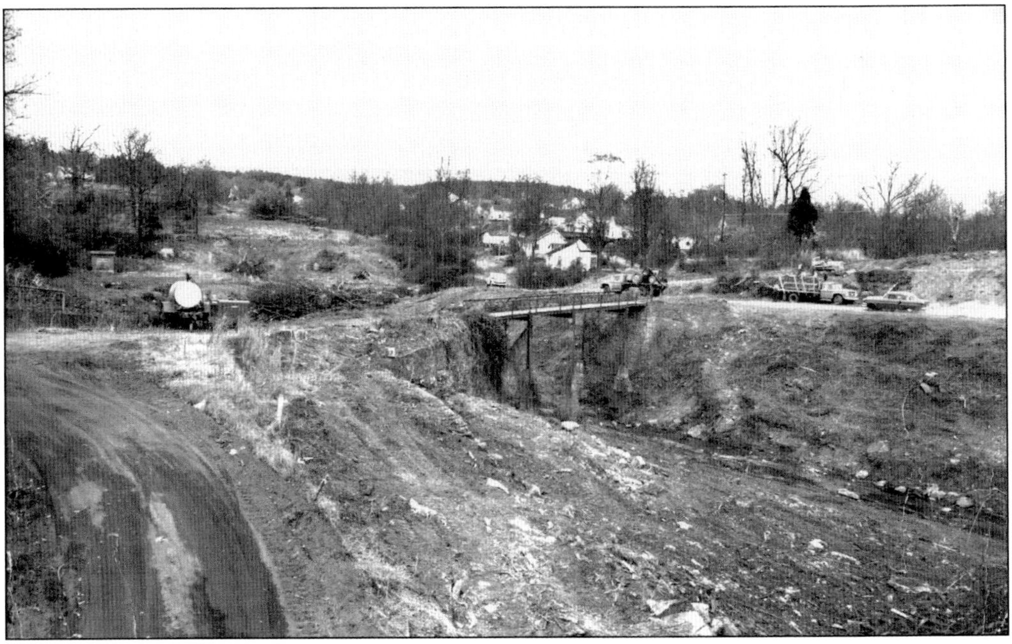

Devastation. As if by a glacier, a good part of the housing district was scoured off the hills to make way for the bypass that rerouted traffic away from the town square, leaving downtown on a dead end street—definitely not good for business. This sad vista shows the area formerly occupied by Reservoir Street and all its intersecting avenues. (Courtesy Larry McDaniel.)

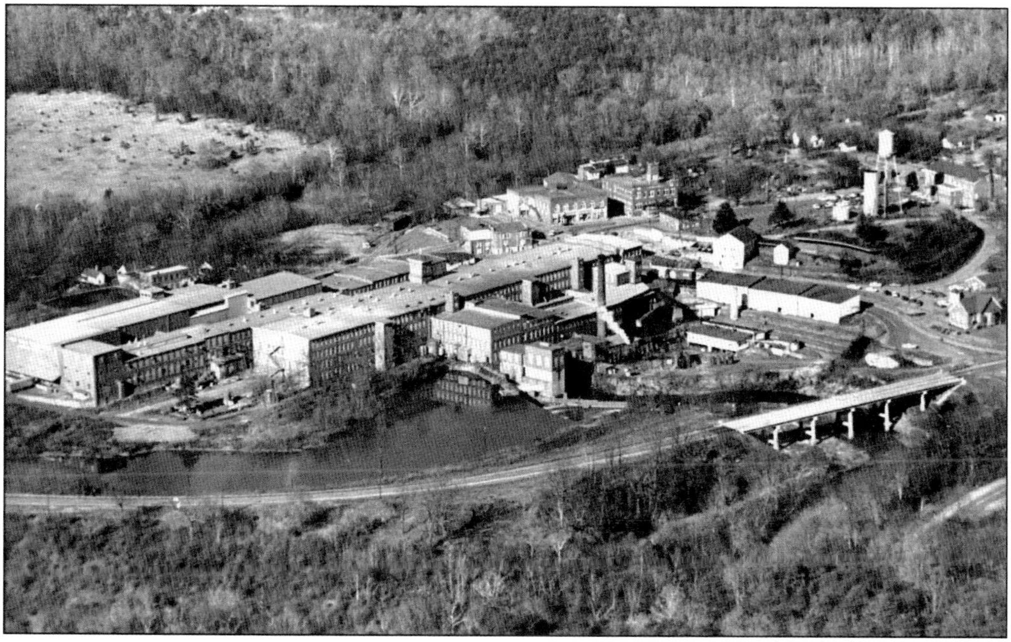

HANGING ON. After the bypass was completed, it was time for the commercial enterprises to die. The garage has been removed, but the store buildings have so far survived; however, with no residents—most houses are now gone—there are no customers to keep the businesses alive. River Street, in the foreground, was formerly home to about 50 families; it is once more a country road. (Courtesy Jim Scancarelli.)

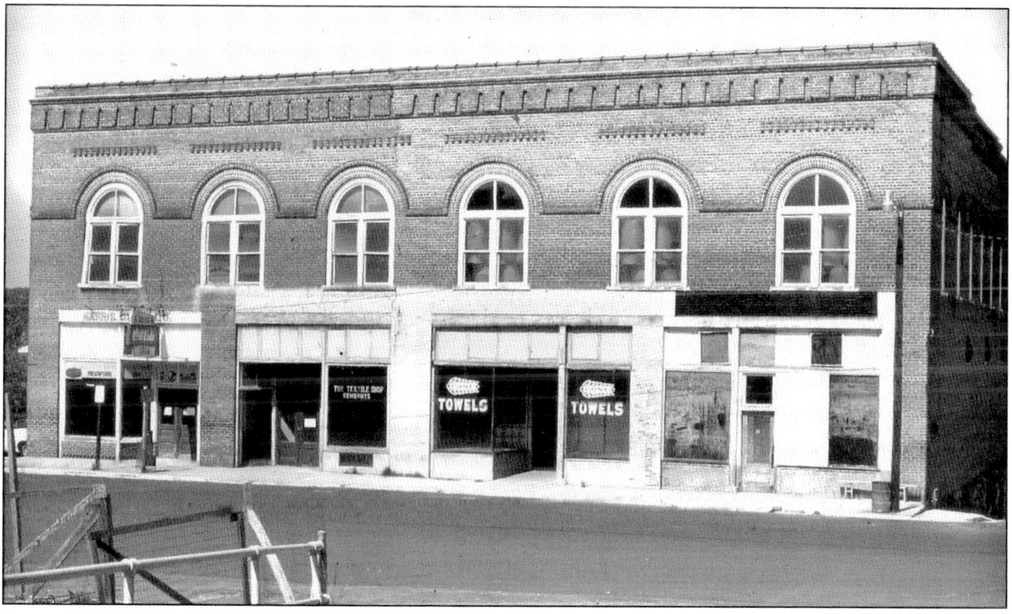

EMPTY STOREFRONTS. The old store building has been abandoned. Signs on the windows indicate a last futile attempt to survive. What was once Jackson's Department Store was recently a place that sold "Cone Towels." The little nook between the drug store (far left) and the department store is still a cloth store. Ironically, it advertises "remnants." The whole town has become a remnant. (Courtesy James M. Walker.)

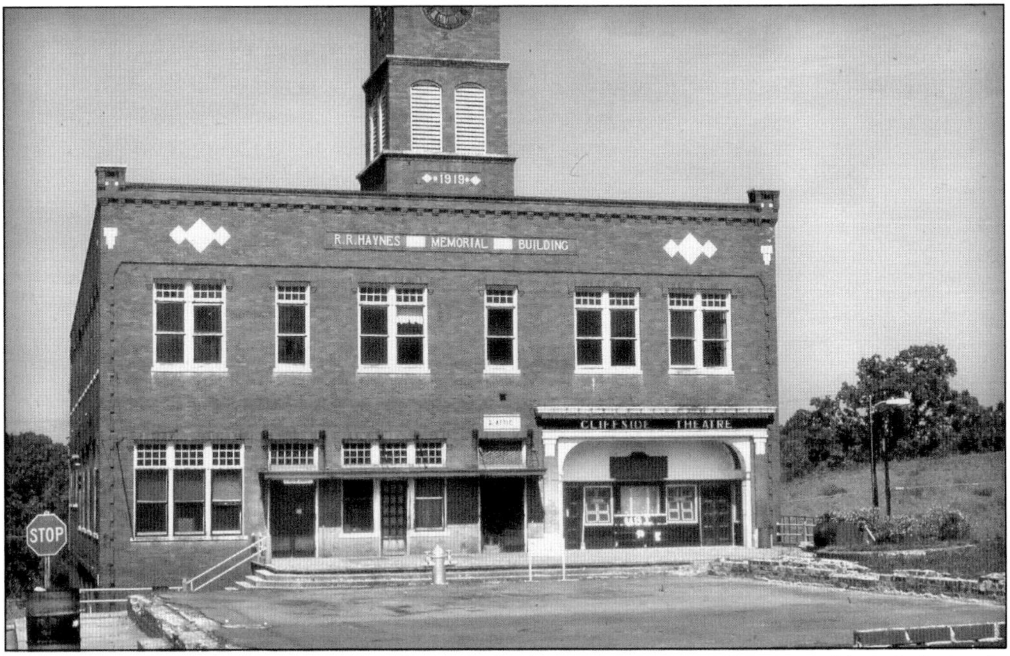

SAD AND TIRED. The Memorial Building of which we were so proud is now old and obviously in the way. A tattered window shade waves goodbye from an upstairs window. The expanse of concrete in the foreground was once the floor of the recently demolished C. P. Hamrick's Grocery. (Courtesy James M. Walker.)

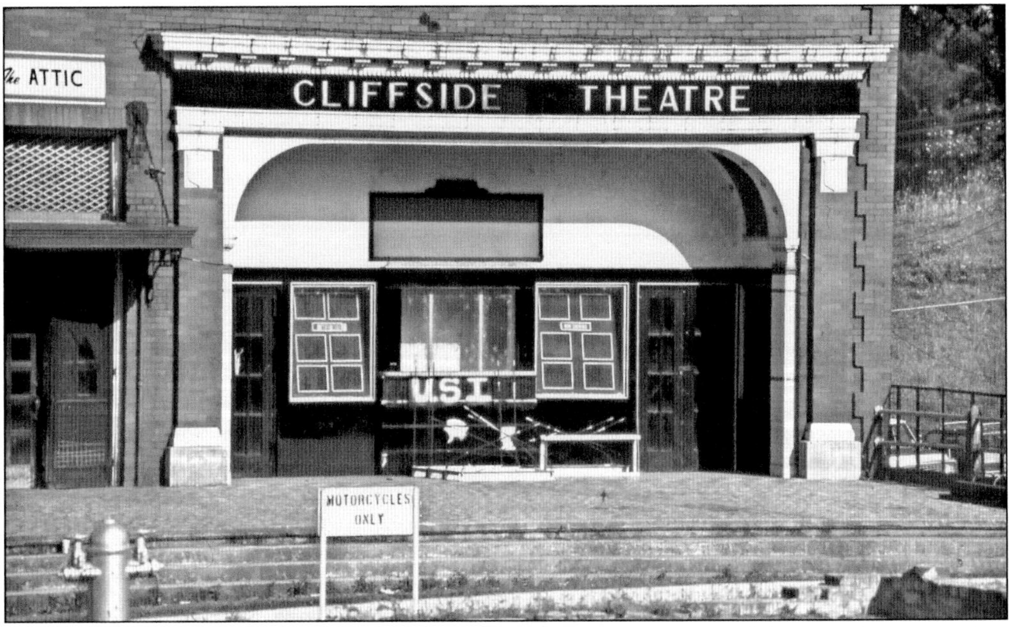

NOT SHOWING. Now silent and dark, this 417-seat theater opened on March 2, 1922. The last picture was shown here in 1970 or 1971 and, fittingly enough, was a horror movie: *Dracula Has Risen From the Grave*. Over the door to the Memorial Building second floor is a sign for a club called "The Attic," a last-ditch effort to provide a diversion for the few remaining teenagers in town. (Courtesy James M. Walker.)

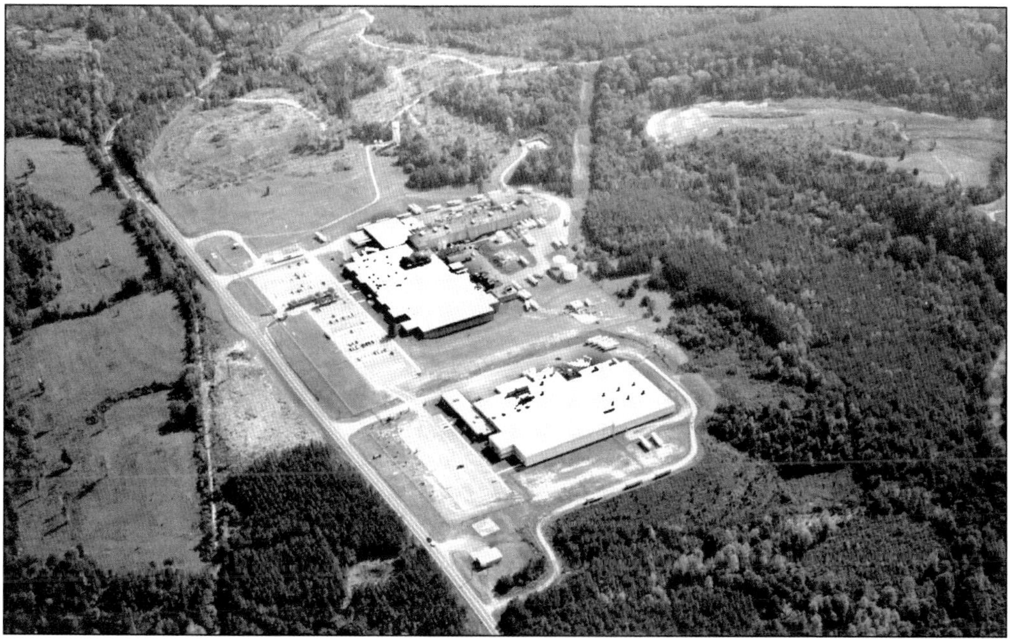

THE NEW MILLS. One factor causing the decline of the downtown area was the construction of a two new plants a couple of miles north of town to replace the original mill (which by this time had switched from terry cloth to denim). Slowly most of the manufacturing moved to the new facilities, leaving behind only the finishing plant and a much-reduced workforce. (Courtesy Gene Meade and Sam Davis.)

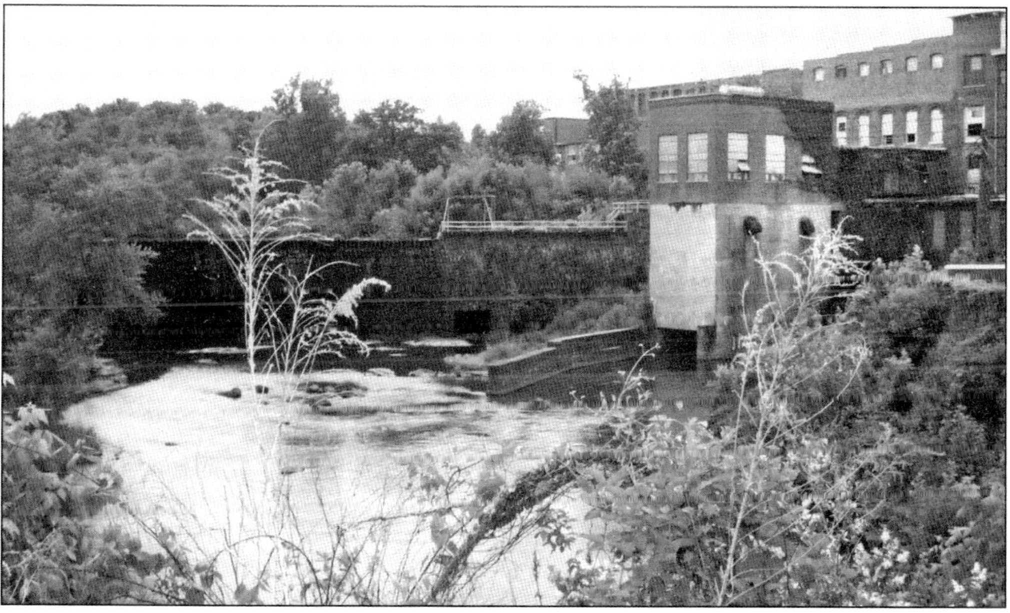

LEFT BEHIND. The old mill began to look scruffy and neglected. A few service departments still located here continued to provide support for the finishing plant and the new mill, but, for all practical purposes, the grand old building was useless except as a storage facility. Back in the 1960s, most of its windows had been bricked up to accommodate air conditioning, ruining its original architectural style. (Photograph by the author.)

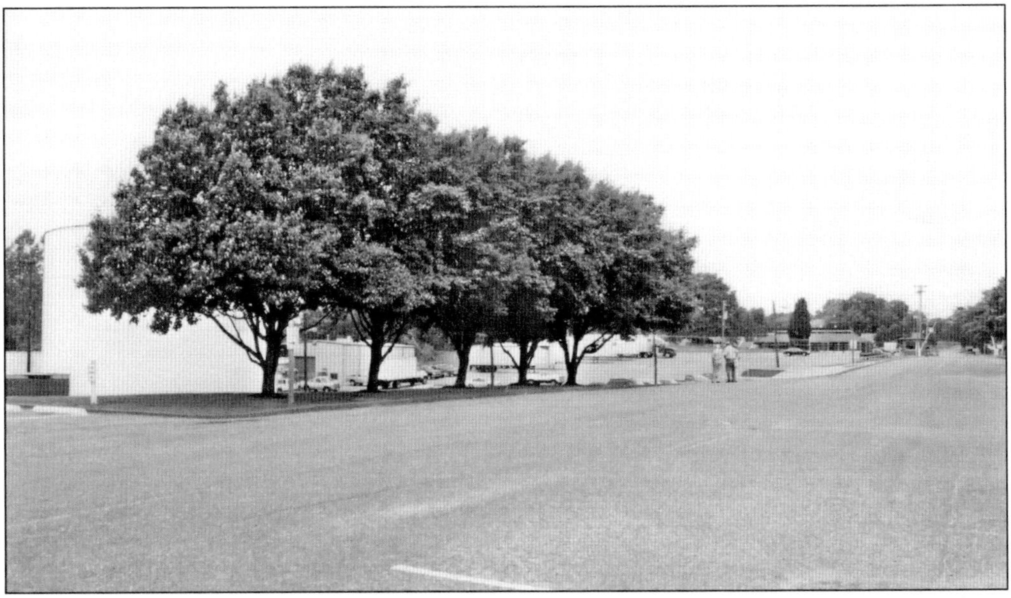

WITHOUT A TRACE. Not much remained of the square by 2002. A row of pear trees grows where once shoppers strode on the store building's sidewalk. Beyond the men is a depression where the Memorial Building once stood. It is now a parking lot. The photographer stands about where the charming little fountain and fish pool used to be, which was ripped out and sold for scrap. (Photograph by the author.)

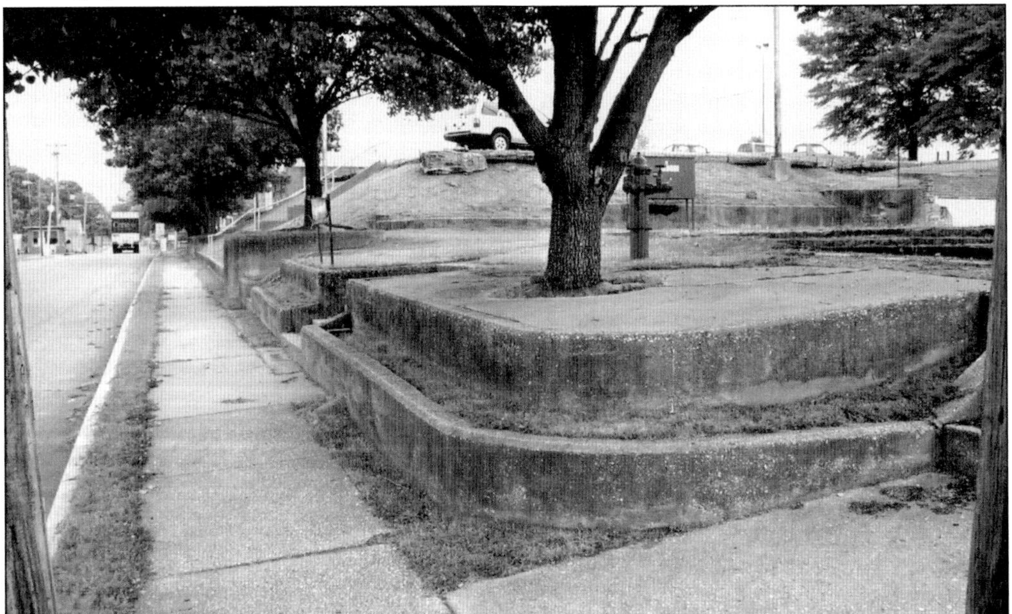

IF THESE WALLS COULD TALK. Men would sit on this wall in front of Hamrick's Grocery enjoying conversation and a last cigarette before their shift began. Outrageous tales were told here; practical jokes were plotted, likely to be played in the mill in the next few hours; plans were hatched, perhaps to go fishing; radio shows were relived—"Did you hear that Charley McCarthy last night?" (Photograph by the author.)

NEW HOME. After the Memorial Building was demolished in 1976, the old clock lay silent, but on December 19, 1978, it rang again at the dedication of its new tower. The nine surviving grandchildren of Raleigh Haynes who attended are, from left to right, Grover Haynes Jr., Edna Love Adams, Sadie Jenkins Harrill, Hazel Haynes Bridges, Betty Shull Griffin, Beth Caldwell Padgett, Mary Jenkins, Margaret Haynes Spoon, and Joe Shull Jr. (Courtesy Hazel Haynes Bridges.)

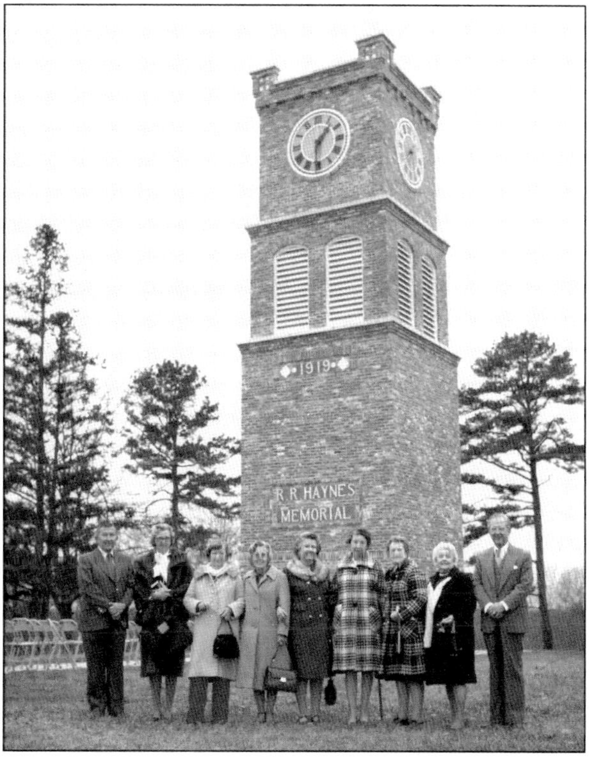

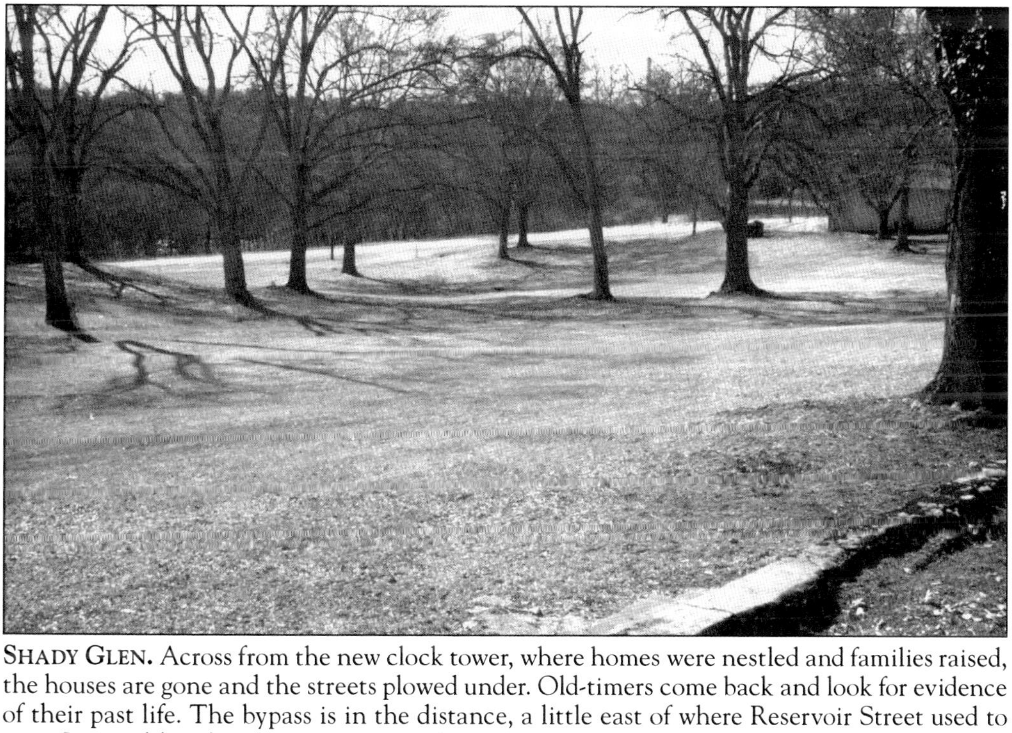

SHADY GLEN. Across from the new clock tower, where homes were nestled and families raised, the houses are gone and the streets plowed under. Old-timers come back and look for evidence of their past life. The bypass is in the distance, a little east of where Reservoir Street used to run. Cars sail by, their occupants probably unaware of what once was here. (Photograph by the author.)

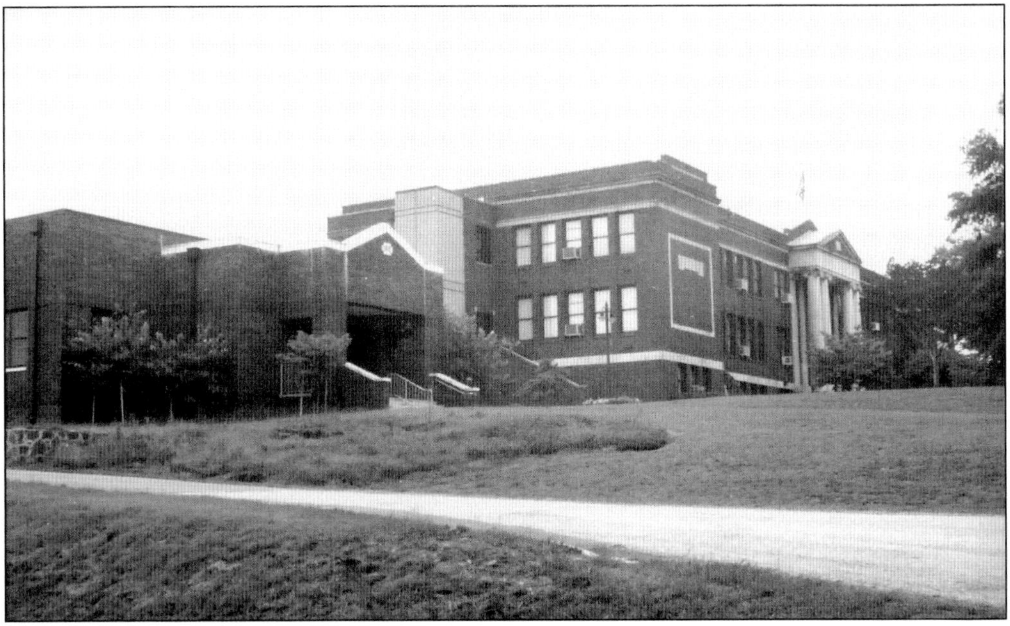

CLIFFSIDE SCHOOL TODAY. It ceased being a high school when the class of 1959 graduated, but it is still a proud and vital landmark where elementary students learn. Thanks to principal Phillip White, who has devoted his life to the school and the town, the old schoolhouse is on the National Register of Historic Places, which means the wrecking ball will not come around anytime soon. (Photograph by the author.)

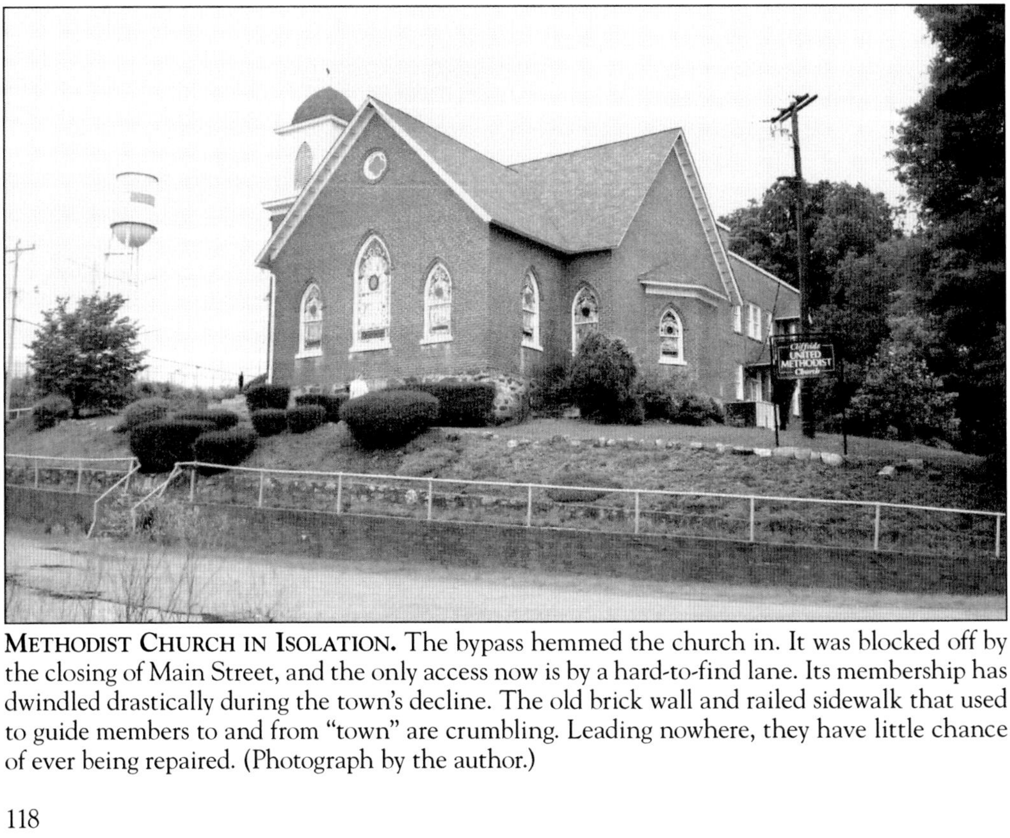

METHODIST CHURCH IN ISOLATION. The bypass hemmed the church in. It was blocked off by the closing of Main Street, and the only access now is by a hard-to-find lane. Its membership has dwindled drastically during the town's decline. The old brick wall and railed sidewalk that used to guide members to and from "town" are crumbling. Leading nowhere, they have little chance of ever being repaired. (Photograph by the author.)

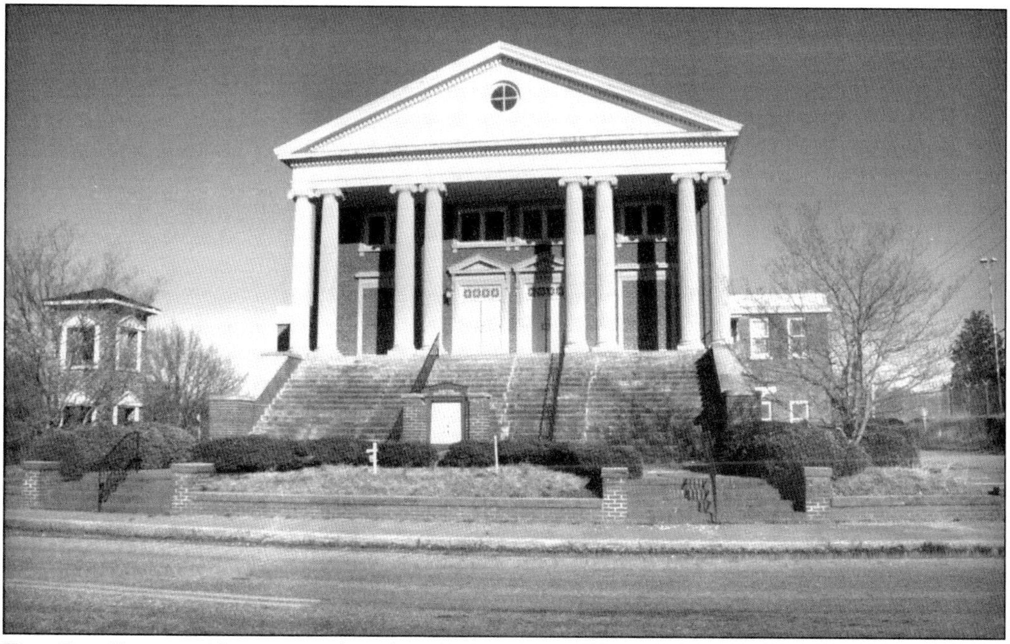

The Old Baptist Church. This church served for 76 years before the congregation voted to move to a new church across the street. Among other problems, it was becoming increasingly difficult for the aging membership to reach the second floor sanctuary. It is now owned by Joe Strahl and Ellen Varner, who use the building to house their businesses. They plan to restore it to its former state. (Photograph by the author.)

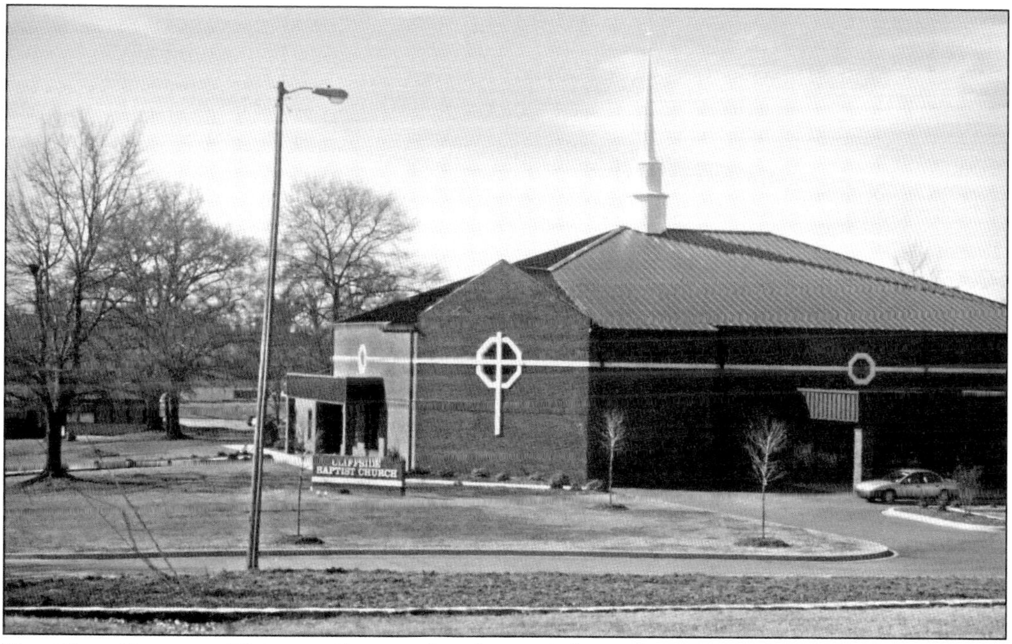

The New Church. This new Baptist church was dedicated in 2000. Located just south of the Clock Tower, it is more comfortable and better suited to its 550 members' needs. Its fellowship hall, built in 1986 on Cone-donated land adjacent to the church, has become the center for Cliffside's religious and civic functions. (Photograph by the author.)

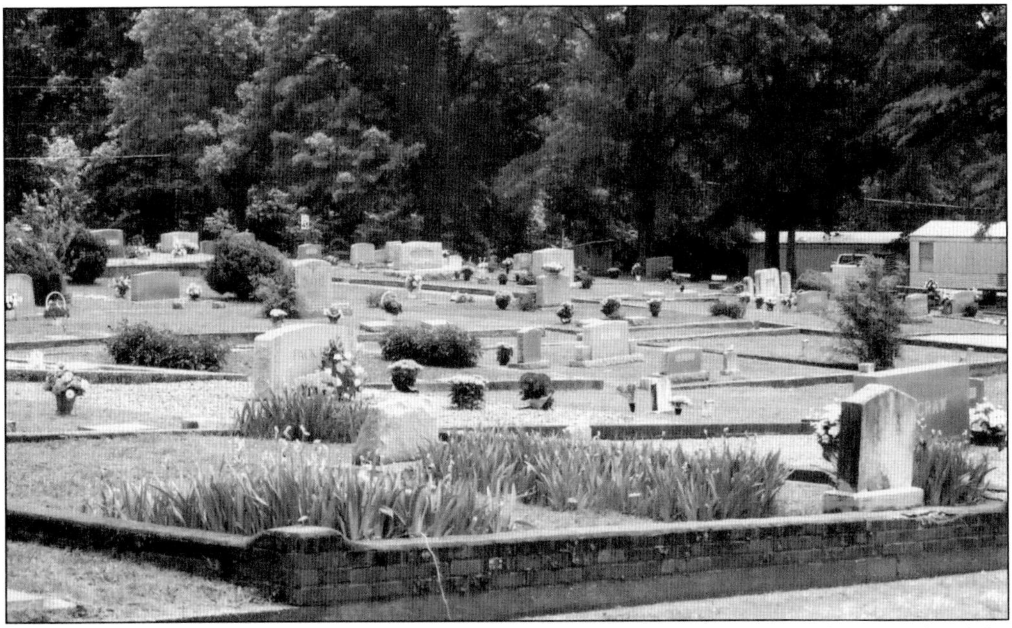

THE CEMETERY. There was an earlier cemetery prior to 1910, located somewhere south of the square. Mr. Haynes established this one in the second decade of the 20th century on a hillside behind the original Baptist church and moved the graves from the old burial ground to the new. In the early 1980s, the company ceded the land to The Cemetery Project, an entity comprised of all plot owners. (Photograph by the author.)

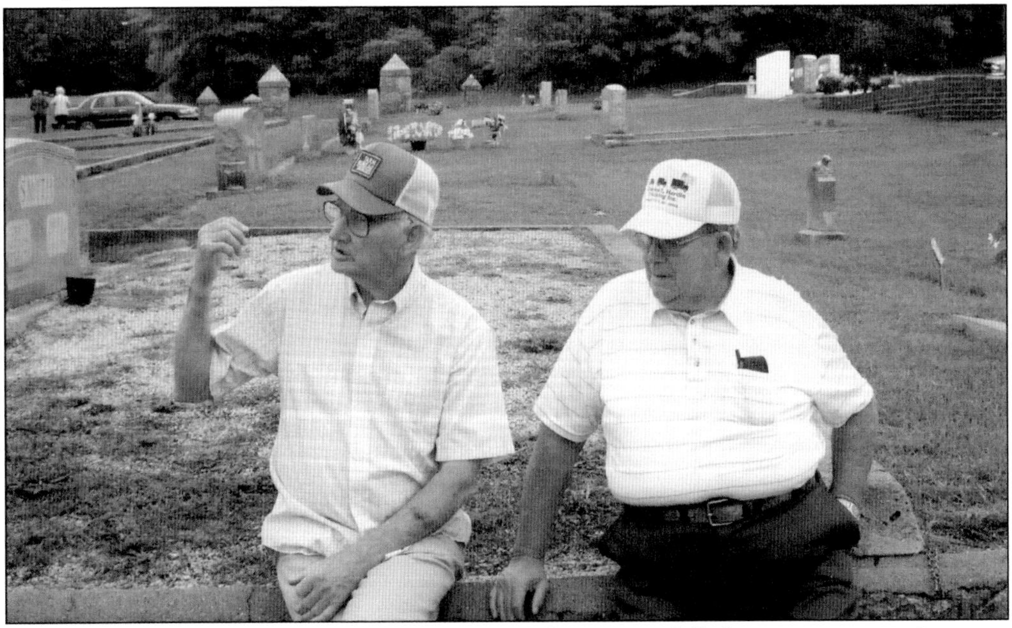

MEMORIAL DAY. Each year on the second weekend in May, Cliffside natives past and present come home, decorate the graves of their relatives, walk through the graveyard, and meet old friends. They talk of the past and remember those buried here. Here Bill Rollins and Glenn "Doc" Pearson sit on a cemetery wall recalling some detail from yesteryear. On Sunday, many attend services at Cliffside's churches. (Photograph by the author.)

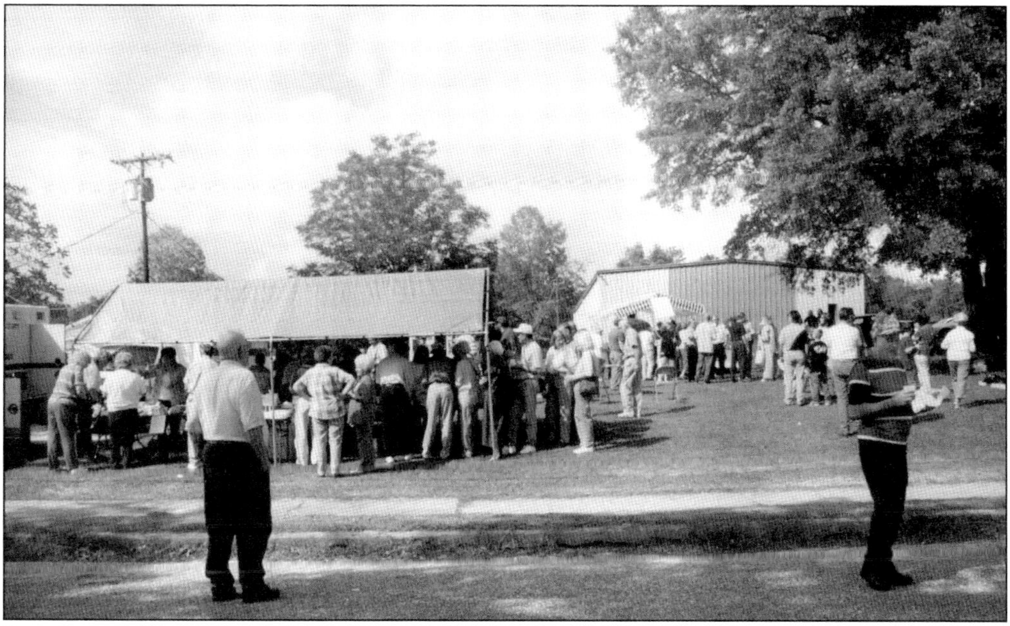

REUNIONS. Several homecoming events have been scheduled in the last couple of decades, drawing large crowds and reviving interest in the town's past. In recent years, the Masonic Lodge has organized a "Cliffside Day," a one-day festival held in early October on the grounds along old Main Street. The attractions are old photograph collections, music, antique cars, and memories. (Photograph by the author.)

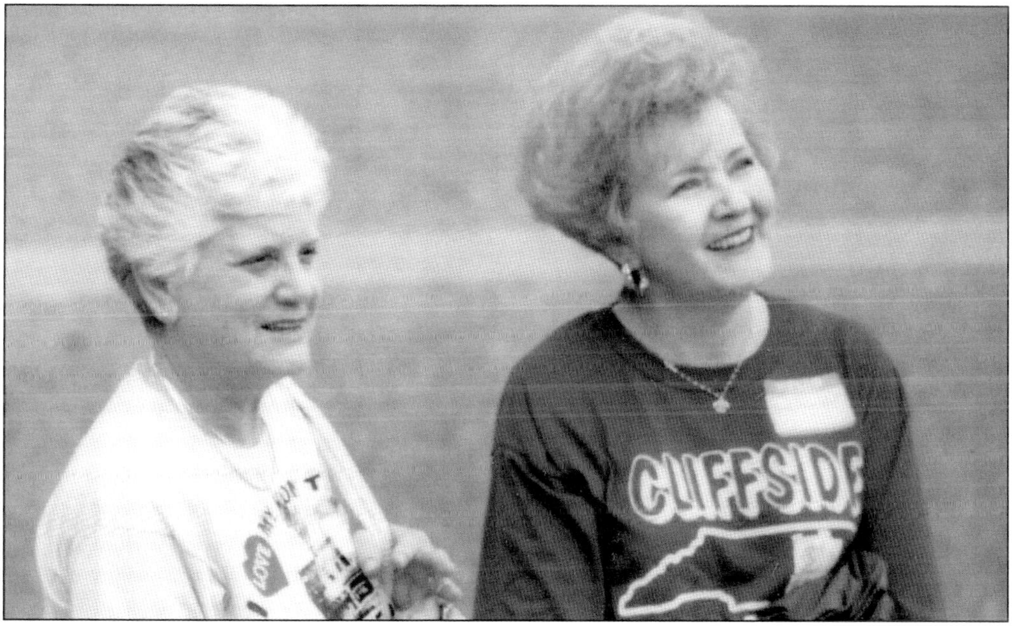

CHEERLEADERS. At any reunion or homecoming, there will always be a dedicated few, like Madeline Scruggs Hardin (left) and Ginny Greene Reid, who will never let the memory of Cliffside fade. If even a wisp of memorabilia floats by, they will capture it for posterity. Ginny is the "picture lady" at these events, displaying dozens of picture-filled albums. (Courtesy Louise Wall Price.)

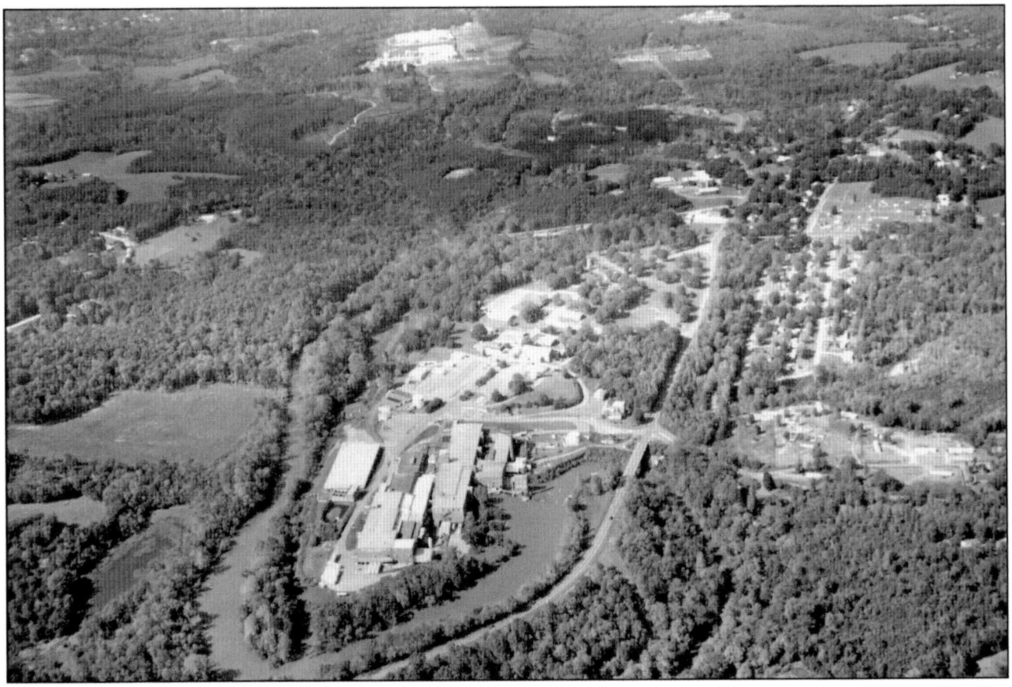

Diminishing Returns. An aerial shot of "greater" Cliffside confirms it: the area with the greatest growth in recent decades has been the cemetery (upper right). The clearing below it is a cluster of mobile homes along Cliffside Street. The new mills (top center) always seemed so far away they might as well be in China, and soon may be. (Courtesy Gene Meade and Sam Davis.)

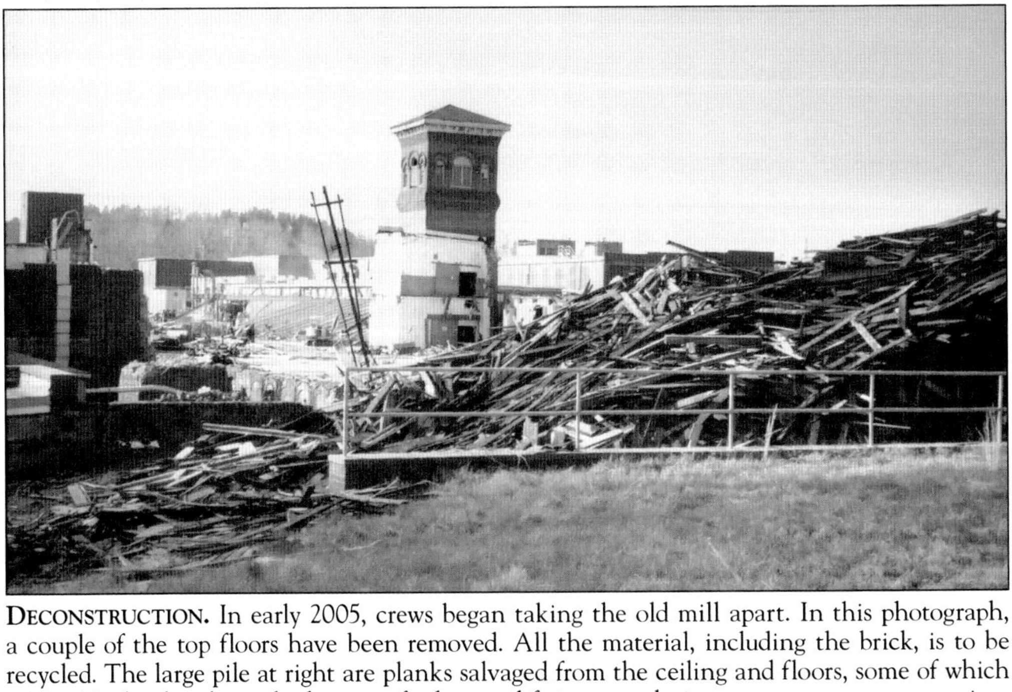

Deconstruction. In early 2005, crews began taking the old mill apart. In this photograph, a couple of the top floors have been removed. All the material, including the brick, is to be recycled. The large pile at right are planks salvaged from the ceiling and floors, some of which is New England rock maple that may find a new life in an exclusive new restaurant or mansion. (Photograph by Todd Putnam.)

GROUND ZERO. The salvage teams slowly work their way down, a floor at a time, until most of the mill is gone. Parts of the structure will be left standing, including the rope tower (upper right), the smokestack and power plant, and—for now—the newest section of the mill, the finishing department and bleachery, built in 1926. (Photograph by Todd Putnam.)

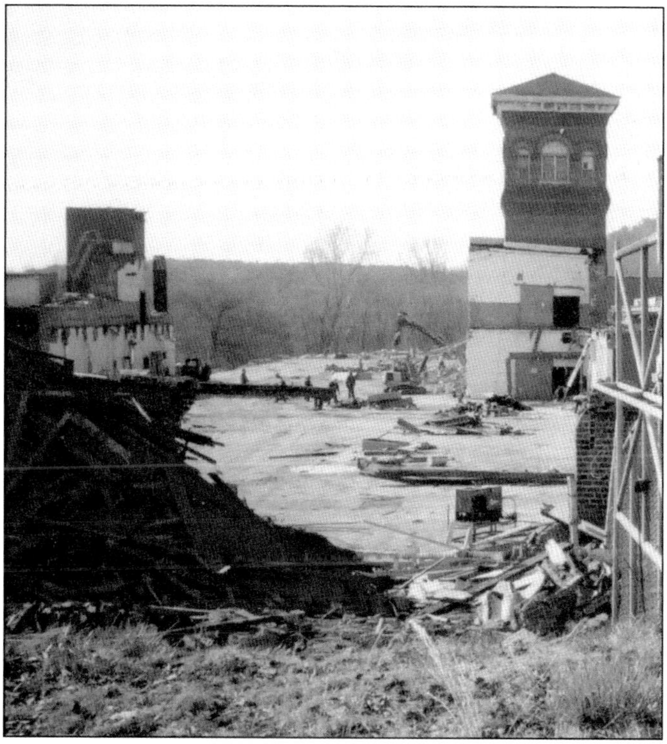

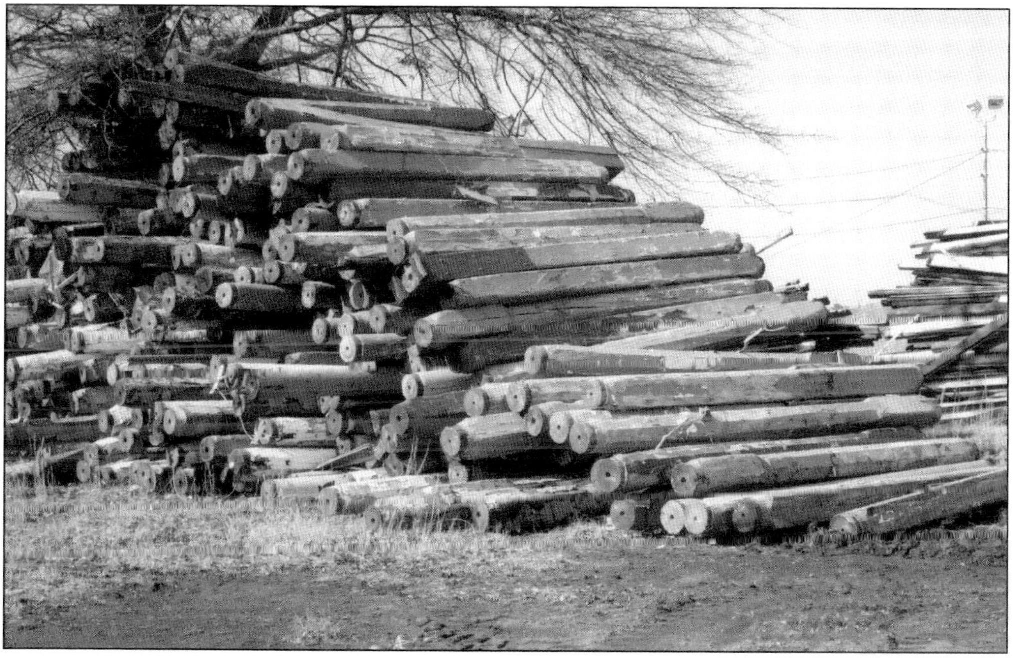

OLD POSTS. About the time these old pine support posts were sawed and shaped, William McKinley was president, "The Maple Leaf Rag" was a hit of the day, and Henry Ford unveiled his first car. There were thousands of these posts all over the mill, each one scarred and nicked by 100 years of abuse by rolling carts and boxes and the steel tips of runaway shuttles. (Photograph by Todd Putnam.)

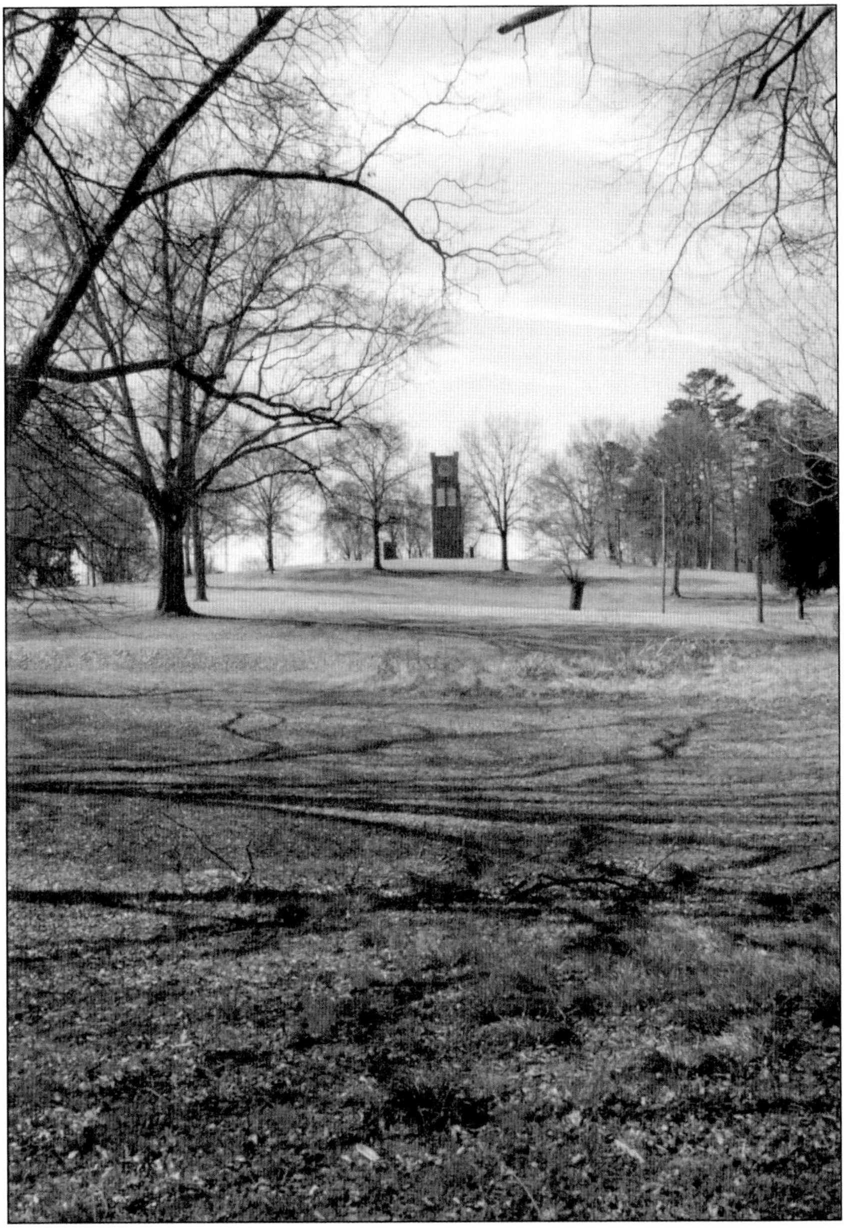

TOMORROW. This glimpse shows the clock tower and the empty acres along old Main Street. The tower and a small patch of land around it now belong to Rutherford County. Marc and Janice Swing recently bought the company's remaining acreage on either side of Main Street and are working on plans to revitalize the town. One day there will hopefully be homes and businesses on these vacant slopes. Another group has purchased the old mill and the downtown area. More changes will occur there, too. Cliffside will never again be what it was in the 1940s and 1950s, the so-called golden years, but it can be something else. The industry that started it is all but gone, as are most of the relics of the town's past, but there was far less here in 1895 when Raleigh Haynes came along. Look at what one man can do. As Jan Glidewell said, "You can clutch the past so tightly to your chest that it leaves your arms too full to embrace the present." (Photograph by the author.)

INDEX